COVER THE BIBLE

Dr. Ralph W. Neighbour, Jr.

ACKNOWLEDGEMENT
Special thanks to Joe Wilson, Natalie Goodhart,
Jan Matthews, Barbara Littlefield,
Joey and Bill Beckham, and Johnson Lim
for their hours spent in proof reading
this book.

Published by TOUCH Publications
P.O. Box 19888
Houston, TX 77224-9888, U.S.A.
(281) 497-7901 • Fax (281) 497-0904

International Standard Book Number: 1-880828-58-8

TOUCH Publications is the book-publishing division of
TOUCH Outreach Ministries, a resource and consulting ministry for
churches with a vision for cell-based local church structure.

For more information on other
TOUCH Publications or CellGroup Journal
Call 1-800-735-5865 or 281-497-7901.
Find us on the World Wide Web at
http://www.touchusa.org

Printed in the Republic of Singapore
by BAC Printers

This book is dedicated to

D. Dean Rhoads

The closest earthly friend I have ever had.

PREFACE

For twenty years, perhaps longer, I have helped new Christians learn about the Bible. Many hundreds have told me that they profited most from my ministry through sitting under the teaching of this course.

I write these materials with the earnest prayer that a lifetime of study and preparation might help both those who are not yet believers, and those who are, to know more about this inspired book, the Bible. Fifty-six hours of audiotapes, containing the lectures as I have given them through the years, are also available. They will be useful to teachers, to small groups, or to individuals who study using this handbook.

For a very long time, I kept folders on each book in the Bible. Each time COVER THE BIBLE was taught, I added a few notes to each folder. As a result, I confess there is no way I can give credit to all the books, sermons, conversations, and student suggestions which are included in these pages.

Thus, some material has been unconsciously "plagiarized" without proper credit being given. If writers recognize their material and notify me, I shall be glad to include credits in later editions. And, if they are like me, they will probably just smile and thank the Lord that their thoughts were valuable enough that someone else felt they should be shared.

It's my deep desire that, at the end of this course, you will have penned marginal notes throughout your Bible, including suggested comments included at the close of each Unit. This year of study could change not only your life, but also your eternity. Know you are prayed for as you study each unit! I welcome response from you. As my Chinese brothers say when temporarily parting, *Tsai Tsien, Tsai Tsien!*

COVER THE BIBLE IN ONE YEAR
SCHEDULE

First Quarter

UNIT	BOOKS AND CHAPTERS
1	General Introduction
2	The Bible's Outlines and Themes
3	Genesis 1-12
4	Genesis 13-28
5	Genesis 29-45
6	Genesis 46-50; Exodus 1-13
7	Exodus 14-18; 19-23 with Deuteronomy 4-13; Exodus 24-28 & 39; Exodus 29 with Deuteronomy 17 & 18
8	Exodus 30-38 & 40
9	Leviticus 1-10; 11-15 with Deuteronomy 14-15; Leviticus 16-20; Numbers 1-10
10	Leviticus 21-24 with Numbers 28-29 & Deuteronomy 16; Numbers 11-12; Numbers 13-14 with Deuteronomy 1
11	Numbers 15-19; Numbers 20-21 with Deuteronomy 2-3; Numbers 22-25; Numbers 26-36 with Deuteronomy 19; Deuteronomy 20-34
12	Joshua 1-14; Judges 1-12
13	Judges 13-21; Ruth; 1 Samuel 1-12

NOTE: Your study will touch upon all Biblical materials, combining chapters that discuss the same periods in Israel's history. This is the reason for combining references in these first 13 Units. This will end with our study of the Kings and Chronicles. You may find it convenient to use two Bibles while reviewing these Units, allowing you to view parallel passages simultaneously.

COVER THE BIBLE IN ONE YEAR
SCHEDULE

Second Quarter

UNIT	BOOKS AND CHAPTERS
14	1 Samuel 13-31; 2 Samuel 1-5 with 1 Chronicles 1-12
15	2 Samuel 6 with 1 Chronicles 13-16; 2 Samuel 7 with 1 Chronicles 17; 2 Samuel 8-12 with 1 Chronicles 18-20; 2 Samuel 13-18; 2 Samuel 19-24 with 1 Chronicles 21
16	1 Kings 1-4 with 1 Chronicles 22-29; 1 Kings 5-8 with 2 Chronicles 1-7; 1 Kings 9-11 with 2 Chronicles 8-9; 1 Kings 12-16 with 2 Chronicles 10-17
17	1 Kings 17-19; 1 Kings 20-22 with 2 Chronicles 18-20; 2 Kings 1-5; 2 Kings 6-8 with 2 Chronicles 21-22
18	2 Kings 9-13 with 2 Chronicles 23,24; 2 Kings 14-17 with 2 Chronicles 25-28; 2 Kings 18-20 with 2 Chronicles 29-32; 2 Kings 21-23 with 2 Chronicles 33-35; 2 Kings 24-25 with 2 Chronicles 36
19	Ezra; Nehemiah; Esther
20	Job; Psalms 1-72
21	Psalms 73-150; Proverbs
22	Ecclesiastes; Song of Solomon; Isaiah 1-44
23	Isaiah 45-66; Jeremiah
24	Lamentations; Ezekiel; Daniel; Hosea
25	Joel; Amos; Obadiah; Jonah
26	Micah; Nahum; Habakkuk; Zephaniah; Haggai; Zechariah; Malachi

COVER THE BIBLE IN ONE YEAR
SCHEDULE

Third Quarter

UNIT	BOOKS AND CHAPTERS
27	The Interbiblical Period; The "Synoptic" Gospels
28	Matthew
29	Mark
30	Luke
31	John
32	Acts 1-14
33	Acts 15-28
34	Romans
35	1 and 2 Corinthians
36	Galatians
37	Ephesians
38	Philippians
39	Colossians

Fourth Quarter

UNIT	BOOKS AND CHAPTERS
40	Philemon; 1 and 2 Thessalonians
41	1 and 2 Timothy; Titus
42	Hebrews
43	James
44	1 and 2 Peter
45	1, 2, and 3 John; Jude
46	Revelation 1-3
47	Revelation 4-11
48	Revelation 12-16
49	Revelation 17-22
50	The First 300 Years After The Bible Was Written
51	How To Use Your Own Reference Library
52	Principles of Biblical Interpretation Summarized

**"He is no fool
Who gives what he
Cannot keep
To gain what he
Cannot lose!"**

- Jim Elliott, Martyr

Unit One

THE INSPIRATION AND AUTHORITY OF THE BIBLE

I. ITS CLAIM FOR ITSELF

A. 2 TIMOTHY 3:14-17
   "God-breathed"—"inspired"
   Man did not *create*; he only *transcribed!*

B. 1 PETER 1:10-12
   ...And men *transcribed,* not knowing fully the full meaning of what they wrote! Yet, the prophets knew they were writing for *us!*

C. LOOK AT *THESE* CLAIMS:
   Psalm 19:7-11

   Psalm 37:29-31

   Psalms 119:89-91, 98-101, 130, 160

   Isaiah 40:6-8

   Mark 13:31

1

II. THE BIBLE MORE VALID THAN PERSONAL EXPERIENCE

A. 2 Peter 1:16-21 with Matthew 17:1-13

B. Note how Paul depended on it:
1 Cor. 15:3-7

Acts 18:24,28

C. Note the powerful words of Hebrews 5:12-14:

D. Now, see this *special* truth in 2 Peter 1:19-21:

TWO THINGS THE BIBLE IS NOT:

- **A PRIVATE OR INDIVIDUAL INTERPRETATION OF TRUTH.**
- **THE RESULT OF AN ACT OF THE HUMAN WILL.**

III. NOTE ITS AMAZING PROPHECIES:

A. Micah 5:2 with Matthew 2:1-6—Bethlehem predicted as His birthplace...

B. Isaiah 53:5, 7, 9—description of death on the cross prior to the use of crosses...

C. COMPARE THIS WITH:

John 19:34—soldiers pierced Jesus...

John 20:27—Thomas saw the wounds...

John 19:1-2—Jesus beaten, crown of thorns...

Matthew 27:14—He did not respond...

Matthew 27:38—crucified between two robbers...

Matthew 27:57-60—body of Jesus in tomb with stone over entrance...

John 19:4—Pilate said there was no charge against Jesus...

IV. CONSIDER JESUS' PREDICTION OF THE FUTURE:

A. John 14:2-3:
(CAN YOU *COUNT* ON IT?)

B. Matthew 25:31:

V. CONCLUSION

The Bible is not just inspired in parts; it's a fully "God-breathed" volume! It's a perfect book, a treasury of truth. Not one part of it—as we shall see during this course—is without meaning and value!

Therefore, as you read it during these next months, be certain of this fact: *the very passage you decide to be irrelevant is hiding a special truth for your blind eyes!*

HOW WE GOT OUR BIBLE

Word of Mouth

Stone Tablets

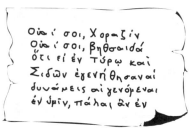

Early Paper

Woodcuts of Bible Events

Scrolls of Animal Skins

Hand Lettered Copies

With the coming of the printing press in 1517, a new era in Bible knowledge began. The printed word of God was translated into many languages.

But translations of the scriptures began much earlier! Let's look at some of them...

THE SEPTUAGINT—Third to First Century B. C.
The Old Testament was translated from Hebrew to Greek—for Jews who could not read their native language any more.

LATIN VULGATE—About 400 A. D.
The work of Jerome; for centuries, the major Bible used by the Roman Catholic church.

WYCLIFFE BIBLE—1383

TYNDALE NEW TESTAMENT—1526

COVERDALE BIBLE—1535

THE GREAT BIBLE—1539

GENEVA BIBLE—1560

RHEIMS NEW TESTAMENT—1582

DOUAY OLD TESTAMENT—1610

KING JAMES VERSION—1611

ENGLISH REVISED VERSION—1881-1885

AMERICAN STANDARD VERSION—1901

MOFFATT BIBLE—1913-1924

SMITH-GOODSPEED TRANSLATION—1923-1927

REVISED STANDARD VERSION—1946-1952

PHILLIPS NEW TESTAMENT—1958

BERKELEY VERSION—1959

NEW ENGLISH BIBLE—1951-1970

TODAY'S ENGLISH VERSION NEW TESTAMENT—1966

THE LIVING BIBLE—1971

NEW AMERICAN STANDARD VERSION—1974

NEW KING JAMES VERSION—1979

NEW INTERNATIONAL VERSION—1979

Note the periods of history when Bible translations were being produced. Over and over, the need for a modern translation which could be clearly understood by the people caused new versions to be prepared.

Literally *hundreds* of early manuscripts, not yet discovered at the time the King James Version was translated, have been used by translators of more recent versions. Thus, modern versions like the New International Version are quite dependable.

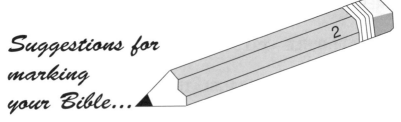

Suggestions for marking your Bible...

Each Unit will end with a page like this one.

It will suggest verses you might wish to underline in your own Bible. It will also provide brief notations for you to write in the margins of your Bible.

Taking the few moments to do this will make *your* Bible a very special study book. You will get much more from the course if you will do so!

THIS UNIT...

Underline some or all of the verses you have studied which reveal your Bible is inspired by the Holy Spirit.

A WORD ABOUT UNDERLINING...

If you have a fine Bible with very thin paper, be careful to select a pen which will not bleed through the paper. Often, humidity will cause this to take place over a period of months—even though at the time you mark your Bible it seemed to be all right.

Best way is with India ink and a pen used by draftsmen. There are also special Bible marking pens, available at many Christian book stores. Colored pencils are also satisfactory, as are a limited number of the "highlighters"on the market. Test your pen on a back page of your Bible before using it. (India ink is impossible to remove if pen leaks in your pocket! Beware of airplanes...pressure in cabin makes it leak.)

Unit Two
THE BIBLE'S OUTLINES AND THEMES

I. ITS BOOKS

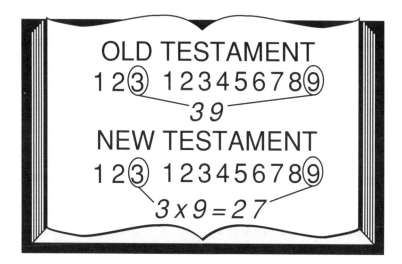

A. There are 66 books in your Bible.

B. They are divided into two major divisions:
    The Old Testament and the New Testament.

C. Some Bibles (Catholic and New English) may also include
    a section between these two divisions, called *The Apocrypha*.
    This section is so placed because it deals with the historical
    period between the Old and New Testaments, called *The
    Interbiblical Period*. At the appropriate place in our study,
    we will discuss these "extra" books, and why they are
    not considered to be inspired—although a few of them
    are excellent historical records.

II. THE "STORY LINE" OF THE BIBLE

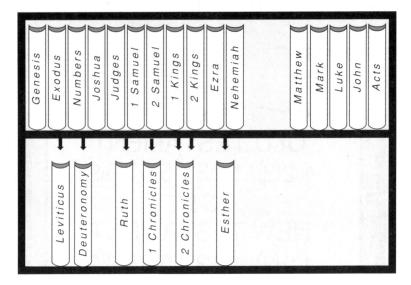

A. In his excellent book *Bible Panorama,* Terry Hall rightly points out that only sixteen of the Bible's books carry its chronological record. These are pictured on the top shelf of this book case.

B. The books on the lower shelf reflect those which enlarge the story of the Bible, and which run parallel to the "Story Line" books.

C. These books take us from Creation to the end of the period of history in which it was recorded.

D. The Book of Revelation takes us *beyond* our present time in history, accurately predicting the coming events which will take place before God establishes His eternal Kingdom. Most other books in your Bible will also prophesy of these coming events, with books such as Daniel and Ezekiel taking a prominent part in prophetic records.

III. THE OLD TESTAMENT BY SECTIONS

A. THE BOOKS OF THE LAW
   (Also called The Books of Moses; The Pentateuch)
   Genesis, Exodus, Leviticus, Numbers, Deuteronomy

B. THE BOOKS OF HISTORY
   Joshua, Judges, Ruth, 1 and 2 Samuel,
   1 and 2 Chronicles, 1 and 2 Kings,
   Ezra, Nehemiah, and Esther

C. THE BOOKS OF POETRY *(Jewish style)*
   Job, Psalms, Proverbs,
   Song of Solomon, Ecclesiastes

D. MAJOR PROPHETS
   Isaiah, Jeremiah, Ezekiel, Daniel

E. MINOR PROPHETS
   All the rest of the Old Testament

Note: The "Major" prophets are so called for only one reason—their size! They are not more "important" than the Minor Prophets. In ancient days, scrolls were shaped from animal skins. To accommodate the size of these leather rolls, the smaller writings were gathered to comprise one scroll. Thus, the "Minor" Prophets were collected by their size—not by their importance, or even by the dates of writing. Thus, you will want to treat them with the same respect as the larger documents.

IV. THE NEW TESTAMENT BY SECTIONS

A. THE SYNOPTIC GOSPELS
1. *"Synoptic"*—same root as the word "synopsis." These Gospels tell the chronological history of the life of Jesus.
2. Matthew, Mark, Luke *(Mark is the earliest one)*

B. THE FOURTH GOSPEL
1. *"Fourth"*—A simple way of separating it from the Synoptics, since it is the fourth Gospel.
2. John

C. HISTORY OF THE CHURCH
Acts

D. PAUL'S LETTERS
Romans, 1 and 2 Corinthians, Galatians, Ephesians, Philippians, Colossians, 1 and 2 Thessalonians, 1 and 2 Timothy, Titus, Philemon
(Note: Luther is responsible for putting them in this order. He put Romans first because of his regard for the book.)

E. HEBREWS
Placed here because the authorship is in question. Did *Paul* write it, or did one of the *other* apostles? So placed, it could be the *last* of Paul's letters, or the *first* of the General Epistles, a collection of letters written by men other than Paul.

F. GENERAL EPISTLES
James, 1 and 2 Peter, 1,2,3 John, Jude

G. THE REVELATION OF JESUS CHRIST

V. THE BIBLE'S THEMES

A. MAN'S FALLEN CONDITION
1. Two lines extend from Adam's children
2. The "God Seekers"—grace is provided
3. The "God Rejecters"—no provision for them!

B. GOD'S PLAN OF REDEMPTION
1. Jesus Christ— *"No man comes to the Father except by me."*
2. He is not only the Savior of the world, but also the King of the Jews.

C. ISRAEL, A CHOSEN PEOPLE
1. A nation with a *spiritual purpose!*
2. They are called to witness to the nations about Jehovah, the only true God.
3. They become a disobedient people, scattered among the nations in judgment.
4. Nevertheless, God's covenants with them are to be fulfilled, and they *will* become a witness to the nations!
5. KEY PERSONS:
    Abraham, the father of the nations
    Moses, the deliverer of God's people
    Joshua, the conqueror of the Land
    David, the beloved King
    Prophets, the spokesmen of God

D. THE CHURCH, A CHOSEN WITNESS

1. After the default of Israel, God created a witness to carry the message of His love to the nations of the world: *Jesus Christ, His Son.*

2. His presence on earth was first felt as He lived in a body miraculously created in a virgin, Mary.

3. He came to the Jews, offering Himself as their King. They rejected Him, finally crucifying Him.

4. They did not know that His death would be the only connecting link between *all* men and Himself.

5. After His death, He arose, lived 40 more days on the earth, and then ascended into the clouds as his followers watched in amazement.

6. Ten days later His Holy Spirit returned. First, He occupied the lives of 120 persons. Quickly, as these 120 shared what had happened to them, thousands of others said, "We want Him to live in us, too!" As they invited Him to do so by repenting of a self-owned life, accepting His death as their connecting link to God, He also came to live in them!

7. *All those people who have been occupied by the Spirit of Christ make up His present Body on earth today.* These people are called "The Church, the Body of Christ."

8. The expression of His Body on earth are *local churches.* It is not possible to be a practicing Christian and develop as God intended unless you are a part of a local Body of Christ. If you do not understand why, take a moment to read 1 Corinthians 12.

14

E. THE KINGDOM OF GOD

1. "Kingdom" means *"reign, rule."*
2. Scripture refers to a time when Christ will reign over the earth, and a time when He will turn His reign over to His Father for the establishment of an eternal Kingdom (1 Corinthians 15:20-26).
3. However, Jesus taught that "the Kingdom of God is in your midst" (Luke 17:21). Thus we see that while the Kingdom is *future,* it's also *present.*
4. Presently, the *Kingdom*, or *Reign*, of our God is within the lives of those who have declared themselves to belong to His "territory."
5. This is a deeply *personal* commitment. No one makes it for you, and no one gives it to you. You must do it for yourself! Romans 10:9-10 gives the simple, yet life-changing, commitment God requires us to make. When we do so, we are a part of the Kingdom of God on earth today. We are "the citizens of the Kingdom," and Jesus *now* reigns over us.
6. But there's another powerful truth: when Jesus died on the cross, His death gave Him the right to claim ownership of *everything!* Abraham Kuyper has said, "There is no sphere of this earth over which Jesus Christ does not say, **'MINE!'** "
7. Thus, when you have become a member of His Kingdom, you live in *two worlds* at the same time. One of them is the "kingdom of this world," and the other is the "Kingdom of our Christ."
8. In order to live in that spiritual world, the Kingdom of our Christ, you are given special faculties to hear, see, and function in it. Your physical faculties of hearing, seeing, etc., are not adequate for life in this spiritual Kingdom. Thus, God's Holy Spirit provides *spiritual gifts* which function in His Kingdom.

15

9. Prophecies about the Kingdom we will study...
   - A coming age for Israel's covenant relationship with God to be completed.
   - A renovation of the earth and its structures.
   - A judgment of the God-Rejecters.
   - A servant-rule assigned to the people of God.

VI. DISTINCTION BETWEEN THE OLD AND NEW TESTAMENTS

OLD TESTAMENT

- PROMISE
- Deep longing
- God OVER us
- Sacrifices—lambs
- Priests—Between man and God; mediators
- Prophets— ("Nabi'"—Those who "speak with their mouths")
- Judgment Suffering of Israel for their sin
- Endless bondage

NEW TESTAMENT

- FULFILLMENT!
- Awareness: God is WITH us
- One sacrifice— THE Lamb
- One Priest—Jesus, our Mediator
- One Prophet—Jesus, who spoke with His entire life
- Judgment—Jesus became our substitute, paying in full the terrible price of our sin

NOTES

VII. TWO TYPES OF PEOPLE IN THE BIBLE

THE GOD REJECTERS	THE GOD FOLLOWERS
GENESIS 4:16-26	*GENESIS 4:25-5:24*
ADAM	ADAM
Cain	Seth
Enoch	Enosh
Irad	Kenan
Mehujael	Mahalalel
Methushael	Jared
Lamech	Enoch

A. THE GOD REJECTERS
   "The nations rage!"
   Death caused by them; after death, torment
   Totally self-centered life style
   Gain significance by what they *DO*
   Length of their lives totally ignored

B. THE GOD FOLLOWERS
   "He gives peace!"
   Death is a *promotion* to a greater life
   God-centered life style
   Gain significance by whom they WORSHIP
   Length of their lives carefully recorded

VIII. BIBLICAL REVIEW:
ISRAEL, A CHOSEN NATION

- Abraham: The Covenant
- Isaac
- Jacob
- Joseph
- Bondage
- 500 Years in Egypt
- Moses
- Joshua
- 12 Tribes, In the Land
- Judges
- "We want a King!"
- David—the Golden Years
- Civil War: Israel, Northern Kingdom
  Judah, Southern Kingdom
- Captivity: Israel to Assyria
  Judah to Babylon
- Judah returns, resettles
- Old Testament concludes
- Revolt of Maccabees: Israel an independent nation
  Romans smash Israel's independence;
  guerilla warfare by Zealots
- Promised Messiah Arrives—rejected!
- Jerusalem barricades itself; seiged; a smashed
  Israel; distributed among the nations
- Vision of future—"The Golden Age"
- "In that day" passages, in both Testaments
- The Remnant: Israel to be restored!
- Unfulfilled covenant; prophecies to be completed!

IX. BIBLICAL REVIEW:
THE CHURCH, A CHOSEN WITNESS

- Jesus, fully God, becomes fully Man
- He offers Himself as King to Israel; rejected
- Offers Himself as King of Kings to all the nations
- Began His life by living inside Israel's culture
- Chooses 12 Jews to be His disciples
- Spends 3 years revealing truth
- Describes "the church" to His disciples
  Church = *Ecclesia* (Greek), *"Called Out Ones"*
  The Church is the "second" Body of Christ!
- Jesus' atonement on the cross *("At-one-ment")*
- His resurrection
- His ascension
- His entrance into His new Body
- His continued activity among men through His Body
- The spread of His Body and His activity from Jews to all the nations of the earth
- The Church is a "grafted limb" into the Tree of Israel, *but in no way replaces Israel!*
- The Future: His personal return in His resurrected Body, establishing His Kingdom
- He completes His work in His 1,000 year reign as King of Kings and Lord of Lords
- The Church reigns with Christ: those who were faithful over much, or little, serve accordingly
- Through Jesus, the Jews enter the "Golden Age"
- The covenant promises of God are fulfilled to His chosen People
- The Kingdom of Our Christ Becomes The Kingdom Of Our God
- Total renovation of all things
- Eternal Kingdom of God: "And He shall reign forever and ever!"

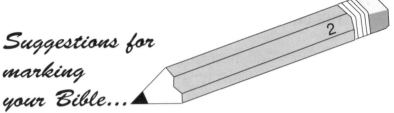

Suggestions for marking your Bible...

1. On the **Title Pages** of the 16 "Story Line" Books, write *A STORY LINE BOOK.*

2. On the **Table of Contents page** in the front of your Bible, write the information about the *sections* of the Old and New Testament books in the margin:

   EXAMPLE:

"The Law" *Also called...* *"The Pentateuch"* *"The Books of Moses"*	Genesis............... Exodus................ Leviticus.............. Numbers............... Deuteronomy..........

3. Mark the secondary books of history, (see page 10) by writing at the head of these books:

Connects to Exodus and Numbers	Leviticus...............
Connects to Numbers and Joshua	Deuteronomy..........
Parallels Judges	Ruth.....................

4. Mark the columns of your Bible with the notes about Genesis 4:16-5:24. Underline the names of the seven men in each category.

5. Find and mark some *"In that day..."* passages in Amos 8:11 and 13, and Micah 4:6-8.

6. Read and underline significant verses in John 1 which speak of Jesus as (1) God; (2) Messiah; (3) Savior of non-Jews.

Unit Three
THE BOOK OF GENESIS
INTRODUCTION
CHAPTERS 1-12

AUTHOR: Moses
THEME: "The Book of Beginnings"
OUTLINE:
(Look for the phrase, "These are the generations of...")

Introduction: The Story of Creation—1:1-2:3
Generations of the Heavens and the Earth—2:4-4:26
Generations of Adam—5:1-6:8
Generations of Noah—6:9-9:29
Generations of the Sons of Noah—10:1-11:9
Generations of Shem—11:10-26
Generations of Terah—11:27-25:11
Generations of Ishmael—25:12-18
Generations of Isaac—25:19-35:29
Generations of Esau—36:1-37:1
Generations of Jacob—37:2-50:26

MAJOR PLACES IN ORDER (Genesis 1-12):
Earth, Eden, Ararat, Babel, Ur of Chaldea, Haran of
Mesopotamia, Canaan, Egypt

MAJOR PEOPLE IN ORDER:
Adam, Eve, Abel, Seth, Noah, Ham, Shem, Japheth,
Abraham, Sarah

AMOUNT OF TIME COVERED:
At least 2,000 years

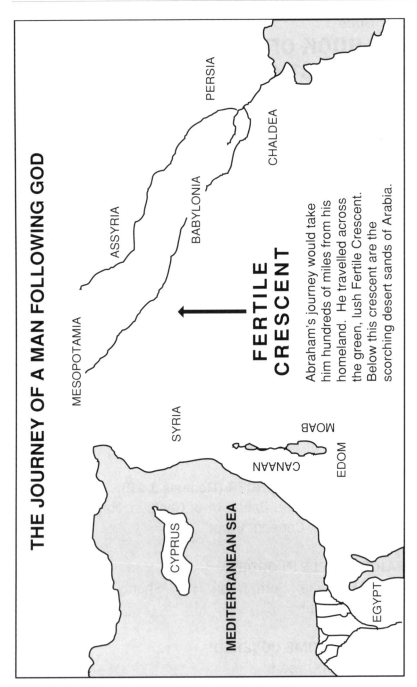

THE JOURNEY OF A MAN FOLLOWING GOD

FERTILE CRESCENT

Abraham's journey would take him hundreds of miles from his homeland. He travelled across the green, lush Fertile Crescent. Below this crescent are the scorching desert sands of Arabia.

MESOPOTAMIA

ASSYRIA

PERSIA

BABYLONIA

CHALDEA

SYRIA

CANAAN

MOAB

EDOM

CYPRUS

MEDITERRANEAN SEA

EGYPT

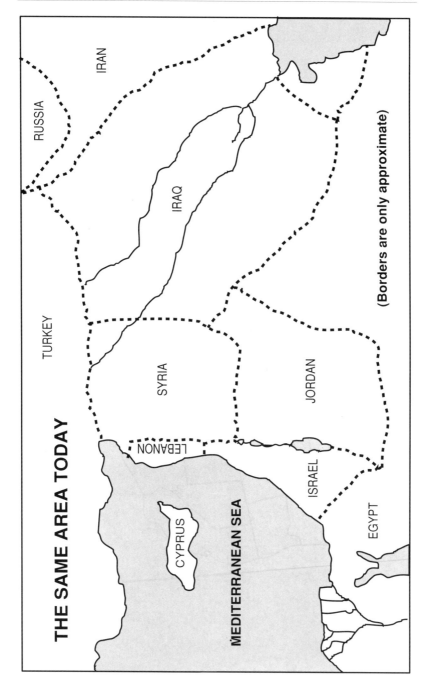

THE SAME AREA TODAY

(Borders are only approximate)

RUSSIA

IRAN

IRAQ

TURKEY

SYRIA

JORDAN

LEBANON

ISRAEL

CYPRUS

MEDITERRANEAN SEA

EGYPT

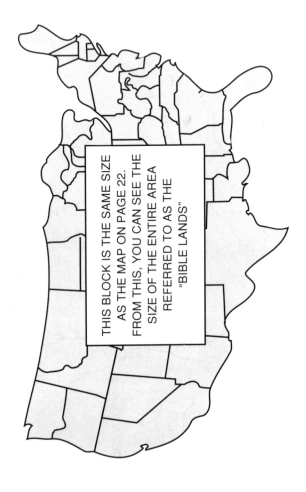

THE LAW OF RECURRENCE

As Author of the Scriptures, the Holy Spirit will use this law over and over, especially in the Prophets:

- **THE OUTLINES OF A SUBJECT ARE GIVEN**

- **THE OUTLINE IS REPEATED; NEW DETAILS ARE ADDED**

EXAMPLE:

GENESIS 1: The account of creation is given in outline
GENESIS 2: The same account repeated, details added:
    2:7:   The nature of man's being
    2:8-14:   The location where man was placed
    2:15-17:   The moral test laid on man
    2:18-25:   The help-mate provided for him

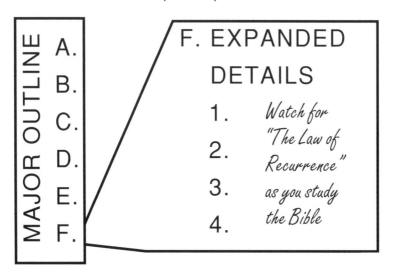

MAJOR OUTLINE
A.
B.
C.
D.
E.
F.

F. EXPANDED DETAILS
1.
2.
3.
4.

Watch for "The Law of Recurrence" as you study the Bible

THE WORD OUTLINE FOR THIS SECTION:

USE THIS OUTLINE TO TAKE NOTES...

- **CREATION (1 and 2)**

- **FALL (3)**

- **DELUGE (5—9)**

- **NATIONS (10 and 11)**

- **ABRAHAM (12)**

How to apply the word of God to your own life...

THE *FACTS* PRINCIPLE

1. Rehearse the story. Get the details in mind.
2. What do these facts suggest?
   - About the *character* of the person?
   - About the *nature* of the person?
3. How do you identify that person's character and nature with your *own*?
4. How can you learn from this person's *good* trait, or squarely challenge that person's *bad* trait which exists in your own life?

EXAMPLE

CHAPTER 12: THE STORY OF ABRAHAM

FACTS OF THE STORY. . .

• God led Abram	• God leads men
• Abram obeyed	• Obedience is the result of faith
• Lot went along	• Abram's insecurity; against God's directions!
• Abram worshipped	• Developed relationship with Jehovah
• Egypt	• Left Promised Land; an act of unbelief
• Passed off Sarai as sister	• Compromised, wanted personal safety; unbelief
• Sarai	• Obeyed her husband (amazing!)
• Abram expelled from Egypt	• Humiliation, the result of disobedience

27

WHAT ARE MY PERSONAL CONCLUSIONS?

1. Every *good* thing is the result of faith.
2. Every *bad* feature in a man is the result of unbelief.
3. God always leads! How do I hear His voice?
4. Those living with a person acting in unbelief will be hurt by it.
5. What a wierd mixture of faith and unbelief in this man! I, too, am such a mixture!
6. How can I squarely face my unbelief and do something about it?
7. What can I do to "stick" where God put me, and not run when *my* "spiritual famine" comes?
8. How has my own reputation been tarnished by my faithless behaviour?

MEDITATION

What could Abraham *ever again* do in Egypt?

Where have I cut myself off from people/areas by my own behavior?

What is the best way to handle such problems?

Is this part of what Paul meant in Philippians when he wrote, **"forgetting those things which are behind..."** ?

(If you *don't forget things which are behind,* the memories could destroy you!)

28

(See the next page for instructions about doing this study...)
LEARNING FROM A STUDY OF ADAM...

STUDY GENESIS 2 and 3

FACTS ABOUT ADAM:

- First Man

- Created in God's own image

- Adam was to have dominion, subdue, replenish, dress, and keep...

- Eve was created from Adam

- Adam was not aware of sin

- Adam lived in total communion with God

- Adam was provided for...every need met by God; the result of total communion was total provision

- Adam was tested...and failed

THESE ARE MY PERSONAL CONCLUSIONS...

Suggestions for marking your Bible...

1. Copy the 10 divisions of Genesis into your Bible. Underline the key phrase *"These are the generations of..."* or its corresponding paraphrase of that term in your translation. Then, print in the margin beside the phrase the title of the Division.

   EXAMPLE:

   Generations of Adam 5:1-6:8   1 This is the book of...
   God created man, He...
   2 He created them...

2. Write this note about "The Law Of Recurrence" in the bottom margin of the page where Chapter 2 begins...

   "The Law Of Recurrence:"—The outline of a subject is given; then, the outline recurs and details are added. Chapter 2 is an excellent example of this.

3. In the margin beside Genesis 3:15, write:

   The Protevangelium: first promise of Jesus' coming in the Bible!

4. Add any other notes from the explanations which you wrote in your notebook and now wish to preserve in your Bible.

5. Do a study of *ADAM*, like the one we did in this lesson on Abram, using Genesis 2 and 3.

Unit Four
THE BOOK OF GENESIS
CHAPTERS 13-28

OUTLINE:

Abram renews his worship—13:1-4
Separation from Lot—13:5-14:24
God "cuts a covenant"—15:1-21
Ishmael, the child of faithlessness—16:1-16
The Abrahamic Covenant—17:1-27
The Angel of the Lord and a promised son—18:1-15
Sodom, Lot, and incest—18:16-19:38
Abraham's weakness recycles—20:1-18
Isaac, Hagar, and Abimilech—21:1-34
Isaac sacrificed—22:1-14
Abrahamic Covenant renewed—22:15-19
Nahor's Sons—22:20-24
Death of Sarah—23:1-20
Isaac and Rebecca—24:1-67
Abraham's death—25:1-11
Ishmael's descendants—25:12-18
Jacob and Esau—25:19-34
Isaac copies his father's deception—26:1-34
Jacob deceives Esau—27:1-28:9
Abrahamic Covenant renewed with Jacob—28:10-22

MAJOR PLACES IN ORDER (CHAPTERS 13-28)

Bethel—Sodom—Gerar—Beersheba—
Nahor, Mesopotamia—Beerlahairoi—Gerar—Haran

MAJOR PEOPLE IN ORDER

Abraham, Sarah, Isaac, Jacob

AMOUNT OF TIME COVERED:

About 120 years

THE WORD OUTLINE FOR THIS SECTION:

ABRAHAM—13-20

ISAAC—21-28

THE HISTORY OF ABRAHAM IN OUTLINE FORM:

His call and move to Canaan—12:1-9
His life in Egypt—12:10-20
His separation from Lot—13-14
His Covenant with God—15
His relationship with Hagar—16
His circumcision as a sign of the Covenant—17
His intercession for Sodom—18
His life at Gerar—20
His blessing in the birth of Isaac—21
His sacrifice of Isaac—22
His choice of a bride for Isaac—24
His child by Keturah—25
His death—25

Note: The missionary heart of God is revealed in this section of scripture. Abraham longs to fully follow Jehovah, longs to be in deeper fellowship with Him. Would we not expect God would send him to a quiet beach, or a lovely mountain retreat where communion would be uninterrupted? Oh, no! His Lord sends His servant to a land inhabited by the vilest tribes imaginable! Human sacrifices, sexual perversion, and cruelty were their way of life. God says to us as well, "Go where the need is great!"

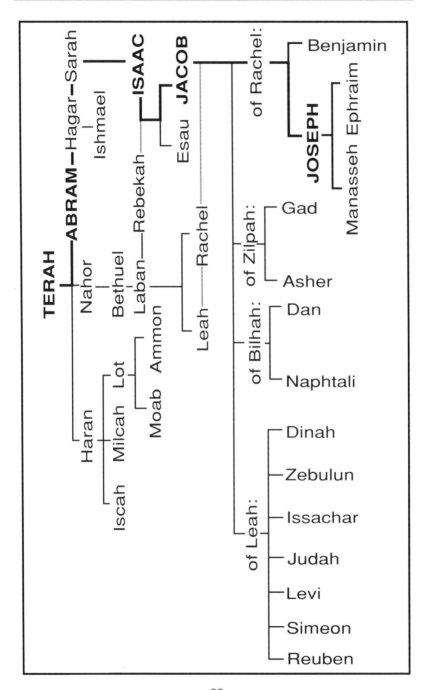

THE "BLESS AND TEST" PRINCIPLE

Abraham's life is a classic illustration of how God works with us. First, He *BLESSES*. Next, He stretches us by *TESTING*. If we pass that test, He *BLESSES* again. If we fail it, we are *TAUGHT SOME MORE,* then *TESTED* again.

EXAMPLES:

- TEST: Will Abraham leave His homeland? PASSES
- TEST: Will he leave *ALL* his relatives? FAILS
- *BLESSED: GIVEN THE LAND*
- TEST: Will he trust during the famine? FAILS
- TEST: Will he trust God for his safety? FAILS

- *RETURNS, WORSHIPS GOD. CYCLE STARTS AGAIN...*

- TEST: Will he give up Lot? PASSES
- *BLESSED: GIVEN ALL THE LAND HE CAN SEE*
- TEST: Will he believe God for a son? FAILS
- *ETC., ETC. ...*

A basic principle of God's working within lives of the "God Followers" is *"BLESS AND TEST."* It is unknown by the "God Rejecters!" God honors our faith by blessing us. At the same time, He does not take away our *freedom!* When we choose a non-faith path, He lets His natural laws operate, causing us to learn the consequences of faithlessness for ourselves—*the hard way!*

Abraham learned a definition of faith:
FAITH IS BELIEVING IT'S SO
    WHEN IT'S NOT SO
      BECAUSE YOU KNOW
        GOD'S GOING TO MAKE IT SO!

JHWH—THE PERSONAL NAME FOR GOD

This name is used for the first time in Genesis 4:1. It is one of the primary names of God used in the Old Testament.*

In Hebrew scripture, when God's activity is that of the all-powerful *Creator,* He is called *ELOHIM.* But when His *personal name* is used, He is called *JHWH. JHWH* means: **"I will always be what I have always been; He Who causes to be; Giver of Life."**

This name is always associated with our God's *personal* relationship with man, not His *impersonal* attributes. Why is His personal name written without vowels? Ancient Jewish scribes considered His personal name too sacred to be spoken by human lips. Therefore whenever this name appeared in scripture which was to be read aloud, they would say, *"Adonai"* (Lord). In the English Bible, this is also done: where the Hebrew says *JHWH,* your Bible says "LORD." Thus, for centuries, the name was never spoken aloud.

In Hebrew, only consonants were written in texts. Vowels were added when the words were spoken. Thus, each generation had to learn the vowels of words by *hearing them,* not *reading them.* It was many centuries after the time of Moses before Hebrew writing was "pointed"—which means vowels were added as "jots and tittles" beneath the strings of consonants. Here is a rough example, using English *consonants* only:

FRGDSLVDTHWRLDTHTHGVHSNLYBGTTNSN

"Pointed" (vowels added), this line would become:

F$_O$R G$_O$D S$_O$ L$_O$V$_E$D TH$_E$ W$_O$RLD

TH$_A$T H$_E$ G$_A$V$_E$ H$_I$S $_O$NLY B$_E$G$_O$TT$_E$N S$_O$N

---

* Scholars use the term "YHWH," or "Yahweh," rather than "JHWH," or "Jehovah." For our study, we will use the popular term, "JHWH." If you proceed into deeper Bible study in the years to come, be aware of these two ways of converting this Hebrew word into the English transliteration.

Here are the possible vowel inserts for JHWH:

J_eh_ov_ah J_ahv_eh J_ah_ov_eh

Usually, we say, "Jehovah."

When, in your Bible, you find phrases similar to these:
   "and the LORD said..."
   "and the LORD caused..."
...the word *Adonai*, LORD, is being used as a substitute for *JHWH (sometimes spelled, JHVH)*. Consider the nature of God as being *very personal* in all these passages.

Where *ELOHIM (a plural noun)* appears in the Hebrew text, the word "GOD" (all in capital letters) is used in our English bible. In these references, the emphasis is upon His power as a *Creator,* rather than upon His deep and personal relationship with men expressed by *JHWH.*

Many adjectives are added to *JHWH,* to further describe His precious nature. Thus, He will be called:

JHWH-JIREH: Jehovah will see or provide or heal
   (Genesis 22:14)
JHWH-NISSI: Jehovah is my banner (Exodus 17:15-16)
JHWH-SHALOM: Jehovah is my peace (Judges 6:23-24)
JHWH-SHAMMAH: Jehovah is coming again (Ezekiel 48:35)
JHWH-TSIDKENU: Jehovah is my righteousness
   (Jeremiah 23:6)
JHWH-ROPHE: Jehovah is my healer

"THE ANGEL OF THE LORD" IN THE BIBLE

In Genesis 16:7, 21:17-18, etc., we are introduced to a very important phrase: *"The Angel of the Lord."* A careful study of the term reveals it to be God Himself, in bodily form, relating personally to men. This is called a *THEOPHANY.*

Carefully study 16:9-13:
> v. 10: Only God could make such a statement!
> v. 11-12: Only God could make such a forecast!
> v. 13: The "Angel of the Lord" was identified by Hagar as God Himself.

In Genesis 18, we again see God in human form, as one of "three men" (verses 2, 13, 14, 33).

In Genesis 22:11 and 15, the "Angel of the Lord" calls to Abraham from heaven.

See also Genesis 31:11, 13; Exodus 3:2,4;
> Joshua 5:13-15 and 6:2;
> Zechariah 1:10-13 and 3:1-2

In Exodus 32:34 and 33:14, along with Isaiah 63:9, the presence of the *Angel of Jehovah* is equivalent to Jehovah's presence. The *Angel of the Lord* thus appears as a manifestation of Jehovah Himself!

Perhaps this will help you understand more clearly all Jesus meant when He said, "Before Abraham was, *I AM"* (in Hebrew, the letters for the word JHWH).

Some Bible scholars thus consider *The Angel of JHWH* to be none other than the pre-incarnate Christ, who is the "Word" described as being "in the beginning" (John 1:1).

COVENANT RELATIONSHIPS

When an ancient Covenant was created, the term *"cut a covenant"* is used in the Old Testament. This describes all or part of these activities:

1. An animal was halved, cut from nose to tail along the spine.
2. The two halves were laid out on the ground, with the blood on the ground between the halves.
3. The two men stood facing each other upon the blood, with the halves of the animal on either side.
4. They pledged their lives to each other.
5. They committed all their wealth to each other.
6. They exchanged belts and swords.
7. They named their relatives, each becoming personally responsible as a *"GO'EL" (Near-Kinsman)* for the relatives of the other person in the event of an untimely death.
8. They pledged their *HESED, "loving-kindness,"* to one another. This meant that they would remain committed to each other regardless of what evil deed the other might commit in the future!
9. They walked in a "circle 8" around the halved animal, so each man stood in the place of the other one at the end of the walk.
10. They cut their wrists with a knife, grasped hands, and mingled their dripping blood as a sign of their oath.
11. They exchanged their *very names,* each adding to his own the name of the other person.
12. They rubbed charcoal into their cuts, making them permanently visible to all.
13. Finally, they planted a tree upon the blood, to mark the place where the Covenant had been cut.

A *MOST* UNUSUAL "COVENANT CUTTING!"

GENESIS 15:12-21...

V. 12: "A deep sleep" in Hebrew refers to a *trance*. God had put Abram into a non-participative state for this Covenant-cutting. It is a "one way" Covenant, in which God provides everything in the Covenant *without any qualifications to be met by Abram!*

V. 13-16: The terms of this Covenant are clearly set forth. It is what God will do for Abram. Nothing in return is required.

V. 17: A "smoking pot" and a "flaming torch" make the "figure 8" around the animals. They remind us of the smoking cloud by day and the pillar of fire by night (God Himself!) that will lead Israel in the wilderness journey.

V. 18: The Covenant promise of God to Abram is given!

GENESIS 17:1-8 . . .

God now reviews this Covenant with Abram. One significant Covenant event is the exchange of names! The "HA" from J**HA**WEH, the root of JHWH, is added to Abram: Abra**HA**m.

And, note this well! From this time on, JHWH will describe Himself as **"THE GOD OF ABRAHAM."**

In addition, Sar**ai** will have a new name...Sar**HA** (Sarah), as explained in 17:15. The Covenant with this man and his wife is irrevocable, and becomes the foundation for our later prophetic studies.

THE IMPORTANCE OF THE ABRAHAMIC COVENANT

Note its terms in Chapter 17. . .

This is an *unconditional* covenant, and it is still in effect. Because it is, and because it has not yet been fulfilled, there are future things which we know will happen. This will strongly shape the way we read the rest of the Bible—looking for prophecies in which God's Covenant to Israel will be kept.

THE RITE OF CIRCUMCISION

Nothing will become a more important reminder of God's Covenant with every Son of Abraham than the rite of circumcision! In every Covenant, there was the cutting of the skin of the wrist, and a permanent scar to remind all of the commitment made by two men.

In this case, the source from which every new Jewish child will be sired by a Jewish man is to be "cut and scarred" by the Covenant sign, circumcision. In the fathering of *each new child,* God will remind the parents again of His Covenant with Abraham. And, soon after birth, this rite of circumcision will remind each *new generation* of its special Covenant with God. To this day, there are virtually no Jewish men who are not circumcised, thus keeping the everlasting reminder of the Covenant!

In Exodus 4:24-26, Moses almost dies from God's judgment because he has yielded to his non-Jewish wife and has *not* circumcised his sons. Only their circumcision saved his life! His sons had to bear "the scar of the Covenant."

Suggestions for marking your Bible...

1. Copy the outline for this Unit into your Bible.

2. Write beside Genesis 16:7:

   First use of JHWH as the personal name for God.

3. In the margin beside Genesis 16:7, write:

   First use of "The Angel of JHWH"

4. Add any notes from the explanations about Covenants which you now wish to preserve in your Bible.

5. Do a study of *LOT,* like the one we did on Abram, using Genesis 13 and 14.

   (See the next page for the outline for this study...)

(See the previous page for instructions about doing this study...)
LEARNING FROM A STUDY OF LOT...

Study GENESIS 13 and 14:

FACTS ABOUT LOT:

THESE ARE MY PERSONAL CONCLUSIONS:

Unit Five
THE BOOK OF GENESIS
CHAPTERS 29-45

OUTLINE:
Jacob's years at Haran—29:1-31:10
Parenthesis—The call back to Bethel—31:11-13
The flight of Jacob—31:14-55
Jacob becomes Israel—32
Jacob meets Esau—33:1-17
Jacob's worship in self-will—33:18-20
Jacob reaps the harvest of his evil years—34
Jacob's return to Bethel—35:1-15
Death of Rachel, birth of Benjamin—35:16-26
Death of Isaac—35:27-29
The generations of Esau—36
Joseph, the beloved of his father—37:1-7
Joseph sold into slavery—37:8-36
Parenthesis—The shame of Judah—38
Joseph's character tested—39-40
The dream of Pharaoh—41:1-13
Joseph exalted in Egypt—41:14-57
Joseph faces his brothers—42-44
Joseph reveals himself—45

MAJOR PLACES IN ORDER (Genesis 29-45):
Haran of Mesopotamia, Canaan, Egypt

MAJOR PEOPLE IN ORDER:
Jacob, Joseph, Judah

AMOUNT OF TIME COVERED:
About 80 years

THE WORD OUTLINE FOR OUR SECTION:

Jacob, 29-36

Joseph, 37-45

THE HISTORY OF JACOB:

Birth—25
Purchase of the birthright—25
Deception of his father—27
Flight to Haran—28
Marriage and prosperity—29,30
Return to Canaan—31-35

JOSEPH, A TYPE OF CHRIST

JOSEPH	**CHRIST**
30:24—Took away Rachel's reproach	Romans 8:1—Took away sin's reproach
Father's love for him	See Matthew 3:17
Suffering caused by hatred of brothers	See John 15:25
Deliverance; exalted to the throne	See Acts 2:22-24
Reveals himself to his brothers	See Zechariah 12:10

ELECTION IN THE BIBLE: 1 PETER 1:2

Esau and Jacob a classic illustration of Election
- Jacob: election unto salvation
- Esau: election unto condemnation

"Chosen according to the foreknowledge of God the Father..."

The word to Rebekah was a prophecy. Its purpose was to create long-term faith within these parents, which would carry them through the heartaches caused by their own wrongdoings and those of their children. They had the assurance that right and truth would prevail in the end.

Note: Because God foreknows, it does not mean He is the cause of what He knows! If you see a child run into the street, and foreknow a speeding car will hit the child, you have not caused the child to be hurt.

"...by the sanctifying work of the Spirit..."

God, knowing those whose hearts are bent toward Him in the line of the "God-Followers," *sanctifies,* or *sets apart,* these special people. Even when a person has not yet made the free choice to follow God and live righteously, God knows that time will come, and responds to that life accordingly.

ELECTION, CONTINUED

"...that you may obey Jesus Christ and be sprinkled with His blood..."

Obedience resulted from faith on Jacob's part. God's response was to honor his obedience by providing redemption through the blood of Jesus Christ.

HERE IS AN ANSWER TO A THORNY QUESTION!

How were the people of the Old Testament "saved," since they lived before the coming of Christ and before His atoning death on the cross? Was there a different way of faith for them? No!

Luke 18:7: "Shall not God bring about justice for His elect, who cry to Him day and night...?"

Ephesians 1:4-7: "Just as *He chose us in Him before the foundation of the world,* that we should be holy and blameless before Him. In love He predestined us to adoption as sons *through Jesus Christ* to Himself, according to the kind intention of His will, to the praise of the glory of His grace, which He freely bestowed on us in the Beloved. In Him we have redemption through His blood, the forgiveness of our trespasses, according to the riches of His grace..."

The giving of salvation came to every Old Testament person in exactly the same way it comes to us: *through faith in the Redeemer,* promised to mankind in Genesis 3:16!

ELECTION, CONTINUED

Those God knew would seek His face *(called in this study the "God-Followers")* were "elected" unto salvation. Those God knew would use their freedom of choice to reject His fellowship were "elected" unto condemnation. The important thing to remember is that each person is free to make the choice. God, knowing the future, acts upon His knowledge of what that choice will be, long before it has been made.

WHAT IS GOD'S CHOICE FOR EVERY MAN?

Exactly the same for all: "He was not willing that any should perish, but that all should come to salvation." God no more damns some people to hell and capriciously chooses others for heaven, than a judge in a courtroom condemns some to be hung and others to be set free! Your free choice *causes* the consequences you will face.

37:35—SHEOL

This is the first use of this term, used 65 times in the Old Testament. It is described as the place of the departed spirits. It is often spoken of as simply the grave, where all activities cease.

Without revelation from God, the natural man sees the grave as the end of everything (see Ecclesiastes 9:5, 10). In Ecclesiastes, this is the case. Beware of the cults (Mormonism, Christian Science, Jehovah's Witnesses) which take passages like this one and try to prove the Bible teaches there is no life after death for the unbeliever!

SHEOL, CONTINUED

Scripture reveals SHEOL as a place of sorrow (2 Samuel 22:6, Psalm 18:5, 116:3), into which the wicked are sent (Psalm 9:17), and where they are fully conscious (Isaiah 14:9-17).

The SHEOL of the Old Testament and the HADES of the New Testament (Luke 16:23) are identical.

NOTES FROM LECTURE:

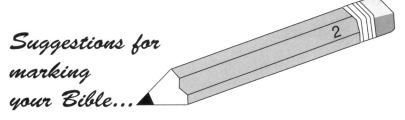

Suggestions for marking your Bible...

1. Copy the outline into your Bible.

2. Write beside Genesis 37:35:

    First use of Sheol

3. Add any notes about Election or Sheol, which you want to keep, in the margins of your Bible.

4. Add any other notes from the explanations which you wish to preserve in your Bible.

5. Complete the Study of Jacob on the following page, using the helps for personal study you have been given in the course.

LEARNING FROM A STUDY OF JACOB...

GENESIS 29—33

FACTS ABOUT JACOB:

THESE ARE MY PERSONAL CONCLUSIONS:

Unit Six

THE BOOK OF GENESIS CHAPTERS 46-50

THE BOOK OF EXODUS CHAPTERS 1-13

Genesis 46-50:

OUTLINE:
Jacob's journeys to Egypt: 46
Jacob and his descendants exalted: 47:1-26
The last days of Jacob: 47:27-50:14
The fear of Joseph's brothers: 50:15-21
The last days and death of Joseph: 50:22-26

MAJOR PLACES IN ORDER (Genesis 46-50):

Egypt, Mamre in Canaan

MAJOR PEOPLE IN ORDER:

Jacob and Joseph

AMOUNT OF TIME COVERED:

17 years

NOTES:

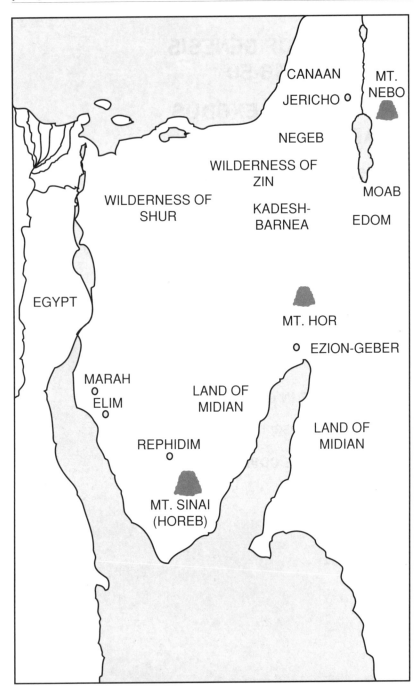

CANAAN
JERICHO o
MT. NEBO

NEGEB

WILDERNESS OF ZIN

WILDERNESS OF SHUR

KADESH-BARNEA

MOAB

EDOM

EGYPT

MT. HOR

o EZION-GEBER

MARAH
ELIM

LAND OF MIDIAN

REPHIDIM

LAND OF MIDIAN

MT. SINAI (HOREB)

Exodus 1-13

OUTLINE:

Israel in Egypt—1
The coming of Moses—2
The call of Moses—3, 4:1-18
The return of Moses to Egypt—4:19-31
The contest with Pharaoh, part 1—5:1-23
Jehovah answers Moses' prayer—6:1-13
The families of Israel—6:14-27
The renewed commissions—6:28-7:13
The contest with Pharaoh, part 2—7:14-11:10
The Passover—12:1-36
First stage of the Journey—12:37-51
The firstborn set apart for Jehovah—13:1-19
Second stage of the journey—13:20-22

MAJOR PLACES IN ORDER (Exodus 1-13):

Egypt, Midian, Egypt

MAJOR PEOPLE IN ORDER:

Moses, Pharaoh

AMOUNT OF TIME COVERED:

215 Years

THE WORD OUTLINE FOR OUR SECTION:

MOSES, 1-6

CONTEST WITH PHARAOH, 7-13

A QUICK LOOK AT EXODUS:

Seventy Jewish people entered Egypt.

During 400+ years, they multiplied to about 3 1/2 million.

They were enslaved.

God selected Moses to deliver them.

Pharaoh resisted the request of Moses to free the people.

Ten plagues were required to break his rebellion.

The Passover, crossing of the Red Sea, manna, quail from heaven, water from rocks, follow.

Wilderness journey takes Israel to Mt. Sinai, where God gave His law.

It involved 613 commandments,
    instructions for building the Tabernacle,
        and assignment of priestly duties.

NOTES:

THE EXCUSES OF MOSES

3:11:   Personal inadequacy in light of past.

3:13:   Religious experience considered inadequate; knowledge and experience limited.

4:1:   Others would reject him as a spiritual man.
Felt his personal testimony would be discounted.

4:10:   Did not possess talent equal to the task.

THE DISCLOSURE OF GOD'S NAME

(See earlier notes on *JHWH*)

Exodus 3:13-14— *JHWH:* the verb form for *"I will be"* is identical to this. The use of the double verb here, "I AM WHO I AM" means, *"I shall continually be that which I have always been;"* or, *"I will be all that is necessary as the occasion will arise."*

Note verse 15: "This is My name forever, and this is My memorial name to all generations."

NOTES:

THE TEN PLAGUES

WATER TURNS TO BLOOD

FROGS

LICE

FLIES

DEATH OF CATTLE

BOILS

HAIL

LOCUSTS

DARKNESS

DEATH OF THE FIRSTBORN

NOTE:

The significance of these plagues is not their uniqueness.
Every single one of these plagues were already known in Egypt.
Their significance is in the fact that God "made the clock speed
up," compressing the equivalent of *years* of plagues into just
a few hours.

In addition, **these plagues attacked the areas of sacred beings and objects worshipped in the religion of Egypt!**

The waters of the Nile were most sacred...

Frogs, gnats, and insects were worshipped...
Intricate jewelry was fashioned after them, using gold and precious stones. (We still have scarab or beetle jewelry from the Middle East being sold today).

Bulls were worshipped...
so much so that they were mummified! Apis, the Black Bull, was worshipped in the second largest temple in Egypt, located in Memphis.

The boils were caused by the soot...
(9:8) taken from kilns where gold was smelted. The soot caused boils. *Gold was also considered a sacred object,* an object of actual worship.

Hail was unknown...
Less than an inch of rain per year fell in Cairo. Judgment fell upon their fields, their possessions, *all that they cherished!*

Locusts were carved in gold on the crown of Pharaoh, and were actually worshipped.

The Sun was an object of particularly significant worship in Egypt; it was blotted out!

The Pharaoh was considered a Divine God...
his son, his heir, *also Divinity.*

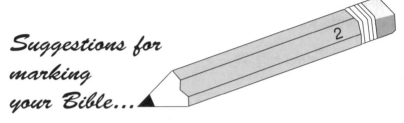

Suggestions for marking your Bible...

1. Copy the outline into your Bible.

2. Write beside Exodus 3:13:

   Means "I shall continually be that which I have always been."

3. Add any notes about Moses' excuses, which you want to preserve, in the margins of your Bible.

4. Add any other notes from the explanations which you want to preserve in your Bible.

Unit Seven
EXODUS 14-18; EXODUS 19-23
with DEUTERONOMY 4-13;
EXODUS 24-28 and 39;
EXODUS 29
with DEUTERONOMY 17 and 18

OUTLINES
Exodus 14-18; 19-23
13:17-15:21—At The Red Sea
15:22-26—At Marah
15:27-16:36—At Elim And The Wilderness Of Sin
17:1-7—At Rephidim
17:8-16—Victory Over Amalek
18:1-27—Visit Of Jethro
19:1-6—The Offer Of A Covenant
19:7-23:33—The Specifications Of The Covenant

Deuteronomy 4-13 (parallels Exodus 19-23)
4:1-40—Pleas For Trust And Obedience
4:41-43—Cities Of Refuge East Of Jordan
4:44-49—Historical Note
5:1-2—Pleas: Concerning Conditions Of Possession
5:3-6:9—Plea: Keep The Law Because Of Promises
6:10-25—Plea: Keep The Law Because Of What The
    Future Will Be
7—Plea: Keep The Law Because Of Necessary
    Separation From Idolatry
8—Plea: Keep The Law Because Of Trials
9-10—Plea: Keep The Law Because Of The
    Intercession Of Moses
11:1-7—Plea: Keep The Law Because Of Deliverance At
    Red Sea

11:8-25—Plea: Keep The Law Because Of Dependence
  On Jehovah For Rain
11:26-32— A Blessing And A Curse Set Before Them
12-13—Living As A "Holy People," Part 1

Exodus 24-29
24:1-11—The Ratification Of The Covenant
24:12-18—Moses Called To The Mount
25:1-27:21—The Tabernacle
28—The Priestly Garments
  (see 39: Making the Priestly Garments)
29—The Priestly Installation

Deuteronomy 17 and 18 (parallels Exodus 29)
17—Commands about Kings
18—Maintaining of the Levites

MAJOR PLACES IN ORDER (Exodus 14-29):

Red Sea, Wilderness, Sinai

MAJOR PEOPLE IN ORDER:

Moses, Aaron, Joshua

AMOUNT OF TIME COVERED: 1 Year (?)

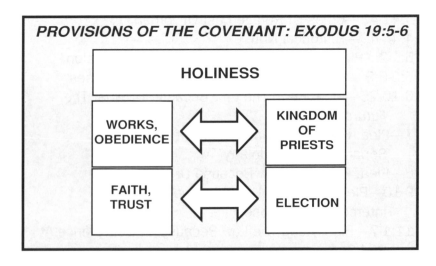

PROVISIONS OF THE COVENANT: EXODUS 19:5-6

HOLINESS

WORKS, OBEDIENCE ⟺ KINGDOM OF PRIESTS

FAITH, TRUST ⟺ ELECTION

THE TEN COMMANDMENTS:

Note the two divisions:

1. _____

2. _____

Note there is nothing new in the Law. *Conscience* has already forbidden each area.

Forbidden by conscience, because already forbidden by *the nature of things,* and the nature of things is...*God!*

The Law is written as *negatives,* for it presupposes the existence of sin and evil desire in *every human heart!*

Chapter 21: SLAVERY IN THE BIBLE

God tolerated it for one reason only..."*because of the hardness of men's hearts*" (Matthew 19:8). He never endorsed it!

It was useless for God to forbid it until after man's heart was sensitized to Christ's Lordship. Christianity *alone*, in the history of the world, was able to stop this practice. No other political or social structure ever dealt effectively with it (See Galatians 3:28). In the day of Jesus, it is estimated that as many as *half* of all the people in the Roman Empire were slaves.

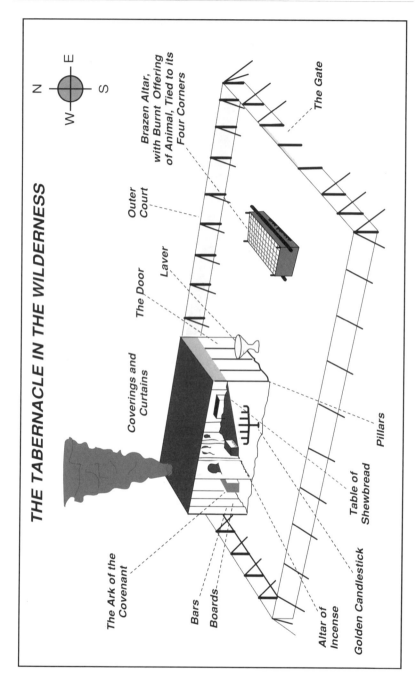

THE TABERNACLE IN THE WILDERNESS

The Gate

Brazen Altar,
with Burnt Offering
of Animal, Tied to its
Four Corners

Outer
Court

Laver

The Door

Coverings and
Curtains

The Ark of the
Covenant

Bars

Boards

Altar of
Incense

Golden Candlestick

Table of
Shewbread

Pillars

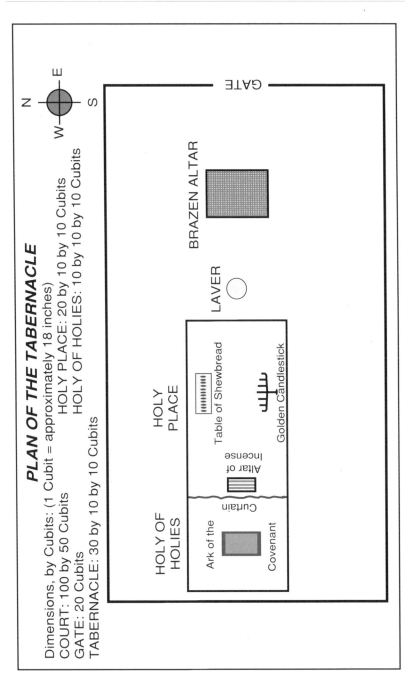

PLAN OF THE TABERNACLE

Dimensions, by Cubits: (1 Cubit = approximately 18 inches)
COURT: 100 by 50 Cubits
GATE: 20 Cubits
TABERNACLE: 30 by 10 by 10 Cubits
HOLY PLACE: 20 by 10 by 10 Cubits
HOLY OF HOLIES: 10 by 10 by 10 Cubits

GATE

BRAZEN ALTAR

LAVER

HOLY PLACE

Table of Shewbread

Golden Candlestick

Altar of Incense

Curtain

HOLY OF HOLIES

Ark of the Covenant

28:1-30:11: THE MEANING OF ATONEMENT

The Priesthood and Service teach the meaning of the atonement (at-one-ment), or perfect spiritual union.

1. The provision of a covering for sin

2. The privilege of communion with Jehovah

3. The assurance of holiness

THE TABERNACLE, THE TEMPLE, AND THE SACRIFICES

THE TABERNACLE:

THE TEMPLE OF SOLOMON:

THE TEMPLE, REBUILT AFTER THE CAPTIVITY:

THE TEMPLE, REBUILT BY HEROD:

THE FUTURE TEMPLE IN PROPHECY:

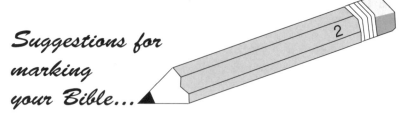

Suggestions for marking your Bible...

1. Copy the outline into your Bible.

2. Write beside Exodus 17:14 and 34:27:

    Note: proof that Moses is the author of Pentateuch

3. Write beside Exodus 23:20-33:

    Note: <u>The Angel Of Jhwh</u> is the Angel of the Covenant: Christ is the assurance of the assurances!

4. Add any other notes from the explanations which you wish to preserve in your Bible.

Unit Eight

EXODUS 30-38 AND 40

OUTLINE

The Altar of Incense—30:1-10

Atonement for Each Person—30:11-16

The Laver of Bronze—30:17-21

The Anointing Oil and Incense—30:22-38

Appointment of Skilled Workmen—31:1-11

The Sabbath—31:12-18

Forty Days and Nights Without God—32-34

The Tabernacle Instituted—35-38

The Tabernacle Erected—40

MAJOR PLACES IN ORDER (Exodus 30-38 and 40):

Sinai

MAJOR PEOPLE IN ORDER:

Moses, Aaron, Bezalel

AMOUNT OF TIME COVERED:

A few months

NOTES ON CHAPTER 30:

THE ALTAR OF INCENSE
Symbolical of the place of prayer.
> *"May my prayer be counted as incense before Thee; The lifting up of my hands as the evening offering."* *(Psalm 141:2)*

THE ATONEMENT MONEY
A special means of reminding each person that he was not his own. Think of it as you would the leasing of a piece of land, which has an annual fee required. The word for "contribution" is literally "heave offering"—an offering freely given by the giver. It was a way of saying, "I recognize I do not own my own life!"

THE PLACE OF CLEANSING
The Laver of Bronze—a type of the word of God. See 38:8 for the source of the bronze. It was a mirror-like, reflecting surface. Unless we wash, our fellowship with God dies! (See John 13:6-10—"If I wash thee not, thou hast no part with me.")

THE ANOINTING OIL AND THE INCENSE
THE OIL—A powerful, oil-based perfume. All objects and all priests were anointed with it. The fragrance revealed the object or person was, in a special way, set apart (sanctified) for the special activity of God among men. Everywhere the anointed ones went, their special fragrance marked them. Because of it, Aaron and his sons were prohibited from sharing in the burial of Nadab and Abihu. One odor—one use!

THE INCENSE

Symbolical of prayer. A beautiful study for you! See Psalm 141:2; Luke 1:10-11; Revelation 5:8 and 8:4,5. *(Be sure to underline these verses as you read them and "key" them with your own marginal reference to "Cf. Exodus 30:22ff.")*

NOTES ON CHAPTER 31:

Where did we get the idea that our skills are self- developed, or came to us from our parents? Verses 1-11 point out that GOD has put the skills we possess into our lives, and they belong to Him. It's not just a preacher who is "special!" Bezalel had both natural and spiritual skills for his life's work.

THE SABBATH

Man is essentially a spiritual being. He must make time to be with God. It is a physical, a family, and a national necessity. The person who secularizes life for weeks at a time is a fool! Note verse 17: even in eternity the Sabbath will be kept!

For the Christian, the day changes from a Sabbath Saturday to Sunday, called "The Lord's Day," to make the resurrection day of our Lord more significant than even the creation of the earth. *However, the special significance of the Sabbath, taught here, does not change as it moves from Saturday to Sunday.* Note verse 14: was it important to God, or an "option" to be remembered by those who are not preoccupied with other things?

FORTY DAYS AND NIGHTS WITHOUT GOD!
(Chapters 32-34)

NOTES:

1. Rejection of _____ leadership

2. Aaron's reasoning: 32:25—_____!

3. Sarcasm—32:4—Shock treatment didn't work.

4. Syncretism—_____

5. Moses' anger—destroyed _____

   (32:19)

6. Forced to _____ their sin—32:20

7. "The furnace made it!"—32:24

8. _____ men died (heads of households)

   Why? _____

9. Moses offered _____ as the sacrifice!—32:30-32

10. "Book"—Custom of that day:

   _____

   _____

11. Chapter 33: God said, "I'll send an _____!"

12. The Tent of Meeting—33:7

13. "Let me know Thy _____!"—33:13

14. Chapter 34: Moses on Sinai, alone with God!

15. Shining _____—34:29

   (His adequacy came from being with God!)

THE INSTITUTION OF THE TABERNACLE

35:5—The "heave" or "wave" offering...
Hebrew is *teruma*—used when personal possessions are freely given to God.

Note there was something for everyone to bring, and something for all to do. Note verse 29—it was a heart relationship which led them to bring their possessions!

THE CURTAINS FOR THE TABERNACLE

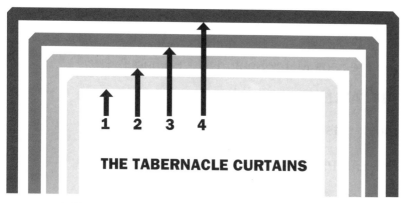

THE TABERNACLE CURTAINS

LAYER 1: Fine linen, colors, gold clasps
LAYER 2: Goat's hair, black, brass clasps
LAYER 3: Ram's skins, red, no clasps
LAYER 4: Porpoise skins, grey, no clasps

Standing inside, looking up, you see blue, purple, scarlet, with woven cherubim: Christ's deity pictured. The second layer was Goat's hair: Christ's humanity pictured. The third layer, red, depicts Christ, our Substitute (see Genesis 22:13-14). See Isaiah 53:2-3 to understand the drab, grey outer covering: *what does it represent about Christ?*

THE BOARDS OF THE TABERNACLE

One cubit=about 18 inches

The size of the outer courtyard fencing was about 175 feet long, 87 1/2 feet wide, and 8 1/3 feet high.

The size of the tabernacle building was about 45 feet long, 18 feet wide, and 18 feet high. All boards were overlaid with pure gold. All sockets were of pure silver.

THE VEIL

Inside that veil, in the Holy of Holies: one man, alone with God! That veil was the thickness of a man's fist...

THE ARK

The precious Mercy Seat: see 1 Samuel 6:19

THE TABLE OF SHEWBREAD

The priests fed on that bread daily.

THE LAMPSTAND

Six=Man; *One*=God
Pictures the church!
Seven branches, one candlestick: See Matthew 5:14-16

THE ALTAR OF INCENSE

The place of prayer in the life of the believer

THE BRAZEN ALTAR

The sacrificed lamb took away the sin of one man; and each lamb, without spot or blemish, was a sign of The Lamb of God, Who would take away the sin of the world! Later, the writer of Hebrews would make this clear.

THE SIGNIFICANCE OF THE TABERNACLE . . .

1. This place of worship was manufactured from the items contributed by the worshipers. They bought nothing; only what they *gave* was used for its construction!

2. It was in the *center* of the camp, not on its edge. Their worship was the central point of all they did.

3. It was mobile. Wherever they went, their worship was to remain central to their lifestyle.

4. The way to God always began with a sacrifice for sin. There was no thought that man had a "spark of goodness" in him that might make it possible to bypass the brazen altar.

5. The Laver reminds us that we must be cleansed before entering into the place of priestly service (1 John 1:9).

6. Trace the fire which is used in the Tabernacle: first, it is used under the sacrifice. Where does it go from there? Do you see the significance of this? What does this say to your heart?

7. The veil—thick as a man's fist—would one day be ripped in half, from the top down. This barrier between men and God would be torn by the Father, and the "middle wall of partition" separating God and man would be removed. Do you know when this happened? (Read the last chapters of the Gospels to find the answer!)

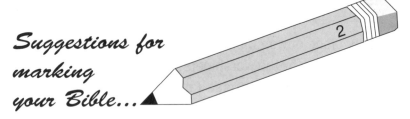

Suggestions for marking your Bible...

1. Copy the outline into your Bible.

2. Write beside Exodus 35:5:
   *Note: Hebrew Tenuphah:,
   used when personal possessions
   are freely given to God,
   not from obligation*

3. Write beside Exodus 35:20:

   *Note: They went home to
   remember what God had
   done for them.*

4. Add any other notes from the explanations which you now wish to preserve in your Bible.

Unit Nine
LEVITICUS 1-10
LEVITICUS 11-15 with
DEUTERONOMY 14-15
LEVITICUS 16-20; NUMBERS 1-10

OUTLINE

Leviticus 1-7—Laws Concerning Sacrifices
    1:1-17—Burnt Offering
    2:1-16—Meal Offering
    3:1-17—Peace Offering
    4:1-7:38—Laws Concerning Offerings
Leviticus 8-10—Historical Interlude: The Institution of the Priesthood
Leviticus 11-15—Laws Concerning Purity and Impurity

(DEUTERONOMY 14 parallels LEVITICUS 11-15)

Deuteronomy 15—The Sabbatic Year
    15:1-11—The Remission of Debts
    15:12-18—The Bondslave Relationship
    15:19-23—Consecration of first-born in the flock
Leviticus 16—The Law for the Day of Atonement
Leviticus 17—The Law for Sacrifice
Leviticus 18:1-19:21—Laws Commanding Holiness and Non-Conformity with Pagan Practices

Numbers 1-4—The Commands for a Census of the People
Numbers 5-10—The Commands for Purity of the People
    5—A Test for Jealousy
    6—The Nazirite Vow and the Aaronic Benediction
    7—The Offerings of the 12 Leaders
    8-9—Levites separated, the Passover observed
    10—The Covering Cloud and the Silver Trumpets

MAJOR PLACES IN ORDER (Exodus 30-38 and 40):

Sinai

MAJOR PEOPLE IN ORDER:

Moses, Aaron, Bezalel

AMOUNT OF TIME COVERED:

A few months, or even weeks

NOTES:

Hebrew title: *"And he called..."*
(the first Hebrew word of the book).

Leviticus means "The Book of the Priests"
Since we as believers are priests, there are *many symbolical truths* waiting for us in the study of this book.

The key to this book is 26:11-12.

AN OVERVIEW OF LEVITICUS

How do we draw near to God?

1-7—Drawing near to God, using the sacrifices.
8-10—Drawing near to God, using the Priesthood.
11-15—Drawing near to God: cleanness demanded.
16—Day of Atonement provided for each one.
17-25—In contrast to the pagan neighbors, the People of God were to be holy in ALL particulars.
26—Israel's choices will bring blessing or curse!
27—Our relationships under God to property.

THE SACRIFICES IN LEVITICUS 1-5

These sacrifices are *only* for those who are in a covenant relationship with God. They sound "odd" to all others!

Let us approach Leviticus remembering Paul's words about the Pentateuch, found in 1 Corinthians 10:11:

> *"Now these things happened to them as an example, and they were written for our instruction, upon whom the ends of the ages have come."*

Note the progression:

BURNT OFFERING
> Total sacrifice. Romans 12:1-2.
> Surrender of my life to Christ.

MEAL OFFERING
> Giving my labors (fruit) to Christ.

PEACE OFFERING
> Part to God, part eaten by Priest, part eaten by giver: *fellowship!*

SIN OFFERING
> For *inadvertent* sins, not *willful!* (See 1 John 5:16-17)

TRESPASS OFFERING
> I am to restore, *adding 20%,* to those who have been trespassed against by me.

THE CONSECRATION OF A PRIEST

CLEANSING

GIRDING

CONSECRATING (SETTING APART)

OFFERINGS:

1. THE BURNT OFFERING

2. THE OFFERING OF "FILLING"

3. THE HEAVE OFFERING

PRIEST IS COVERED WITH OIL AND BLOOD!
   Oil=Sacred, set apart
   Blood=Clean, through another's sacrifice

LEVITICUS 10: 1—STRANGE FIRE!

Note these were Aaron's own sons! How tragic was the sorrow caused in the hearts of those who remained after they died. "Strange Fire" always leaves pain in the lives of others.

THE DAY OF ATONEMENT

Note the occasion—16:1
Two offerings: one for salvation, one for sanctification: 16:3
The "scapegoat"—16:10 (Literally, the goat of removal). *16:15 ties to Hebrews 9:25,* which tells us something significant about the sacrifice of Christ on the cross.

THE LAW FOR SACRIFICE

17:4—Note the place for sacrifice: ONLY ONE DOOR!

17:10-12—Eating Blood

Cf. Genesis 9:4 and Acts 15:19-20
> The blood is for God, and is to be held in deepest reverence.
> It is *from* God, and is a substitute for our sin.

Why were they not to eat blood?
> To do so was a sign of self-redemption. Ingesting it was
> to take from it the sacredness of the truth that *the blood
> is for God, not man!*

*Note 1 Peter 1:18-19—the blood is God's only price of
redemption.*

NUMBERS: ORGANIZED AS A CONQUERING ARMY

Leaving Sinai, Israel marches forth as Jehovah's conquering
army, with God himself leading them! The book graphically
portrays Israel as the servants of God. They are to establish
His Kingdom. They have His power to do so.

At the same time, we are told how Israel broke the covenant
relationship God had established with them. The opportunity
to serve was available—and the freedom to *not* serve was
also available. Israel was organized as an army, but they didn't
have the desire to do battle in Jehovah's name. Thus, as
we read through the book we are saddened by the results
of disobedience.

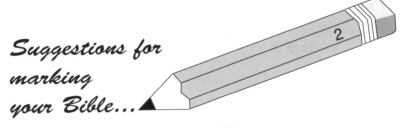

Suggestions for marking your Bible...

1. Copy the Outline into your Bible.

2. Underline Leviticus 26:11-12. Write beside them:
   Note: Key to Leviticus

3. Write marginal comments beside the offerings which are described in the first five chapters of Leviticus.

4. Add any other notes from the explanations which you now wish to preserve in your Bible.

Unit Ten
LEVITICUS 21-24 with NUMBERS 28-29 and DEUTERONOMY 16; NUMBERS 11-12; NUMBERS 13-14 with DEUTERONOMY 1

OUTLINE

PART 1: LAWS FOR LIVING CLOSE TO GOD

Leviticus 21-22—Laws For The Priesthood
    21—Laws For Personal Purity
    22—Laws For Eating and Offering Sacrifices
Leviticus 23—Laws Of The Sacred Calendar
Leviticus 24—Laws For The Tabernacle and Camp

(NUMBERS 28-29 parallels LEVITICUS 21-24)

Numbers 28:1-8—The Daily Offerings
Numbers 28:9-15—The Sabbath and Monthly Offerings
Numbers 28:16-29:40—The Offerings At The Appointed
    Feasts

(DEUTERONOMY 16 parallels LEVITICUS 21-24)

Deuteronomy 16—The Feasts
    16:1-9—The Feast Of The Passover
    16:10-12—The Feast Of Weeks
    16:13-17—The Feast Of Booths

PART 2: THE NEGATIVE SIDE OF LIVING UNDER LAW

(See Romans 8:13-16)

Numbers 11:1-9—The Complaining People

Numbers 11:10-15—The Complaining Leader

Numbers 11:16-35—God's Method Of Dealing With
   Complainers

Numbers 12:1-9—Miriam And Aaron Complain Against
   Moses

Numbers 12:10-16—Miriam Smitten With Leprosy

Numbers 13—Twelve Spies Sent To Canaan

Numbers 14—The Rebelling People Pay...*And Pay...*

(DEUTERONOMY 1 SUMMARIZES NUMBERS 11-14)

MAJOR PLACES IN ORDER:

Sinai, Wilderness of Paran, Kadesh-Barnea

MAJOR PEOPLE IN ORDER:

Moses, Aaron, The 70 Elders, Eldad and Medad,
Miriam, The 12 Spies

AMOUNT OF TIME COVERED:

A few months in B. C. 1490.

NOTES

SANCTIFICATION SHOWN IN THE PRIESTLY LAWS

LEVITICUS 21:8—Illustrates the Old Testament concept of sanctification. Every Christian is to be "set apart" for the service of God.

LEVITICUS 21:17-23—Restricted any man with a physical blemish or imperfection from serving as a priest. Not *only* the sacrifice, but *the one offering it,* had to be without blemishes. See Hebrews 4:15 and 1 John 3:5.

LEVITICUS 22:18-25—Refers to special types of Peace Offerings—the *Votive* and the *Free Will* Offerings.

The *Peace Offering* expressed peace and fellowship between the offerer and God. It included a communal meal.

There were three kinds of Peace Offerings:

THANK OFFERING—showed gratitude for a special blessing or deliverance.

VOTIVE OFFERING—showed gratitude for a special answer when a vow had accompanied the petition.

FREE WILL OFFERING—Expressed gratitude to God without regard to any specific blessing or deliverance.

THE FEASTS OF THE SACRED CALENDAR

There were 7 religious festivals ordained of God for Israel's year, mentioned in LEVITICUS 23:

THE PASSOVER—v. 5.
Deliverance by Christ from sin's bondage.

THE FEAST OF UNLEAVENED BREAD—vv. 6-8
Unleavened bread a type of Christ and the Church.

THE DAY OF FIRST FRUITS—vv. 9-12
Always a Sunday. Jesus resurrected from the dead on this day, a guarantee of our resurrection (See 1 Cor. 15:20-23, 1 Thess. 4:13-18).

THE FEAST OF WEEKS (PENTECOST)—vv. 15-22
Always a Sunday. Day of the outpouring of the Holy Spirit. Two loaves represent Jew and Gentile, contained leaven, because sin is yet present within the Church.

THE DAY OF TRUMPETS—vv. 23-25
The blowing of the trumpets is associated with the coming of our Lord.

THE DAY OF ATONEMENT—vv. 26-32
The only fast day among the festivals. On this day annual atonement was made for the sins of the priests, the people, and the tabernacle. Points to the redeeming work of Christ more than any other festival.

THE FEAST OF TABERNACLES (BOOTHS)—vv. 33-43
Foreshadows the millennial reign of Christ.
(See Zechariah 14:16)

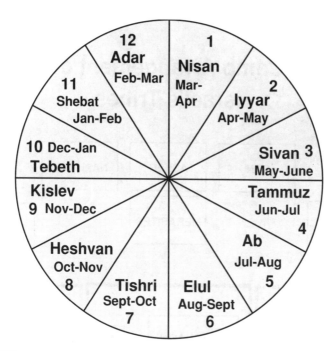

NOTES

Nisan is also called *Abib.* Passover is in this month.

Iyyar (Ziv) is the month of the Feast of Unleavened Bread, followed by the Day of First Fruits.

Seven weeks later, in **Sivan**, is the Feast of Pentecost.

Tishri is the month of the following festivals:
- The Day of Trumpets
- The Day of Atonement
- The Feast of Tabernacles

Camp Arrangement of Israel's Tribes

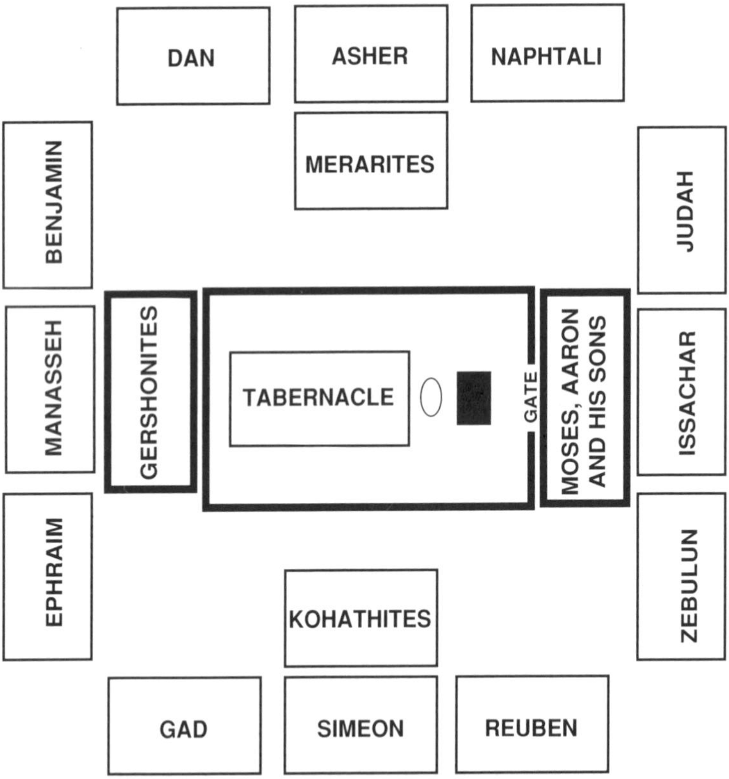

| DAN | ASHER | NAPHTALI |

MERARITES

BENJAMIN

JUDAH

MANASSEH

GERSHONITES

TABERNACLE

GATE

MOSES, AARON AND HIS SONS

ISSACHAR

EPHRAIM

KOHATHITES

ZEBULUN

| GAD | SIMEON | REUBEN |

STUPID IS FOREVER!
THE HIGH COST OF COMPLAINING

Numbers 11:1—Fire is a sign of God's presence and
      judgment.

11:6—Manna means, "What is it?"
      See John 6:31-35, 48-58!

11:26—*NABI':* means "Prophesied"
      Noting the difference between *NABI'* and the New
      Testament concept of *"prophet"* is important...

CLASS NOTES ON NUMBERS 11-14:

1. No one who rebelled will live to see the land: 14:23

2. They must return to the wilderness: 14:25

3. Forty years will pass: 14:34

4. The ten spies who misled the people will die: 14:37

5. The people will have no success in military
    encounters with the people of the land: 14:33

6. Only Joshua and Caleb will enter!

*Does this press upon us the terrible result of unbelief? Why
are we so prone to recycle, over and over, the learning of this
lesson?*

Suggestions for marking your Bible...

1. Copy the Outline into your Bible.

2. Write beside Leviticus 21:8, and underline the verse:

    Note: Description of Sanctification

3. Write comments of your choice beside the Feasts, as described in your notes.

4. Add any other notes from the explanations which you now wish to preserve in your Bible.

Unit Eleven
NUMBERS 15-19
NUMBERS 20-21 with
DEUTERONOMY 2-3
NUMBERS 22-25
NUMBERS 26-36 with
DEUTERONOMY 19
DEUTERONOMY 20-34

OUTLINE

Laws Concerning Offerings—Numbers 15:1-31
The Stoning Of A Sabbath Breaker—Numbers 15:32-36
Fringes On Garments—Numbers 15:37-41
Korah's Rebellion—Numbers 16:1-40
Ravages Of The Plague—Numbers 16:41-50
Aaron's Rod—Numbers 17
Provision For The Priests and Levites—Numbers 18:1-24
The Heave Offering—Numbers 18:25-32
Purification With Heifer Ashes—Numbers 19
Miriam's Death—Numbers 20:1
Water From The Rock—Numbers 20:2-21
Aaron's Death—Numbers 20:22-29
The Canaanites Attack—Numbers 21:1-3
The Fiery Serpents—Numbers 21:4-9
Detour Around Moab—Numbers 21:10-20
Israel Conquers Foes—Numbers 21:21-35

(Note: Deuteronomy 2-3 summarizes the above material)

Balaam, The Surprised Prophet—Numbers 22-24
Israel Worships Baal-peor—Numbers 25
Israel Takes A Census—Numbers 26
The Law Of Inheritance—Numbers 27:1-17

(Continued on next page)

Joshua Appointed Moses' Successor—Numbers 27:18-23

The Daily Offerings—Numbers 28-29

The Law Concerning Vows—Numbers 30

The Midianites Conquered—Numbers 31

Reuben, Gad Inherit East Of Jordan—Numbers 32

The Wilderness Journeys—Numbers 33:1-49

Orders To Expel Canaanites—Numbers 33:50-56

Partitioning The Land—Numbers 34:1-35:8

Laws Concerning Murder—Numbers 35:9-36

Female Inheritance And Marriage—Numbers 36

The Cities Of Refuge—Deuteronomy 19

Laws Concerning War—Deuteronomy 20

Settlement For An Unknown Murderer's Crime;
    Miscellaneous Laws—Deuteronomy 21-25:16

Command To Destroy Amalek—Deuteronomy 25:17-19

Offerings—Deuteronomy 26

Mount Ebal: Signs Of Blessings And Curses—
    Deuteronomy 27-30

Joshua Commissioned—Deuteronomy 31

The Law To Be Placed In The Ark—Deuteronomy 31:24-29

The Song Of Moses—Deuteronomy 31:30-32:47

Moses Permitted To See Canaan—Deuteronomy 32:48-52

Moses Blesses The Tribes—Deuteronomy 33

The Death Of Moses—Deuteronomy 34:1-8

Joshua Succeeds Moses—Deuteronomy 34:9-12

MAJOR PLACES IN ORDER

Kadesh-Barnea, Moab, Mount Nebo

MAJOR PEOPLE IN ORDER

Moses, Aaron, Korah, Baalam, Joshua

AMOUNT OF TIME COVERED

About 39 years

THE BOOK OF NUMBERS

PREPARATION	THE JOURNEY	AT THE GATE
CHAPTERS 1-5	CHAPTERS 10-18	CHAPTERS 22-36
Inventory and Assignments Cleansings, Preparations, Final Admonitions	Sinai to Kadesh-Barnea *WANDERING, WANDERING, UNTIL ALL ARE... DEAD!* On to Moab	At the gate of the Land New Problems Final Tasks
MOUNT SINAI	**MOUNT HOR**	**MOUNT NEBO**

KEY VERSES: 10:9; 10:29

DEUTERONOMY: "BOOK OF REMEMBRANCE"
Key Verses: 4:23; 5:29; 8:11; 10:12-13; 11:26-28; 28:1; 29:1

INTRODUCTION	THE WORD OF THE COVENANT	CONCLUSION
1-4: Remember, Lest you forget...	4:44-26: Commandments for the present 27-30: Options Affecting the future	31-34: Parting Words of Moses

ISRAEL'S HISTORY BY PERIODS

PENTATEUCH (BOOKS OF MOSES)	JOSHUA JUDGES RUTH	1, 2 SAMUEL 1, 2 KINGS 1, 2 CHRONICLES	EZRA NEHEMIAH ESTHER
IN EGYPT IN THE WILDERNESS	IN CANAAN, UNDER THE JUDGES	IN CANAAN, UNDER THE KINGS	IN CAPTIVITY, IN ASSYRIA and BABYLON
660 YEARS	360 YEARS	460 YEARS	160 YEARS

WE HAVE COME THIS FAR IN OUR STUDY...

KORAH'S REBELLION: NUMBERS 16

Korah was joined by 250 leaders who challenged the authority of Moses.

They tried to establish a priestly order without God's permission. God dealt harshly with them!

THE RED HEIFER: NUMBERS 19

A type of the sacrifice of Christ in cleansing the believer:
1. The sacrifice is killed
2. Sevenfold sprinkling of blood
3. Sacrifice turned into ashes
4. Ashes become a memorial
5. Used to cleanse from defilement

Water is both a type of the Holy Spirit and the Word of God (John 7:37-39). The Holy Spirit uses the sacrifice of Christ to bring the forgiveness of the believer, and cleansing! (See 1 John 1:9)

Always remember that everything you will ever need in your Christian life comes from the CROSS! There are *NO* "second sources!"

MOSES' SIN: NUMBERS 20:7 ff.

Why was God so hard on Moses? The rock was a symbol of Christ (1 Corinthians 10:4). Moses had already struck the rock once (Exodus 17:6), and his striking it the second time said the one sacrifice was not enough (Hebrews 9:26). His act exalted himself (v. 10). His frustration and anger at the people cost him...*everything!*

BAALAM, THE HIRELING PROPHET: (Numbers 22 ff.)

This passage is important because of 2 Peter 2:15, Jude 11, and Revelation 2:14. He sought to "sell" his spiritual gift, and was a false teacher. He reasoned that a holy God would be glad for him to curse a people as corrupt as Israel. He disregarded God's willingness to justify believing sinners.

CITIES OF REFUGE: DEUTERONOMY 19

A beautiful picture of our safety in Christ, where we are free from the retaliation of our sins. Later, we will see Abner die "as a fool" because he did not stay in the city of refuge. *What about you?*

Have you taken your refuge in Jesus Christ? There are so many folks in our age who take their refuge in church membership. Joining a church no more makes you a *Christian* than entering a garage makes you an *auto-mobile!*

John 1:12-13: *"But as many as received Him, to them He gave the right to become children of God, even to those who believe in His name,* **who were born not of blood, nor of the will of the flesh, nor of the will of man, but of God."**

We did not make ourselves the children of our parents by what we accomplished. We are the product of their activity. So it is with becoming a child of God. We are not the product of our own deeds (even joining a church!), but rather the product of the activity of God. He so loved us that He sent His son to the cross. The "birthing" of our spiritual sonship comes not from the blood and water of physical birth, but from Christ's death on the cross. (See John 19:34.)

A FAREWELL TO THE WILDERNESS...

Don't miss the sheer horror of how the Pentateuch ends! Because of *unbelief,* an entire generation of Israelites spent their lives wandering aimlessly, never getting any meaning out of life. Is that not *always* the result of life apart from God? Their environment was not pleasant. Their lives had no destiny except dusty graves. Their investment in history was to serve only as a lesson of the futility of unbelief.

WHY DID THE WILDERNESS LIE BETWEEN EGYPT AND CANAAN FOR THESE PEOPLE?

The answer to that question is appropriate for each one of us. Egypt stands for a land of carnal, lustful lifestyle. To leave the habits and foods of that land behind and to immediately enter into the promised land would have left a lesson unlearned! *The people of Israel had to learn that all their sufficiency, all their supply, came from God and God alone.*

Had they slipped out of Egypt to reside at once in the promised land, where abundance was everywhere, would have created a self- centered people. They would have taken their environment for granted. Because of the wilderness, there was a stark realization that land without God's blessing—*without God's provision*—life is barren and dry.

In our Christian lives, we sometimes wonder why God allows the "desert experiences." It is obvious: *sin* creates this barrenness. Living in the midst of sin, there is only one valid supply—*God.* When we trust Him, we find the reality of life. It's not in the environment, but in *Him!*

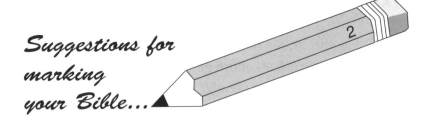

Suggestions for marking your Bible...

1. Copy the Outline into your Bible.

2. Underline the key verses for Numbers and Deuteronomy.

3. Write marginal comments beside the scriptures explained in your notes.

4. Add any other notes from the explanations which you now wish to preserve in your Bible.

Unit Twelve
JOSHUA 1-24
JUDGES 1-12

OUTLINE OF JOSHUA

PART ONE: CONQUEST OF THE LAND
(Joshua 1:1-11:15)

Chapters 1-5—Preparation
    Charge to Joshua—Joshua 1
    Spying Jericho—Joshua 2
    Crossing Jordan—Joshua 3
    Memorial Stones—Joshua 4
    Circumcision and Passover—Joshua 5
Chapters 6-11:15—Conquest
    Chapters 6-8—Central Campaign
        Jericho—Joshua 6
        Ai Defeats Israel—Joshua 7
        Israel Defeats Ai—Joshua 8
    Chapters 9-10—Southern Campaign
        Pact With Gibeon—Joshua 9
        Five Kings Slain—Joshua 10
    Chapter 11:1-15—Northern Campaign
Chapters 11:16-23—Summary

PART TWO: DIVISION OF THE LAND (Joshua 13-21)

PART THREE: JOSHUA'S FINAL YEARS (Joshua 22-24)

MAJOR PLACES IN ORDER

Jericho, Ai, and the territories of the South and the North in
the Promised Land

MAJOR PEOPLE IN ORDER

Joshua

AMOUNT OF TIME COVERED

Approximately 7 years

OUTLINE OF JUDGES

PART ONE: WILL THEY NEVER LEARN? (Judges 1-16)

Incomplete Obedience—Judges 1
"As The Wheel Turns:"—Judges 2
The Roster of Players—Judges 3:1-6
First Cycle: Othniel—Judges 3:7-11
Second Cycle: Ehud—Judges 3:12-31
Third Cycle: Deborah—Judges 4
Parenthesis: The Song of Deborah—Judges 5
Fourth Cycle: Gideon—Judges 6:1-8:32
Fifth Cycle: Abimelech Made King, Tola—
    Judges 8:33-10:5
Sixth Cycle: Jephthah—Judges 10:6-12:15

MAJOR PLACES IN ORDER:

The Land of Israel

MAJOR PEOPLE IN ORDER:

Judges: Othniel, Ehud, Deborah, Gideon, Abimelech, Tola, Jephthah

AMOUNT OF TIME COVERED:

Judges covers approximately 400 years
    (1500-1000 B. C.)

NOTES

JOSHUA

In the Jewish Old Testament, this is the first of the Historical Books.

It took 7 years to conquer Canaan. The secret of Joshua was OBEDIENCE!

The spiritual message of this book is victory over the POWER of Sin.

The Summary of Joshua is found in 21:42-45.

JOSHUA 7: THE SIN OF ACHAN

When we are defeated, we must root out OUR Achan and utterly destroy that area in our life style!

JUDGES:

The 5 Spokes of the "Wheel:" (see page 103)

1. 2:5—"They sacrificed to the Lord"
2. 2:11—"The sons of Israel did evil in the sight of the Lord, and served the Baals"
3. 2:14—"And the anger of the Lord burned against Israel, and He gave them into the hands of...their enemies around them"
4. 2:15—"They were severely distressed"
5. 2:16—"Then the Lord raised up judges who delivered them from the hands of those who plundered them"

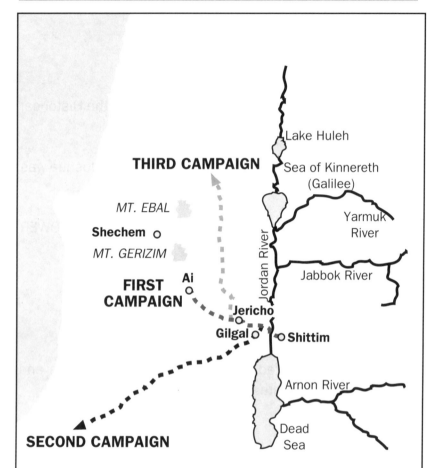

JOSHUA'S MILITARY CAMPAIGNS

Following the directions of Jehovah, the Israelite army saw victory at Jericho. Disobeying Jehovah, they suffered defeat at Ai. In the Second and Third Campaigns they were able to defeat their enemies, but through their disobedience created serious problems for the future...problems which would eventually destroy their nation.

Partial obedience is not enough! Compromise with what is God's best doesn't bring "almost best." It brings disaster.

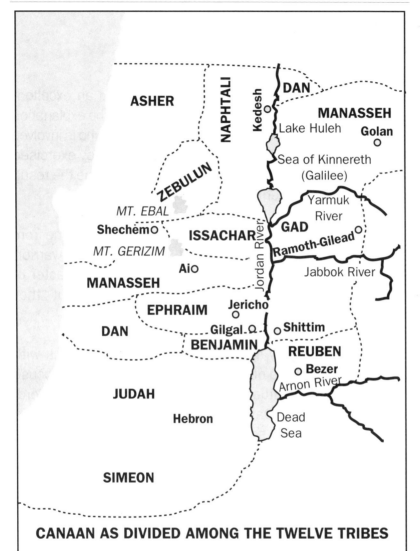

CANAAN AS DIVIDED AMONG THE TWELVE TRIBES

Hebron, Bezer, Shechem, Ramoth-Gilead, Golan, and Kadesh were set apart as Cities of Refuge to receive and protect accidental manslayers. Note Dan and Manasseh occupy two portions. The Sidonians were to the North. The Philistines occupied the coastal territory in Judah.

USING YOUR ZONDERVAN PICTORIAL BIBLE ENCYCLOPEDIA...

In volume 3 of the Encyclopedia, you will find an excellent article on page 756 about Israel's judges. Note the explanation that the word "judge" means more here than one who is involved with legal affairs. Besides judicial functions "they exercised a saving, liberating activity that was conceived to be the result of a direct endowment from Jahweh."

The article goes on to explain that all these judges came from three classes of men: High priest, wise man, and warrior. Note that these men frequently fell below the character of other great men or women in the Old Testament, but "they were men of faith."

Someone has rightly said, "The Lord hits many a lick with a crooked stick!" One of the Devil's tricks with us is to accuse us of not being "spiritual enough" to do anything for the Lord. That's just not true. David was a murderer and an adulterer, and God used him in spite of these things. It's true that his personal life was wretched because of his sin, *but his sin did not make him useless.*

The old joke has two men meeting on the street. One says to the other, "How's your wife?" He replies, "Compared to what?" How *pure* do you have to be for the Lord to use you? *"Compared to what?"*

The point is this: you and I will never become RIGHTEOUS ENOUGH to be God-like. Therefore, He gives us *His* righteousness. It is always adequate when our own is not. This is not a license to SIN; instead, it's a license to SERVE!

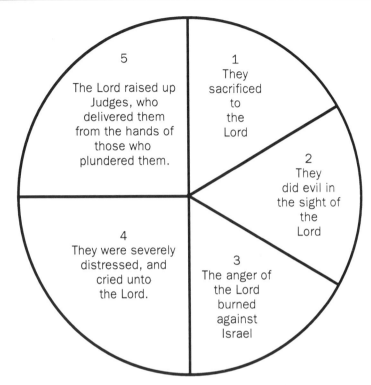

THE "WHEEL OF LIFE" IN THE BOOK OF JUDGES

Chapter 2 is an excellent place to review this cycle. It is obsrved throughout the book.

FIND AND UNDERLINE THESE POSITIONS ON THE WHEEL:

2:5-10: Position 1—but note last part of verse 10.
2:11-13: Position 2—note their rejection and substitutions.
2:14-15a: Position 3—note God's hand was *against* them.
2:15b: Position 4—*Finally,* they began to cry out for help.
2:16: Position 5—The Lord raised up Judges to deliver them.
CONTINUE TO TRACE THE WHEEL IN VERSES 17-23...

Is it not tragic that we have never learned for ourselves that disobedience causes misery? Note: God was always ready to deliver them if they would turn to Him. So it is today. NEVER believe you have passed out of the love and grace of our God.

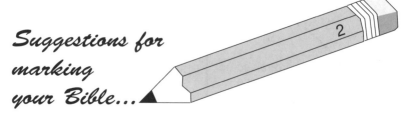

Suggestions for marking your Bible...

1. Copy the outline into your Bible.

2. Write beside Joshua 21:42-45:

   Note: Summary Statement of Joshua

3. Write beside Joshua 10:12-13:

   Note: The sun and the moon replaced God as objects of worship to these people!

4. Add any other notes from the explanations which you now wish to preserve in your Bible.

Unit Thirteen
JUDGES 13-21
RUTH
1 SAMUEL 1-12

OUTLINE

JUDGES 13-21:

Seventh Cycle: Samson—Judges 13-16
Idols in Israel—Judges 17
Tribe of Dan Seeks An Inheritance—Judges 18
Tragedy: A Levite and A Harlot—Judges 19
Israel At War—Judges 20
Benjamites Barely Squeak By—Judges 21

MAJOR PLACES IN ORDER

Israel, Gaza, Gibeah, Rimmon's Rock, Mizpah, Bethel

MAJOR PEOPLE IN ORDER

Samson, Delilah, Micah, "A certain Levite," Phinehas

AMOUNT OF TIME COVERED

Approximately 263 years

NOTES

Key to this book: Judges 21:25—"In those days there was no king in Israel; everyone did what was right in his own eyes."

13:2-5—THE NAZARITE VOW

Why this vow? It was the means by which a "lay priesthood" was established.

It included...
1. No strong drink
2. Hair never to be cut
3. Cannot touch a dead body or eat unclean things

Samson repeatedly violated these vows, including eating honey from a carcass of a dead animal. He is a symbol of those who try to follow God's will without accepting God's values. He is deluded, imprisoned, blinded, degraded, chained, and given a life of drudgery.

THE TRAGEDY OF THE CONCUBINE

Israel had finally yielded to the vulgarity of the religious scene around them, among the Baal worshippers! Even the practice of homosexual activity had penetrated their lifestyles. At Gibeah the homosexuals are called "Sons of Belial" (Satan) in 19:22. In 20:5 we discover the concubine was left dead or dying, her hands on the threshhold of the house where the Levite had stayed. The Levite dramatically publicized their atrocity by dismembering the body of the woman and sending pieces to the tribes.

This period of Israel is the story of people who lived without any mourning for sin, no return to Jehovah. They acted in self-will. 40,000 Israelites and 25,000 Benjamites are killed, cities destroyed, the population decimated.

What a terrible, lawless period!

WHY? WHY SUCH A LAWLESS PERIOD?

There were not enough *models* of Godly living to permeate the families of Israel. The mothers and fathers who bred this generation of Israelites had been born in Egypt or the Wilderness. All of those who first entered Canaan with Joshua were born in the Wilderness.

As they entered the land, they were disobedient. They did not follow the orders God plainly gave to them to create a holy territory. Inside the borders was to be one thing—the worship of Jehovah.

Instead, they endorsed a "pluralistic society," where each person could do what they desired to do, as long as they did not hurt anyone else. The evil of this compromise is that truth no longer exists for anyone. Each person is the final judge of "right" and "wrong." We are experiencing such a life-style in America today. It never brought any meaning or peace to Israel, and it will not bring any peace to us! We may not be able to change all society, but there is one place we can keep sacred...our own lives. We Christians compose a special group of people called the "body of Christ." *Holy living is a necessity.*

AUTHORSHIP OF BOOK:

Probably Samuel.

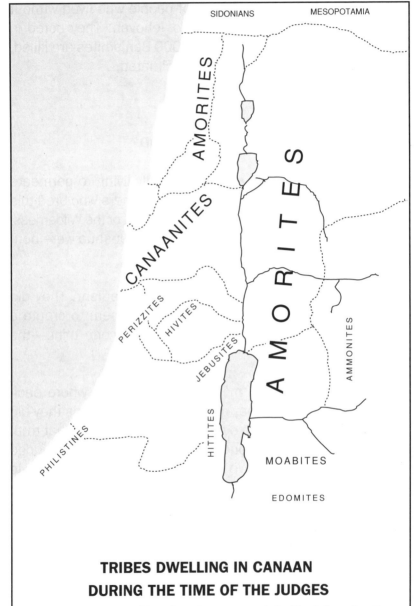

TRIBES DWELLING IN CANAAN
DURING THE TIME OF THE JUDGES

In every case, they should not have been present. God had given directions for them to be cleared out of the land. Israel could no more co-exist with them than WE can co-exist with sin!

NAME	TRIBE	IDENTIFICATION	ENEMY	YRS OF PEACE	YRS OF OPPRES-SION	REFERENCE
Othniel	Judah	Nephew of Caleb	Mesopo-tamia	8	40	3:9-11
Ehud	Benjamin	Left-handed An Assassin	Moabites	18	80	3:12-30
Shamgar	Naphtali	Used Ox Goad	Philistines	?	?	3:31
Deborah	Ephraim	Only woman judge	Canaanites	20	40	4:4-5:31
Gideon	Manasseh	An obscure family	Midianites	7	40	6:11-8:35
Tola	Issachar				23	10:1-2
Jair	Gilead	30 sons, 30 cities			22	10:3-5
Jephthah	Gilead	Made rash vow	Ammonites	18	6	11:1-12:7
Ibzan	Bethlehem	30 sons, 30 daughters			7	12:8-10
Elon	Zebulun				10	12:11-12
Abdon	Ephraim				8	12:13-15
Samson	Dan	Nazarite from birth	Philistines	40	20	13:2-16:31

JUDGES OF ISRAEL
Some of them prove the Lord "hits many a lick with a crooked stick!"

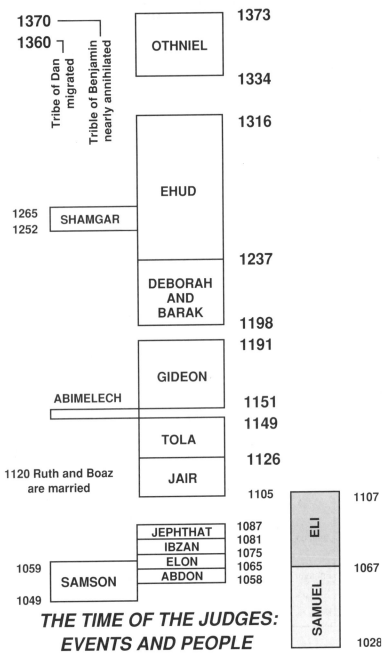

THE TIME OF THE JUDGES:
EVENTS AND PEOPLE

OUTLINE OF RUTH

Elimelech Migrates To Moab—1:1-5
Family Faces Crisis—1:6-21
Naomi Returns To Bethlehem—1:22
Ruth Meets Boaz—2:1-23
Ruth And Naomi Trust Boaz To Be
      Their Kinsman-Redeemer—3:1-18
Boaz And Ruth—4:1-12
Their Son, Obed—4:13-16
Ruth's Part In David's Genealogy—4:17-22

MAJOR PLACES IN ORDER

Bethlehem, Moab, Bethlehem

MAJOR PEOPLE IN ORDER

Elimilech, Naomi, Ruth, Boaz

AMOUNT OF TIME COVERED

Approximately 10 years

NOTES ON THE BOOK OF RUTH

Bethlehem means "House of Bread and Praise"
Elimelech means "My God Is King"
Naomi means "Pleasant"
Mahlon and Chilion mean "Sick" and "Pining"
Orphah means "Fawn"
Ruth means "Friendship"
Boaz means "Fleetness"
Obed means "The Serving One"

THE CONCEPT OF THE KINSMAN-REDEEMER

In Hebrew, *GO'EL*. The nearest kinsman had the right to redeem the forfeited inheritance of the family. Elimelech's death meant the needs of the women were to be met by the *GO'EL*. Involved were:

1. Support and protect the women.
2. Insure their property remained intact for them, even if liens had to be paid.
3. In a childless marriage where there was no heir, the *GO'EL* must marry the widow and sire a child to inherit the land of his father.
4. If the widow's property was put up for sale, the *GO'EL* would buy it at public auction.
5. If the man had been murdered, the *GO'EL* would avenge the death.
6. If the dead man's relatives were sold into slavery or servitude, the *GO'EL* would purchase and free them.
7. If the nearest kinsman-redeemer refused the responsibility to act as *GO'EL,* he lost the right to the inheritance and sometimes suffered the indignity of spit in the face (See Deut. 25:9).
8. The next kinsman was then free to come forward and take over. Taking off the shoe and handing it to another was a symbol of transfer of obligation—"You walk in my shoe!"

OUTLINE OF 1 SAMUEL 1-12:

SAMUEL AS JUDGE AND PROPHET—1:1-8:22
Childhood—1:1-3:21
The Ark—4:1-7:2
Reconsecration at Mizpah—7:3-17
The Call for a King—8:1-22

SAMUEL AND SAUL—9:1-12
Saul Anointed—9:1-10:27
Defeat of the Ammonites—11:1-11
Renewal of the Kingdom at Gilgal—11:12-15
The Farewell Address of Samuel—12

MAJOR PLACES IN ORDER

Mount Ephraim, Shiloh, Ebenezer, Ashdod, Bethshemite, Kirjath-jearim, Mizpeh, Ramah, Gibeah, Jabesh-Gilead, Gilgal

MAJOR PEOPLE IN ORDER

Elkanah, Hannah, Eli, Samuel, Philistines, Joshua the Bethshemite, Abinadab, Saul

AMOUNT OF TIME COVERED

Approximately 76 years

AUTHOR

Not known for certain. Jewish tradition picks Samuel; Gad and Nathan added the sections following his death.

NOTES

SAMUEL combines two Hebrew words meaning, "Heard of God." In 1:20 Hannah explains why she chose that name.

ELI: a good man, a poor father. He humored his children more than he honored God. He ruined both them and himself! When love refuses to be "tough," it's not love...

3:1: "And word from the Lord was rare in those days, visions were infrequent." This condition occurs when there is no receptivity to God's word! He does not talk to those who will not listen—for obvious reasons.

3:7: He needed a personal encounter!

God's call to Samuel: Remember—if He calls, and you do not understand what is happening, He will not FORSAKE you. He will *keep on calling* until you understand what is taking place. Don't worry about "missing" God's message to you.

4:21: *Kabod* = "Glory;" *I-Kabod* = "No Glory"

Shiloh was probably burned following the capture of the ark. Shiloh is never mentioned again.

(Do this Bible study on your own...)

THE LOSS OF THE ARK: 1 SAMUEL 4-7

1. What nation is Israel's enemy at this time?

2. What mistake was made in bringing the Ark into battle?

3. How can the error of trusting in the symbol instead of the One symbolized teach us a powerful lesson?

4. What prophecy was fulfilled in 4:11?

5. What is the meaning of "Ichabod?"

6. Did the Ark bless or curse its captors?

7. How were their idols put to ridicule?

8. How does 6:10-12 attest the supernatural?

9. What judgment befell the Betshemites, and why?

10. Where, and for how long a period, did the Ark then rest?

11. How would you account for the changed conditions of affairs in chapter 7?

Note that Israel's attitude about the ark came not from the counsel of God, but by copying the heathen around them who carried their idols into battle for "luck." God allowed the Ark to be captured to discipline Israel, and to show His power over the silly deities worshipped by other nations.

(This Bible study is adapted from James M. Gray's *Synthetic Bible Studies,* published back in 1906 by Fleming H. Revell Company.)

Suggestions for
marking
your Bible...

1. Copy the outline into your Bible.

2. Write beside Judges 21:25:

   Key to understanding the book.
   People think what they do is
   right! They often do not act
   out of deceit, but out of blindness.

3. Write beside Ruth 1 the meaning of the names of the characters of this lovely story *(see page 118).*

4. Add any other notes from the explanations which you now wish to preserve in your Bible.

Unit Fourteen
1 SAMUEL 13-31
2 SAMUEL 1-5
with 1 CHRONICLES 1-12

OUTLINE OF 1 SAMUEL 13-31:
THE DECLINE OF SAUL and THE RISE OF DAVID

The reign of Saul—13:1-14:52
Saul's great sin—13:1-14
Jonathan's victory—13:15 -14:15
Saul's poor judgment—14:16-52
Enmity between Saul and David—15:1-18:30
     Saul's disobedience—15:1-9
     Samuel hews Agag to pieces—15:10-35
     Samuel anoints David—16:1-23
     David kills Goliath—17:1-17:58
     Jonathan and David—18:1-19
Saul seeks to kill David by indirect means—18:20-30
David's flights and dangers—19:1-23:29
     Saul seeks to kill David directly—19:1-24
     David and Jonathan cut a covenant—20:1-23
     Saul and Jonathan divide over David—20:24-42
     David eats consecrated bread—21:1-6
     David feigns madness—21:7-15
     Saul murders priests and families—22:16-23
     David delivers Keilah—23:1-29
David's mercy to Saul and rising popularity—24:1-31:13
     Deliverance at Engedi—24:1-22
     Deliverance at Hachilah—25:1-26:25
     Suicide provoked by defeat at hands of Philistines—
          27:1-31:13

MAJOR PLACES IN ORDER

Gilgal, Gibeah, Jerusalem, Ramah, Jerusalem, Keilah, Maon, Engedi, Hakilah

MAJOR PEOPLE IN ORDER

Saul, Jonathan, Samuel, Agag, David, Goliath, Michael, Abishai

AMOUNT OF TIME COVERED

Approximately 39 years

NOTES

In the Hebrew Bible, 1 and 2 Samuel appear as one book: *Samuel.* 1 and 2 Kings appear as simply *Kings.* The four books are collectively called *"The Books of the Kingdoms."*

The theme of 1 and 2 Samuel is the establishment of the Kingdom. The theme of 1 and 2 Kings is the taking away of the Kingdom.

The Holy Spirit's purpose running through these books is not to give the history of Samuel, Saul, and David, but rather to interpret the relation of these men to the establishment of the Kingdom.

Samuel laid its foundations;
    Saul tried to establish it and failed;
        David succeeded in establishing it.

SAMUEL: GREATEST BETWEEN MOSES AND DAVID

His principles of statecraft were summed up in 1 Samuel 12:12: *"Jehovah your God was your king."* The responsibility of the human king was outlined in 1 Samuel 12:13-15:

1. You are appointed by JHWH, not the people;
2. If you serve JHWH, it will be well;
3. If not, JHWH will be against you and Israel.

Two significant phrases are then used:
"*The Anointed of Jehovah*"
Used to describe both Saul and David
"*The Servant of Jehovah*"
Never used of Saul, frequently used of David

THE ANOINTED OF JEHOVAH

The anointing with oil symbolized being "set apart" (sanctified) for the work of God. This rite was done to both political and religious leaders. It indicated:
- Divine ordination to office
- Spirit-given power for duties of the office
- Divine protection to fulfill the call to the office

The coming of the Spirit of JHWH upon the anointed one was significant:

1 Samuel 10:9-12—For Saul, it produced ecstatic emotions which caused him to prophesy;

(Continued on next page)

(Continued from previous page)

1 Samuel 11:6-15—It gave him the will to fight Israel's enemies.

1 Samuel 18:1; 20:12-17—For David, it went much further, leading to the love of David and Jonathan, to wise behavior under difficult circumstances, to constant seeking for the guidance of God, to respect for Saul's position, to hymn writing, to devoted planning for the temple and its service, to prophetic insight into the future of Israel.

DAVID'S ATTITUDE TOWARD SAUL

David recognized Saul as God's appointed man. JHWH alone should remove him. Anointing guaranteed God's aid, but not success. Success depended upon the choice of a man to appropriate the aid of God!

SAUL: A STUDY OF A MAN WHO WOULD NOT DEPEND ON GOD

- •Poor judgment (wisdom comes from God)
- •Jealousy
- •Fear
- •Despair
- •Suicide

DAVID: A STUDY OF A MAN WITH A HEART FOR GOD
- • Lust, yes...but always a heart for God
- • Response to God's chastening
- • Restoration

THE SERVANT OF JHWH

David became an outstanding example of a servant:
1. Jerusalem made the capital of a united Israel.
2. He put worship at the heart of the nation.
3. He headed the line ordained to rule Israel forever.
4. He established justice and righteousness in his realm.
5. He learned to bow his will to God's will in all things.
6. He laid the plans for the Temple.
7. He led in preparation of a hymnbook for Israel (the Psalms).

A STUDY OF THE SERVANT OF JEHOVAH:

(Note: the references below give you an opportunity to do some personal, independent study of this subject. Using these scriptures, trace the topic. Jot down your personal conclusions on a note sheet, and insert it in your notebook at this point if you wish.)

- Angels: Job 4:18
- Abraham: Genesis 26:24
- Isaac: Genesis 24:14
- Jacob: Exodus 32:13
- Moses: Exodus 14:31
- Joshua: Joshua 24:29
- Caleb: Numbers 14:24
- Job: Job 1:8
- Hezekiah: 2Chronicles 29:1-5
- Zerubbabel: Haggai 2:23
- Eliakim: Isaiah 22:20-24
- The Prophets: 2 Kings 9:7
- Messiah: Isaiah 49:5-7

OUTLINE OF 2 SAMUEL 1-5:

DAVID BECAME KING OF JUDAH—1:1-4:12
    David made King at Hebron—1:1-2:4
    Men of Jabesh-Gilead blessed for burying Saul—
       2:4-2:7
    Victory over northern tribes—2:8-3:5
    Northern tribes turn to David—3:6-4:12

DAVID BECAME KING OF JUDAH and ISRAEL—5:1-20:26
    Tribes rally to David—5:1-5
    Jerusalem made capital of Israel—5:6-16
    Victories over the Philistines—5:17-25

MAJOR PLACES IN ORDER

Ziklag, Hebron, Jerusalem, Philistia

MAJOR PEOPLE IN ORDER

David, Abner, Ishbosheth, Joab, Asahel, Mephibosheth, Hiram

AMOUNT OF TIME COVERED

Approximately 8 years

NOTE

2 Samuel deals with David.
It pictures a "Theocratic Monarchy."

122

OUTLINE OF 1 CHRONICLES 1-12:

Genealogies—1:1-2:55
David's Genealogies—3:1-24
Judah's Genealogies—4:1-43
Reuben's Genealogies—5:1-26
Levi's Genealogies—6:1-81
Issachar's Genealogies—7:1-5
Benjamin's Sons—7:6-12
Naphtali, Manasseh, Ephraim, Asher's Genealogies—
    7:13-40
Benjamin's Genealogies—8:1-40
Israel/Judah's Genealogies—9:1-44
Saul's overthrow and death—10:1-14
David's mighty men—11:1-47
The men who made David King—12:1-40

NOTES

Like 1 and 2 Kings, there is only one "Chronicles" in the Jewish Bible. They cover the period from the death of Saul to the time of the captivity of Judah and Israel. The document was probably written during the time of the captivity.

Chronicles records this history from an entirely different standpoint than Kings. The outlook is almost totally confined to Judah, the chronicler mentioning Israel only as necessary. Everything is written from the viewpoint of the Davidic line.

The story of the Chronicles centers around the Temple. The chief matter in David's reign is his desire to get it built. For Solomon, the chief matter was the building of it.

SUBTITLE 1 CHRONICLES
"THE LINE OF THE GOD-FOLLOWERS"

The genealogies are very carefully selected. They trace the line of the "God Followers!" The opening verse mentions Seth as the only son of Adam (from him came the "God Followers!"). From Noah, we continue the direct line of this special "faith people" through his son Shem. We then go to Abraham, through Isaac, to David.

Note there are brief "side excursions" to position this line of "God Followers" in parallel to other lineages. However, none of the others are followed very far; in every case, they are mentioned to give perspective, nothing more.

...THIS BRINGS UP AN IMPORTANT POINT!

A quick look at the Kings and Chronicles materials might cause you to think they are dull and repetitious. Or, you might look at a set of genealogies and say, "Ugh! What is that good for?"

God has not breathed inspiration into any portion of His book to bore us. All of it has truth which can guide us, and further reveal the nature of God to us.

"BUT CAN I UNDERSTAND ALL OF IT?"

Yes, you can! H. A. Zimmerman is a classic example of how even an uneducated person can grow from the study of scripture. Raised on a Pennsylvania Dutch farm, he was apprenticed to a Jewish jeweler while in his teens. Early in his life, he began to read the Bible every day. At age 22, he and his bride left the countryside and moved to Shamokin, where they opened a small jewelry store. He made a small stool which would fit under their bed and placed a Bible on it. Each morning he would awaken about 4 A.M., turn on his side and quietly turn on a light near the floor. He spent much time reading his Bible in this way.

His jewelry store prospered as he and his wife worked six days a week, 12-15 hours a day. He became known as the best "watch fixer" in the region. Beside his workbench, always spread with tiny watch parts, was *another* Bible! As he worked into the night on a broken clock, he would meditate on scripture portions. He learned how to remember the locations of passages by ingenious memory devices he created for himself.

For him, the Bible was a *living* thing! This poorly educated watchman became a friend of preachers and Bible scholars, who frequented his workroom on a daily basis. Doctrinal discussions raged in the back of "Zimmie's" jewelry store as travelling evangelists and pastors met with the watchmaker.

H. A. Zimmerman was my grandfather. As a five year old boy, I learned to love scripture in his workroom. At age seven, he gave me my first Bible and began to teach me how to study it. I never had a seminary professor who knew as much about the Bible in a *practical* way as did this Godly jeweler. On Sundays, he drove to all the little "coal patches" in the countryside around Shamokin to teach the miners and their children the truths of the scriptures he had discovered.

He put all the truths he learned into his lifestyle. Literally hundreds of persons accepted Christ because of his loving, caring witness to them in his store.

You, too, can understand your Bible.
All it takes is a love for its truths!

Suggestions for marking your Bible...

1. Copy the outline in your Bible.

2. Write beside 1 Samuel 28:16-19 and 31:2-4:

    Key Verses

3. Underline special passages referred to in the class discussions of Samuel, David, and Saul, etc.

4. Add any other notes from the explanations which you now wish to preserve in your Bible.

Unit Fifteen

2 SAMUEL 6
with 1 CHRONICLES 13-16
2 SAMUEL 7 with 1 CHRONICLES 17
2 SAMUEL 8-12
with 1 CHRONICLES 18-20
2 SAMUEL 13-18
2 SAMUEL 19-24
with 1 CHRONICLES 21

2 SAMUEL	1 CHRONICLES
LIFE OF KING DAVID	
Throne Emphasis	Temple Emphasis
No Genealogies	Nine Chapters of Genealogies
Bathsheba: Key Turning Point	No Mention of Bathsheba
David, A Man	David, God's Man
11-12 1-10 13-24	1-9 10-29

In order to help you correlate these sections of scripture, we are going to parallel portions of each book which cover the same events. As you study in this way, you will begin to see how the different emphases of the writers directed their choice of materials.

If you have *two* Bibles available, it might be helpful to open one of them to the Samuel passages and the other one to the Chronicles passages. Thus, all the materials can be quickly compared.

OUTLINE OF 2 SAMUEL 6 with 1 CHRONICLES 13-16:

2 SAMUEL 6   1 CHRONICLES 13-16

2 SAMUEL 6	1 CHRONICLES 13-16
David brings the ark to Zion—6:1-19	David's desire to remove the ark—13:1-8
David reproves Michal—6:20-23	Uzzah is smitten—13:9-14
	Hiram's kindness to David—14:1-2
	Children born to David in Jerusalem—14:3-7
	David's victories over the Philistines—14:8-17
	David brings the ark to Zion—15:1-29
	David's sacrifices and thanks—16:1-6
	David's Psalm of thanksgiving—16:7-36
	Levites appointed for the ark—16:37-43

OUTLINE OF 2 SAMUEL 7 with 1 CHRONICLES 17:

2 SAMUEL 7   1 CHRONICLES 17

2 SAMUEL 7	1 CHRONICLES 17
David plans to build a temple—7:1-3	God's covenant with David—17:1-15
God's covenant with David—7:4-29	David's prayer and thanksgiving—17:16-27

OUTLINE OF 2 SAMUEL 8-12 with 1 CHRONICLES 18-20:

2 SAMUEL 8-12   1 CHRONICLES 18-20

2 SAMUEL 8-12	1 CHRONICLES 18-20
David extends his kingdom—8:1-13	David extends his kingdom—18:1-17
David's officers—8:14-18	David's messengers humiliated—19:1-5
David's kindness to Mephibosheth—9:1-13	David defeats Ammon—19:6-15
Defeat of Ammonites and Syrians—10:1-19	David defeats the Syrians—19:16-19
David and Bathsheba—11:1-27	Joab and David capture Rabbah—20:1-8
Nathan rebukes David—12:1-12	
David's repentance and sorrow—12:13-25	
David captures Rabbah—12:26-31	

OUTLINE OF 2 SAMUEL 13-18:

Amnon's sin against Tamar—13:1-19
Absalom's revenge—13:20-33
Absalom's flight—13:34-39
Joab's scheme for Absalom's return—14:1-24
Absalom returns to David's court—14:25-33
Absalom revolts against David—15:1-12
David flees from Jerusalem—15:13-37
Ziba's deceit—16:1-4
Shimei curses David—16:5-14
Absalom enters Jerusalem—16:15-23
Absalom receives counsel—17:1-14
Hushai reports to David—17:15-22
Ahithophel commits suicide—17:23-29
Absalom and Israel defeated—18:1-8
Absalom murdered by Joab—18:9-33

OUTLINE OF 2 SAMUEL 19-24 with 1 CHRONICLES 21:

2 SAMUEL 19-24	1 CHRONICLES 21
Joab causes the king to stop mourning—19:1-14	David numbers Israel and Judah—21 :1-6
David returns to Jerusalem—19:15-43	David chooses his punishment—21:7-17
Sheba revolts against David—20:1-13	David builds an altar—21:18-30
Sheba is slain—20:14-26	
Seven sons of Saul hanged—21:1-14	
Abishai rescues David from the Giant—21:15-22	
David's song of deliverance—22:1-51	
The last words of David:—23:1-7	
David's mighty men—23:8-39	
David numbers Israel and Judah—24:1-9	
God punishes David—24:10-25	

MAJOR PLACES IN ORDER

Jerusalem

MAJOR PEOPLE IN ORDER

David, Hiram, Mephibosheth, Bathsheba, Nathan, Joab, Amnon, Tamar, Absalom, Ziba, Shimei, Hushai, Ahithophel, Sheba, Abishai

AMOUNT OF TIME COVERED

Approximately 33 years (2 Samuel 5:5)

NOTES

2 Samuel 6:3—David did a right thing the wrong way. The ark should never have been transported with a cart. God desires us not only to have the right spirit, but to also do His will according to HIS plans, not our own.

7:10-16—Why do we see a prophecy of Christ in this passage? Compare this with Hebrews 1:5...

Nathan announces the term of an unconditional covenant with David. Therefore, this covenant must be fulfilled at some future date during the reign of Christ as King of Kings.

David's sin—read Psalm 51 for insights into him in relationship to this!

Chapter 13—David's weakness for giving in to his lust sets the scene for this sad situation! The tragedy of David's children and their problems is a reflection on him. His own weaknesses were duplicated in their characters.

STUDY: THE LAW OF DOUBLE REFERENCE

On page 25, we learned about "The Law of Recurrence." Now we shall view another law in Bible study, called *"The Law of Double Reference."* This is a passage that applies primarily to a person or event in the present, but used by the Holy Spirit at a later time to apply to the person of Christ or the activities of His kingdom.

The human writers probably did not have this two-fold sense in mind. Instead, the double reference was in the mind of the Holy Spirit as He dictated the passages. It is really important to understand this Law before we study the Psalms and the books of prophecy.

Example: 2 Samuel 7:11ff.

1. What new blessing is promised at the end of v. 11?
2. In v. 12, to whom did this promise apply?
3. But...note v. 13! This is speaking of CHRIST!
4. Now, look at v. 10: this speaks of a yet future event!
5. Look at v. 14: how does Hebrews 1:5 explain it does not refer to Solomon, but to Christ?

COMMENT ON HEBREWS 1:5...

The comment in 2 Samuel 7:14 is here explained as applying to God's son, Jesus. Thus, these words are Messianic prophecies. Thus, while God tells David He will build him a house, He is not referring to a material building, such as David was considering, but a *kingdom*—one that would be set up by Christ, not by Solomon.

An alternate Hebrew rendering for v. 14 is: *"When iniquity is laid upon Him I will chasten Him with the rod of men."* This refers to Christ's substitutionary death!

Suggestions for marking your Bible...

1. Copy the outline in your Bible.

2. Write beside 2 Samuel 7:10:

   Davidic Covenant:
   10-16

3. Underline special passages referred to in the lecture.

4. Add any other notes from the explanations which you now wish to preserve in your Bible.

Unit Sixteen
1 KINGS 1-4 with 1 CHRONICLES 22-29
1 KINGS 5-8 with 2 CHRONICLES 1-7
1 KINGS 9-11 with 2 CHRONICLES 8-9
1 KINGS 12-16 with 2 CHRONICLES 10-17

OUTLINE OF 1 KINGS 1-4 with 1 CHRONICLES 22-29:

1 KINGS 1-4

The last days of David—1:1-2:11
  Abishag ministers to David—1:1-4
  Adonijah usurps the throne—1:5-31
  Solomon anointed king—1:32-40
  Adonijah's reaction—1:41-53
  David charges Solomon—2:1-9
  The death of David—2:10-18

The beginning of the reign of
  Solomon—2:19-4:34
  He ascends the throne—2:12
  He removes his enemies—2:13-3:2
  He prays for wisdom—3:3-28
  His staff and reign—4:1-34

1 CHRONICLES 22-29

David prepares materials
  for the Temple—22:1-19
Preparations for operating
  the Temple—23:1-27:34
The great convocation—28:1-8
The charge to Solomon—28:9-21
David challenges the
  people—29:1-9
David prays—29:10-19
Solomon enthroned—29:20-25
The death of David—29:26-30

OUTLINE OF 1 KINGS 5-8 with 2 CHRONICLES 1-7:

1 KINGS 5-8

Preparations for building the Temple—
  5:1-18
The building of the Temple—6:1-38
The building of the Royal Palace—
  7:1-12
The making of the Temple Vessels—
  7:13-51
The dedication of the Temple—
  8:1-66

2 CHRONICLES 1-7

Solomon's kingdom established—
  1:1-2:18
The erection and dedication of
  the Temple—3:1-7:22

OUTLINE OF 1 KINGS 9-11 with 2 CHRONICLES 8-9:

1 KINGS 9-11	2 CHRONICLES 8-9
God's covenant with Solomon—9:1-9	Solomon's accomplishments—
Solomon's activity and fame—9:10-10:29	8:1-18
Solomon's fall and demise—11:1-43	The praise heaped upon Solomon—
	9:1-31

OUTLINE OF 1 KINGS 12-16 with 2 CHRONICLES 10-17:

1 KINGS 12-16	2 CHRONICLES 10-17
Solomon's successor—12:1-20	Apostasy of the Northern tribes—
Rehoboam made king—12:1	10:1-11:23
Revolt of the 10 tribes—12:2-19	Apostasy and repentance of
Jeroboam made king in Israel—12:20	Rehoboam—12:1-16
The command for Peace—12:21-25	Abijah and Asa's
	reigns—13:1-16:14
Jeroboam's reign over Israel—	Jehoshaphat succeeds Asa—17:1-5
12:26-14:20	Revival under Jehoshaphat—17:6-9
Rehoboam's reign over Judah:—	Jehoshaphat's power increased—
14:21-31	17:10-19
Abijah's reign over Judah—15:1-8	
Asa's reign over Judah—15:9-24	
Nadab's reign over Israel—15:25-32	
Baasha's reign over Israel—15:33-16:7	
Elah's reign over Israel—16:8-14	
Zimri's reign over Israel—16:15-20	
Omri's reign over Israel—16:21-28	
Ahab's accession to the throne—16:29-34	

MAJOR PLACES IN ORDER

Jerusalem, Shechem

MAJOR PEOPLE IN ORDER

David, Solomon, Rehoboam, Jeroboam, Jehoshaphat

AMOUNT OF TIME COVERED

Approximately 90 years

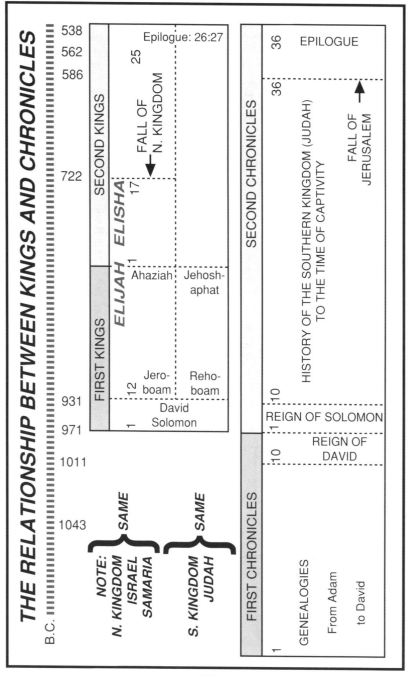

AN OVERVIEW OF 2 CHRONICLES

SOLOMON | THE KINGS OF JUDAH FOLLOWING HIM

← Chapters 1-10 →

			Chapter 12		Chapter 36:17	

| Inauguration | Solomon's Temple | Solomon's Glory | The Kingdom Divided: "Northern" & "Southern" | "Northern"="Israel" / "Southern"="Judah" | The Exile of Judah | 36:22: Order to rebuild it / Temple Destroyed |

These ten chapters focus on the construction of the Temple...

These chapters focus on the decline of the Temple under kings who are not in touch with Jehovah...

KINGS OF JUDAH

NAME OF KING	AGE BEGAN REIGN	YEARS OF REIGN	CHAR-ACTER	RELATION WITH ISRAEL	SCRIPTURE REFERENCE
Rehoboam	41	17	Bad	War	1 Ki 12:1-14:31 2 Ch 10:1-12:16
Abijah	n.a.	3	Bad	War	1 Ki 15:1-8 2 Ch 13:1-22
Asa	n.a.	41	Good	War	1 Ki 15:9-24 2 Ch 14:1-16:14
Jehoshaphat	35	25	Good	Peace	1 Ki 22:41-50 2 Ch 17:1-20:37
Jehoram	32	8	Bad	Peace	2 Ki 8:16-24 2Ch 21:1-20
Ahaziah	22	1	Bad	Alliance	2 Ki 8:25f, 9:27f 2 Ch 22:1-9
Athaliah (Queen)	n.a.	6	Bad	Peace	2 Ki 8:18f, 11:1f 2 Ch 22:1-23:21
Joash	7	40	Good	Peace	2 Ki 11:1-12:21 2 Ch 22:10-24:27
Amaziah	25	29	Good	War	2 Ki 14:1-14 2 Ch 25:1-28
Uzziah	16	52	Good	Peace	2 Ki 15:1-7 2 Ch 26:1-23
Jotham	25	16	Good	War	2 Ki 15:32-38 2 Ch 27:1-9
Ahaz	20	16	Bad	War	2 Ki 16:1-20 2 Ch 28:1-27
Hezekiah	25	29	Good		2 Ki 18:1-20:21 2 Ch 29:1-32:33
Manasseh	12	55	Bad		2 Ki 21:1-18 2 Ch 33:1-20
Amnon	22	2	Bad		2 Ki 21:19-23 2 Ch 33:21-25
Josiah	8	31	Good		2 Ki 22:1-23:30 2 Ch 34:1-36:27
Jehoahaz	23	3 mo.	Bad		2 Ki 23:31-33 2 Ch 36:1-4
Jehoiakim	25	11	Bad		2 Ki 23:34-24:5 2 Ch 36:5-8
Jehoiachin	18	3 mo.	Bad		2Ki 24:6-16 2Ch 36:8-10
Zedekiah	21	11	Bad		2 Ki 24:17-25:7 2 Ch 36:11-21

KINGS OF ISRAEL

NAME OF KING	YEARS OF REIGN	CHAR-ACTER	DETHRONED BY . . .	RELATION WITH JUDAH	SCRIPTURE REFERENCE
Jeroboam	22	Bad		War	1 Ki 11:26-14:20 2 Ch 9:29-13:22
Nadab	2	Bad	Baasha	War	1 Ki 15:25-28
Baasha	24	Bad		War	1 Ki 15:27-16:7 2 Ch 6:1-6
Elah	2	Drunkard	Zimri	War	1 Ki 16:8-10
Zimri	7 days	Murderer	Omri	War	1 Ki 16:10-20
Omri	12	Very Bad		War	1 Ki 16:16-27
Ahab	22	Horrible		Alliance	1 Ki 16:28-27:40 2 Ch 18:1-34
Ahaziah	2	Bad		Peace	1 Ki 22:40, 51-53 2 Ki 1:1-17
Joram	12	Bad	Jehu	Alliance	2 Ki 3:1ff, 9:14ff 2 Ch 22:5-7
Jehu	28	Bad		War	2 Ki 9:1-10:36 2 Ch 22:7-12
Jehoahaz	17	Bad		Peace	2 Ki 13:1-9
Jehoash	16	Bad		War	2 Ki 13:10, 14:8ff 2 Ch 25:17-24
Jeroboam II	41	Bad		Peace	2 Ki 14:23-29
Zechariah	6 mo.	Bad	Shallum	Peace	2 Ki 15:8-12
Shallum	1 mo.	Bad	Menahem	Peace	2 Ki 15:13-15
Menahem	10	Bad		Peace	2 Ki 15:16-22
Pekahiah	2	Bad	Pekah	Peace	2 Ki 15:23-26
Pekah	20	Bad	Hoshea	War	2 Ki 15:27-31 2 Ch 28:5-8
Hosheah	9	Bad		Peace	2 Ki 17:1-41

In 722 B.C., the Northern Kingdom fell...

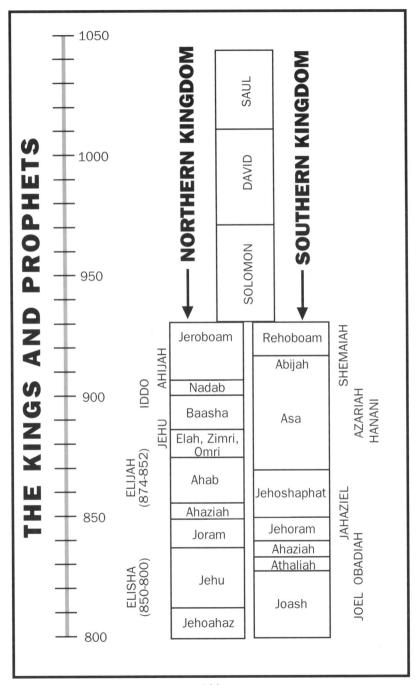

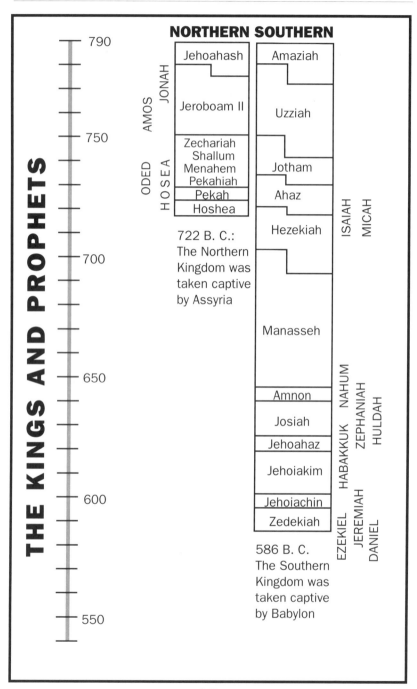

HERE'S WHERE YOUR ZONDERVAN PICTORIAL BIBLE ENCYCLOPEDIA CAN BE MOST USEFUL!

Look up the articles about "Judah" and "Israel." Browse through the various articles on these Kings. Read about the prophets. *Spend a little time digesting the history of this period.* Those who will spend 5 or 6 hours just absorbing the basics for this period in the history of Israel will find many lessons to be learned!

In particular, research the religions of that day. Learn more about *Baal* worship, with its infanticide, vile immorality, and evil practices. Recognize how shocking the conduct of the bad kings really was!

Then, marvel at the patience of God with sinning people. You will find yourself saying, "If I had been God, I would have utterly destroyed Israel!" ...But you are *not* God, and He is astonishingly willing to wait for rebellious men to come to Him. That's the only reason Israel was treated as kindly as it was. Being sent into captivity was the least of all the judgments God could have bestowed on them!

Occasionally, you'll hear some half-enlightened soul saying that the "God of the Old Testament" lacked love and compassion—and that in the "evolution" of the Bible, the "God of the New Testament" has significantly changed. DON'T YOU BELIEVE IT! And, to document this, spend time in understanding Israel during this period of their wicked kings.

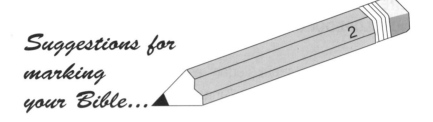

Suggestions for marking your Bible...

1. Copy the outline into your Bible.

2. Using the charts in this lesson, find the passages where the history of each king of Israel and Judah appears. In the margins, write two things about each king: which Kingdom they ruled, and whether their character was good or bad.

   EXAMPLE:

   Abijah
   Judah
   (Bad)

3. Underline special passages you read in your research which you want to remember.

4. Add any other notes from the explanations which you now wish to preserve in your Bible.

Unit Seventeen
1 KINGS 17-19
1 KINGS 20-22
with 2 CHRONICLES 18-20
2 KINGS 1-5
2 KINGS 6-8
with 2 CHRONICLES 21-22

OUTLINE OF 1 KINGS 17-19

Elijah predicts drought—17:1
Elijah fed by ravens—17:2-7
Elijah and widow of Zarephath—17:8-16
Elijah raises the widow's son—17:17-24
Elijah returns to Ahab—18:1-14
The contest on Mt. Carmel—18:20-40
Elijah prays for rain—18:41-46
Elijah flees from Jezebel—19:1-7
Elijah flees to Horeb—19:8-18
The call of Elisha—19:19-21

OUTLINE OF 1 KINGS 20-22 with 2 CHRONICLES 18-20

1 KINGS 20-22	2 CHRONICLES 18-20
Ben-Hadad beseiges Samaria—20:1-12	Jehoshaphat's alliance with Ahab—18:1-3
Ahab defeats the Syrians—20:13-30	Ahab's false prophets—18:4-11
Ahab spares the life of Ben-Hadad—20:31-34	Micaiah's true prophecy—18:12-27
The prophet scolds Ahab—20:35-43	Defeat of Jehoshaphat and death of Ahab—18:28-34
Ahab denied Naboth's vineyard—21:1-4	Jehu rebukes Jehoshaphat—19:1-3
Jezebel plots Naboth's death—21:5-16	Jehoshaphat's additional reforms—19:4-11
Elijah pronounces Ahab's doom—21:17-26	Moab invades Judah—20:1-2
Ahab repents—21:27-29	Jehoshaphat prays for deliverance—20:3-12
Ahab seduced by false prophets—22:1-28	Jehaziel promises a great deliverance—20:13-19
The Death of Ahab—22:29-40	Invading armies die—20:20-25
Reign of Jehoshaphat—22:41-50	Triumphant return to Jerusalem—20:26-30
Ahaziah's reign over Israel—22:51-53	Jehoshaphat reigns over Judah—20:31-37

143

OUTLINE OF 2 KINGS 1-5

Ahaziah of Israel—1:1-18
Elijah translated—2:1-11
Elijah's spirit rests upon Elisha—2:12-18
Elisha heals the poisoned waters—2:19-22
The cursing of the children—2:23-25
Joram reigns over Israel—3:1-3
Elisha predicts victory over Moab—3:4-20
Moab defeated—3:21-27
The widow's oil—4:1-7
Elisha and the Shunamite woman—4:8-37
Elisha's miracles for the prophets—4:38-44
Naaman's leprosy cured—5:1-14
Elisha declines Naaman's gifts—5:15-19
The sin and punishment of Elisha's servant—5:20-27

OUTLINE OF 2 KINGS 6-8 with 2 CHRONICLES 21-22

2 KINGS 6-8	2 CHRONICLES 21-22
The axe head floats—6:1-7	Jehoram reigns over Judah—21:1-7
Elisha and the Syrians—6:8-23	Edom, Libnah revolt—21:8-10
The seige of Samaria—6:24-29	Elijah prophesies against Jehoram—
Ben-Hadad seeks Elisha's life—	21:11-15
6:30-33	Philistines and Arabians invade Judah—
Elisha's prophecy—7:1-4	21:16-17
Flight of Syrians—7:5-15	Jehoram's illness and death—
Elisha's prophecy fulfilled—7:16-20	21:18-20
The Shunamite's land restored—	Ahaziah's wicked reign over Judah—
8:1-6	22:1-6
Hazael becomes King of Syria—	Jehu kills Ahaziah—22:7-9
8:7-15	Athaliah usurps the throne—22:10-12
Jehoram reigns over Judah—8:16-24	
Ahaziah reigns over Judah—8:25-29	

MAJOR PLACES IN ORDER

Israel and Judah

MAJOR PEOPLE IN ORDER

Elijah, Elisha, Ahab, Jehoshaphat, Ahaziah, Jehoram

AMOUNT OF TIME COVERED

Approximately 33 years (874 to 841 B.C.)

NOTES

THE KINGS OF JUDAH

- Protected by their geographical position.
- Prosperity of country gained through control of the trade routes to Egypt and the Red Sea.
- The nation's capitol, Jerusalem, was beseiged by the Assyrians in 701 B.C., and by the Babylonians in 597 and 586 B.C.
- Finally, Nebuchadnezzar destroyed all of Jerusalem and ended the monarchy.
- All the Kings followed the line of David.

THE KINGS OF ISRAEL

- NOT protected by their geographical position.
- Forced to develop an efficient standing army and enough chariots to defend themselves against all too frequent attacks.
- Ahab of Israel provided *2,000 chariots* in a battle held in 853 B. C.!
- Unstable government; army officers caused many internal revolutions.

THE LIFE AND MINISTRY OF ELIJAH

- Remember Elijah's ministry was in ISRAEL, not JUDAH! He had a difficult assignment...

- God sent him to oppose, by *word* and *action*, both Baal worship and those who engaged in it.

- See 1 Kings 17:1—Elijah tells wicked Ahab pointedly that the King does not have his allegiance: *God* has it!

- Note verse 2—God tells him to *leave* Israel! Imagine...a nation without a prophet and only a *wicked* king.

- Note how he is cared for by God, using ravens.

- Meanwhile, in his absence judgment becomes more intense than before...

- 17:7—Read the wonderful story of the Widow at Zarephath...

- 18:16—Read the thrilling story of Elijah on Mt. Carmel...

2 KINGS 2: THE TRANSFER OF THE PROPHET'S MANTLE TO ELISHA—THE CONTINUANCE OF GOD'S ACTS

(Add comments from explanation...)

THE LIFE AND MINISTRY OF ELISHA
(Add comments from explanation...)

Suggestions for marking your Bible...

1. Copy the outline into your Bible.

2. Write beside 2 Kings 4:1:

    *God's way of making our resources **enough!***

3. Write beside 2 Kings 4:23:

    Faith is the victory!

4. Add any other notes from the explanations which you wish to preserve in your Bible.

Unit Eighteen

2 KINGS 9-13
with 2 CHRONICLES 23-24
2 KINGS 14-17
with 2 CHRONICLES 25-28
2 KINGS 18-20
with 2 CHRONICLES 29-32
2 KINGS 21-23
with 2 CHRONICLES 33-35
2 KINGS 24-25
with 2 CHRONICLES 36

OUTLINE OF 2 KINGS 9-13 with 2 CHRONICLES 23-24

2 KINGS 9-13	2 CHRONICLES 23-24
Jehu anointed King over Israel—9:1-13	Joash becomes King over Judah—23:1-11
Jehu kills Joram, King of Israel—9:14-26	Athaliah is slain—23:12-15
	Revival under Jehoiada—23:16-21
Jehu kills Ahaziah, King of Judah—9:27-29	Joash reigns in Judah—24:1-3
Jezebel's Death—9:30-37	Joash repairs the Temple— 24:4-14
Jehu destroys the House of Ahab—10:1-17	Jehoiada the good priest dies—24:15-16
Jehu slays the Baal worshipers—10:18-31	Joash turns to idolatry—24:17-22
Jehu's death—10:32-36	Syrians invade and defeat Judah—24:23-27
Athaliah kills her grand-children to get the throne—11:1	
Joash is saved—11:2-11	
Joash made king (age 7)—11:12-15	
Athaliah killed—11:16-21	
Jehoash reigns over Judah—12:1-21	
Jehoahaz reigns over Israel—13:1-9	
Jehoash reigns over Israel—13:10-13	
Elisha's final prophecy and death—13:14-25	

OUTLINE OF 2 KINGS 14-17 with 2 CHRONICLES 25-28

2 KINGS 14-17

2 CHRONICLES 25-28

2 KINGS 14-17	2 CHRONICLES 25-28
Amaziah reigns over Judah—14:1-22	Amaziah reigns over Judah—25:1-4
Jeroboam reigns over Israel—14:23-29	Amaziah defeats Edom—25:5-16
Azariah reigns over Judah—15:1-7	War between Israel and Judah—
Zechariah reigns over Israel—15:8-12	25:17-28
Shallum reigns over Israel—15:13-16	Uzziah succeeds Amaziah—26:1-5
Menahem reigns over Israel -15:17-22	Uzziah prospers in war—26:6-15
Pekahiah reigns over Israel—15:23-26	Uzziah usurps the priest's office;
Pekah reigns over Israel—15:27-31	his punishment—26:16-23
Jotham reigns over Judah—15:32-38	Jotham reigns over Judah—27:1-9
Ahaz reigns over Judah—16:1-18	Ahaz reigns over Judah—28:1-4
Hezekiah reigns over Judah—16:19-20	War between Ahaz and Pekah—
Hoshea reigns over Israel—17:1-4	28:5-15
THE FALL OF SAMARIA AND THE	Edomites and Philistines invade
CAPTIVITY OF ISRAEL—17:5-23	Judah—28:16-26
Samaria repopulated—17:24-41	Ahaz' death—28:27

OUTLINE OF 2 KINGS 18-20 with 2 CHRONICLES 29-32

2 KINGS 18-20

2 CHRONICLES 29-32

2 KINGS 18-20	2 CHRONICLES 29-32
Hezekiah reigns over Judah—18:1-12	Hezekiah reigns over Judah—29:1-2
Sennacherib invades Judah—18:13-37	Revival under Hezekiah—29:3-19
Hezekiah's message to Isaiah—19:1-7	Temple worship restored—29:20-36
Sennacherib's letter to Hezekiah—	Preparation for the Passover—
19:8-13	30:1-14
Hezekiah's prayer—19:14-19	Passover celebrated—30:15-27
Isaiah's prophecy and Judah's	The idols destroyed—31:1
deliverance—19:20-37	Hezekiah's provision for priests
Hezekiah's sickness and	and Levites—31:2-21
recovery—20:1-11	Sennacherib invades Judah—32:1-19
Hezekiah receive envoys	God delivers Hezekiah—32:20-23
from Babylon—20:12-19	Hezekiah's illness and recovery—
	32:24-26
	Hezekiah receives envoys from
	Babylon—32:27-31
	Hezekiah dies—32:32-33

OUTLINE OF 2 KINGS 21-23 with 2 CHRONICLES 33-35

2 KINGS 21-23

Manasseh reigns over Judah—
   21:1-18
Amon reigns over Judah—21:19-26
Josiah reigns over Judah—22:1-7
The Book of the Law found—22:8-14
Huldah's prophecy—22:15-20
Josiah's covenant—23:1-3
Josiah's reforms—23:4-20
The Passover restored—23:21-23
The Lord's anger against
   Judah—23:24-27
Josiah's death—23:28-30
Jehoahaz reigns over
   Judah—23:31-35
Jehoiakim reigns over Judah—
   23:36-37

2 CHRONICLES 33-35

Manasseh reigns over Judah—
   33:1-10
Manasseh's captivity and restoration–
   33:11-20
Amon reigns over Judah—33:21-25
Josiah reigns over Judah—34:1-2
Josiah's reforms—34:3-7
Josiah repairs the Temple—34:8-13
The Book of the Law discovered—
   34:14-2
Huldah's prophecy—34:22-28
Josiah's covenant—34:29-33
Josiah keeps the Passover - 35:1-19
The death of Josiah—35:20-27

OUTLINE OF 2 KINGS 24-25 with 2 CHRONICLES 36

2 KINGS 24-25

Jehoiakim ruled by
   Nebuchadnezzar—24:1-7
Jehoiachin taken captive
   to Babylon—24:8-17
Zedekiah reigns over Judah—
   24:18-20
Jerusalem falls—25:1-7
THE FALL OF JUDAH; CAPTIVITY IN
   BABYLON—25:8-21
Remnant flees to Egypt—25:22-26
Jehoiachin restored—25:27-30

2 CHRONICLES 36

The reign and dethronement of
   Jehoahaz—36:1-4
Jehoiakim reigns over
   Judah— 36:5-8
Jehoiachin taken captive to
   Babylon—36:9-10
Zedekiah reigns over Judah—
   36:11-16
THE CAPTIVITY OF JUDAH—36:17-21
Decree of Cyrus to build the Temple—
   36:22-23

MAJOR PLACES IN ORDER

Israel and Judah, Assyria and Babylon

MAJOR PEOPLE IN ORDER

Kings of Israel and Judah, from Jehu and Joash to the Captivity; their captors

AMOUNT OF TIME COVERED

Approximately 303 years (841 to 538 B.C.)

NOTES

The theme of this section is the rapid and fearful corruption of God's chosen people. The story alternates between Judah and Israel, and both sections of the nation sink deeper and ever deeper into sin and decay.

The story of Jehu is one of personal failure. He turned himself against Baalism, and broke it with shocking activity. Yet, while an instrument in God's hand, he was a proud spirit. In his private life he was corrupt. He is a reminder that one can be an instrument in the hand of God and yet never be in fellowship with Him.

Athaliah is the lowest of all! She murders her own grandchildren and reigns over Judah for 6 years.

Jehosheba, the daughter of Athaliah, nursed and cared for Joash for 6 years, as he was hidden away in the Temple.

Jehoiada, the high priest, arranged the death of Athaliah and the crowning of Joash.

Joash, in cowardice, buys off Hazael when invaded by giving him all the vessels and treasures of the house of God.

Note that when Jehoash visits Elisha, he addressed him with the exact words Elisha had used with Elijah at the moment he was taken up in God's chariot: "My father, my father, the chariots of Israel and the horsemen thereof!" The king realized the true strength of the nation was not in its military equipment, but in being in the will of God. Yet in this interview, we see the weakness of the king. He lacked that passion and consecration which were necessary to the full accomplishment of his purpose.

Amaziah is another picture of limits in loyalty to Jehovah!

In Israel, Jeroboam II was evil before God, a man of war. Yet, he was used to restore some of the land of Israel that had been lost. Note that Jonah, the son of Amittai, influenced this. This is the same Jonah that went to Ninevah.

Azariah in 2 Kings 15 is the same man who will be called Uzziah in the book of Isaiah. In the main, he tried to obey God, but the people continued in sin. He was smitten with leprosy.

In Israel, at the end one king succeeded another through murder. Zechariah was murdered by Shallum, who one month later, was murdered by Menahem, who reigned evilly for 10 years. During this time the Assyrians invaded the land. Menahem bought them off. He was followed by Pekahiah, his son. After 2 years, he was murdered by Pekah. He occupied the throne for 20 years, during which the Assyrians (under Tiglath-Pileser) invaded. He carried away a section of the people into captivity. Finally, Pekah was murdered by Hoshea.

In Judah, things were also decayed. Ahaz, who was challenged by Isaiah the prophet, was a depraved man. He sought help from the Assyrians, and placed his neck in their yoke. Then he set up a heathen altar in the actual courts of the Temple! Both Isaiah and Micah were delivering the word of God during this time.

Note in 2 Kings 17:7-12 how the writer declares exactly why the people were taken away into captivity:

- Disobedience to Jehovah
- Conformity to the nations around them
- Secret practice of abominations
- Public idolatry

Where did Hezekiah get any spiritual guidance? He was the son of depraved Ahaz! The answer is in a prophet's influence. All his life he was under the influence of Isaiah. The people had made a fetish out of the serpent of brass that Moses had used in the wilderness. Hezekiah called it Nehushtan, "a piece of brass," and broke it in pieces.

It was in the sixth year of his reign in Judah that Israel was carried off into captivity. Yet, before Sennacherib, Hezekiah showed a weakness. Again, later in life, he showed his weakness during the Babylonian's visit, when he showed them all the treasures of his house. Isaiah rebuked him, saying they would eventually carry it all away.

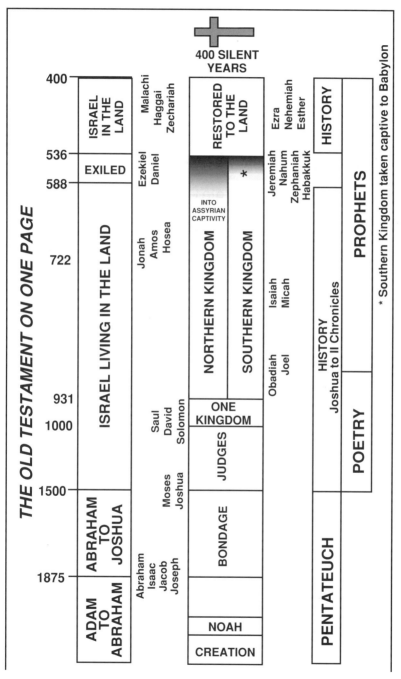

THE OLD TESTAMENT ON ONE PAGE

400 SILENT YEARS

400

ISRAEL IN THE LAND

Malachi
Haggai
Zechariah

RESTORED TO THE LAND

Ezra
Nehemiah
Esther

HISTORY

536

EXILED

Ezekiel
Daniel

588

INTO ASSYRIAN CAPTIVITY

*

Jeremiah
Nahum
Zephaniah
Habakkuk

PROPHETS

ISRAEL LIVING IN THE LAND

Jonah
Amos
Hosea

722

NORTHERN KINGDOM

SOUTHERN KINGDOM

Isaiah
Micah

* Southern Kingdom taken captive to Babylon

Obadiah
Joel

931

Saul
David
Solomon

ONE KINGDOM

1000

HISTORY
Joshua to II Chronicles

JUDGES

1500

Moses
Joshua

POETRY

ABRAHAM TO JOSHUA

BONDAGE

Abraham
Isaac
Jacob
Joseph

1875

ADAM TO ABRAHAM

ABRAHAM

PENTATEUCH

NOAH

CREATION

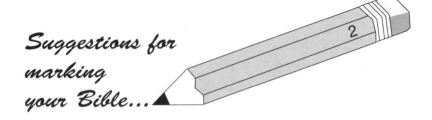

Suggestions for marking your Bible...

1. Copy the outline into your Bible.

2. Write beside 2 Kings 19:31:

> *Mention of the "remnant" important in prophecy.*

3. Write beside 2 Chronicles 28:3:

> *The valley of Hinnom Place where parents offered children as sacrifices to idol Molech. In N.T., "Gehenna" (hell) is the Greek word for this valley.*

4. Add any other notes from the explanations which you wish to preserve in your Bible.

Unit Nineteen
EZRA—NEHEMIAH—ESTHER

OUTLINE OF EZRA

I. THE EARLY RETURN OF THE JEWISH EXILES—1:1-2:70
The royal decree of Cyrus—1:1-4
Reactions to the decree—1:5-11
The return of the first wave of exiles—2:1-70

II. THE REINSTATEMENT OF THE WORSHIP OF JEHOVAH—3:1-6:22
Renewal of the Altar of Burnt Offerings—3:1-3
Observance of the Feast of Tabernacles—3:4-7
Rebuilding of the Temple—3:8-13
Conflict over rebuilding—4:1-5
Continued opposition—4:6-24
Haggai and Zechariah, the prophets, inspire the resuming of rebuilding—5:1-17
Darius searches for Cyrus' Edict—6:1-12
Darius' Decree implemented—6:13-16
The Dedication of the Temple—6:17-22

III. EZRA'S LEADERSHIP AND THE RETURN OF THE EXILES 7:1-10:44
Ezra's activities under Artaxerxes—7:1-10
Artaxerxes' assignment to restore the Temple—7:11-26
The blessing of Ezra—7:27-28
Record of those returning with Ezra—8:1-14
Jewish Chiefs convened at Ahava—8:15-36
Ezra's lament over intermarriage by the exiles—9:1-4
Ezra's deep intercession—9:5-15
Ezra gives the way for reform—10:1-17
The naming of priests guilty of intermarriage—10:18-44

MAJOR PLACES IN ORDER

Persia, Jerusalem

MAJOR PEOPLE IN ORDER

Cyrus, Zerubbabel and Jeshua, Haggai and Zechariah, Darius, Ezra, Artaxerxes

AMOUNT OF TIME COVERED

Approximately 86 years (541 to 455 B.C.)

OUTLINE OF NEHEMIAH

I. THE REBUILDING OF THE WALLS OF JERUSALEM—1:1-7:73
The arrival of Nehemiah in Jerusalem—1:1-2:20
Eliashib the High Priest as leader in the
    restoration of Jerusalem's walls—3:1-6:19
The responsibility of Hanani—7:1-73

II. THE ACTIVITIES OF EZRA AND NEHEMIAH SUMMARIZED—8:1-13:31
Renewal of the Covenant—8:1-10:39
Listing of Jerusalem dwellers—11:1-36
Identification of the Priests and Levites—12:1-26
Dedication of the Walls—12:27-43
Priests, Levites, Singers, Porters, and their method of support—12:44-47
Exclusivism: the prohibition of Ammonites and Moabites—13:1-5
The second return of Nehemiah—13:6-31

MAJOR PLACES IN ORDER

Persia, Jerusalem

MAJOR PEOPLE IN ORDER
Nehemiah, Artaxerxes, Eliashib, Hanani, Ezra

AMOUNT OF TIME COVERED

Approximately 15 years (445 to 430 B.C.)

OUTLINE OF ESTHER

I. ESTHER CHOSEN QUEEN—1:1-2:18
The feasts of King Ahasuerus (Xerxes) in Shushan - 1:1-9
Queen Vashti deposed—1:10-22
Vashti's successor sought—2:1-14
Esther becomes queen—2:15-18

II. ESTHER'S DELIVERANCE OF THE JEWS—2:19-7:10
Mordecai sits in the King's gate—2:19-20
Mordecai saves the King's life—2:21-23
Haman conspires against the Jews—3:1-15
Jews mourn; Esther hears of conspiracy—4:1-9
Esther asked by Mordecai to risk her life
 for her people—4:10-17
Esther's courage; her request—5:1-14
The king's insomnia—6:1-3
Haman forced to honor Mordecai—6:4-14
Esther pleads for herself and her people—7:1-6
Haman hanged on his own gallows—7:7-10

III. THE JEW'S REVENGE UPON THEIR ENEMIES—
8:1-10:3

Haman's conspiracy defeated—8:1-14
Mordecai exalted; Jews rejoice—8:15-17
Jews destroy their enemies; they rest and are glad—
9:1-19
The Feast of Purim instituted—9:20-32
Mordecai's further advancement—10:1-3

MAJOR PLACES IN ORDER

The Persian palace of Shushan

MAJOR PEOPLE IN ORDER

Ahasuerus, Vashti, Mordecai, Esther, Haman

AMOUNT OF TIME COVERED

Approximately 1 year (485 B.C.)

NOTES

Ezra, Nehemiah and Esther conclude the historical books
of the Old Testament. Both Ezra and Nehemiah tell about the
events which occur in Israel at the end of the Captivity. Ezra
and Nehemiah relate to events concerning JUDAH, not ISRAEL.
Connect these stories, then, to 2 Chronicles 36:6: this was
the first deportation of Judah (597 B.C.); the final deportation
is in 36:15-21.

In 538 B.C., Cyrus permitted the Jews to return to the ruins
of Jerusalem.

Ezra emphasizes the rebuilding of the Temple; Nehemiah, the rebuilding of the wall of Jerusalem. Both books contain lengthy genealogies, designed to establish the priesthood as descended from Aaron.

There is a gap of about 50 years between Ezra 6 and 7. Thus, the people who lived in the first half of the book have died by the time Ezra began his ministry in Jerusalem. Esther's story fits into this 50 year gap. Ezra was a priest; Nehemiah was not. They were contemporaries. Be sure to fit Haggai and Zechariah into this period (see Ezra 5).

MORE THAN YOU EVER WANTED TO KNOW ABOUT THE ASSYRIAN, CHALDEAN, AND BABYLON EMPIRES...

It is confusing to tie the captivities of Israel and Judah into the contemporary scene if you do not know something about the huge world powers which surrounded this little nation.

THE ASSYRIAN EMPIRE

The original center of Assyrian power began in 3000 B.C. in Asshur, located 60 miles south of Nineveh on the west bank of the Tigris River. Assyria was founded by colonists from Babylonia.

Tiglath-Pileser (1115 B.C.) made it a great nation. Assyria dominated everything in the region! It declined during the period of David and Solomon (1010-931 B.C.). Otherwise, their Jewish empire would not have been permitted.

The mighty Assyrian Empire lasted from 885-612 B.C. Its capital was Nineveh. (See the book of Nahum.)

A SUMMARY OF THE KINGS OF THAT EMPIRE:

Ashurnasirpal II (885-860). Powerful fighter; extended Assyria to the Mediterranean.

Shalmaneser III (859-824). First Assyrian king to clash with Israel. Ahab fought against him with Benhadad (853). Jehu paid tribute to him.

Shamsi-Adad V (824-815), Adadnirari III (808-783), and several weak emperors through 747, enabled Uzziah of Judah and Jeroboam II of Israel to rule without threat.

Shalmaneser IV (781-772) allowed Jeroboam III to expand the border of Israel while he concentrated on Damascus.

Asshur-Dan III (771-746) suffered a painful defeat in battle, marked by an ominous eclipse in 763 B.C.

Tiglath-Pileser III (745-727), "Pul," carried northern Israel into exile in 734 B.C.

Shalmaneser V (726-722) besieged Samaria.

Sargon II (722-705) conquered Samaria in 722.

Sennacherib (705-681) was a great conqueror, but failed to take Jerusalem.

Esarhaddon (681-668) rebuilt Babylon and conquered Egypt.

Ashurbanipal (669-626), called Asnapper (see Ezra 4:10), was the last great emperor.

The period 626-607 witnessed the disintegration and fall of this cruel empire.

THE CHALDEAN EMPIRE

OLD BABYLONIAN PERIOD (1830-1550). Babel dates from prehistoric times, but did not become the capital of a great empire until this time. Hammurabi (1728-1686) created the first dynasty of Babylon, and lifted it to the height of power. Babylon and Assyria struggled for supremacy until Assyria finally subdued them. This conflict between them lasted from 885-626.

THE CHALDEAN EMPIRE (605-539). This "Neo-Babylonian Empire" was ended when Judah was sent into captivity.

Here is a summary of the Kings of that Empire:

Nabopolassar (625-605), governor of Babylon, threw off the Assyrian yoke and destroyed Nineveh, 612 B.C. He was the father of Nebuchadnezzar II.

Nebuchadnezzar II (605-562). His first deportation of Judah (Daniel 1:2) came in 605 B.C., the second in 597, and the third in 586, when he destroyed Jerusalem. He besieged Tyre (585-573) and also invaded and desolated Moab, Ammon, Edom and Lebanon. He invaded Egypt in 572 and 568 B.C., and died in 562. He was one of the most autocratic and powerful rulers of the ancient world. His capital city of Babylon was awesome in its grandeur!

Evil-Merodach, also called **Amel-Marduk** or "Man of Marduk" (562-560), son of Nebuchadnezzar, was murdered by this brother-in-law Nergal-shar-usur.

Neriglissar (560-556), reigned 4 years.

His son **Labashi-Marduk** was murdered after reigning a few months.

Nabonidus (556-539) was one of the men who usurped the throne. He was also called "the god Nebo (Nabu)."

His oldest son was **Belshazzar** (meaning "Bel, protect the King!"), who was coregent with him when Babylon fell to the Persians (Daniel 5) in October, 539 B.C.

THE PERSIAN EMPIRE (539-331 B.C.)

The Persian kings were humane rulers who permitted the Jews to return and rebuild their temple and city. Persia reversed the cruel policies of Assyria and Chaldea, and repatriated the displaced peoples. Under the two century Persian regime, Judah became a tiny province in the Fifth Persian Satrapy. Its southern frontier fortress was Lachish, and it was controlled from the palace of the Persian administrator.

Here is a summary of the Kings of that Empire:

CYRUS (539-530) united Media and Persia (549), conquered Lydia (546), Babylon (539), ruled at the time by Nabonidus and crown prince Belshazzar. His decree (Ezra 1:1-4) permitted the return of the Jews to Palestine.

CAMBYSES (530-522) conquered Egypt. His death was by suicide (Ezra 4:7,11).

SMERDIS (522) was a Magian usurper who caused civil war (Ezra 4:7,11).

[NOTE: *Magis* were a part of the governmental system, the *Megistanes*, similar to our Senate. Thus, the *"Magis"* visited Jesus when he was a baby.]

DARIUS I THE GREAT (522-486) put down the insurrection under Smerdis and saved the empire. He erected the famous Behistun Inscription on the road from Babylon to Ecbatana which furnished the key to Babylonian-Akkadian cuneiform, as the Rosetta Stone in Egypt proved to be the key to Egyptian hieroglyphics. The temple at Jerusalem was completed under his encouraging reign in 520-515 (Ezra 6:15).

XERXES I, also called **AHASUERUS** (486-465), was the husband of Esther. Mordecai was his Prime Minister. He warred against Greece.

ARTAXERXES I LONGIMANUS (465-424) was a friend of Jerusalem. Ezra returned in 458 B.C.; Nehemiah became Governor (Ezra 7:1, 8; Nehemiah 2:1) in April/May, 445 B.C. The famous Elephantine Papyri from the Jewish military colony, discovered at the Nile in 1903, confirm this period.

XERXES II (424), **DARIUS II** (423-404), **ARTAXERXES II** (404-358), **ARSES** (338-336), and **DARIUS III** (336-331) conclude the Kings of this Empire.

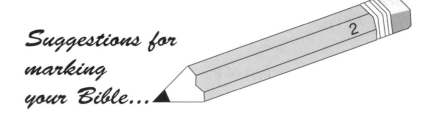

Suggestions for marking your Bible...

1. Copy the outline into your Bible.

2. Write beside Ezra 9:3:

   An idiomatic expression of indignation. His agony over the situation led to confession and intercession.

3. Write beside Nehemiah 5:13:

   "Amen," "Aman" in Hebrew, means "to be firm or sure." Sometimes translated "verily" in New Testament. It signifies that which is truth. Its double use (John. 3:3) increases its intensity that something is true.

4. Add any other notes from the explanations which you wish to preserve in your Bible.

Unit Twenty
JOB
PSALMS 1-72

OUTLINE OF JOB: A PLAY IN SIX ACTS

PROLOGUE—1:1-2:13

Job's Piety—1:1-5
Satan's Challenge—1:6-12
Job's Afflictions—1:13-22
Satan's Pressure Increased—2:1-8
Job's Wife—2:9-10
Arrival of Friends—2:11-13

ACT 1: THE JUSTICE OF GOD—3:1-14:22

SCENE 1:
     Job curses his birth—3:1-26
SCENE 2:
     Eliphaz uses EXPERIENCE to judge Job—4:1- 5:27
     Job's response—6:1-7:21
SCENE 3:
     Bildad uses TRADITION to judge Job—8:1-22
     Job: Complains about God's fairness—9:1-10:22
SCENE 4:
Zophar uses OPINION to judge Job—11:1-20
     Job: Rebukes friends, pleads with God—12:1-14:22

ACT 2: THE FATE OF THE WICKED—15:1-21:34

SCENE 1:
>Eliphaz discusses fate of the wicked—15:1-35
>Job: All have forsaken him!—16:1-17:16

SCENE 2:
>Bildad reemphasizes fate of wicked—18:1-21
>Job: Declares innocence, cries out for
>vindication—19:1-29

SCENE 3:
>Zophar feels insulted by Job; elaborates
>on Fate of wicked—20:1-29
>Job's response—Demands silence, refutes arguments
>of his friends—21:1-34

ACT 3: THE SINFULNESS OF JOB—22:1-26:14

SCENE 1:
>Eliphaz accuses Job of sinning—22:1-30
>Job's response—"Innocent! God is
>indifferent!"—23:1-24:25

SCENE 2:
>Bildad affirms God's transcendence and
>man's sin—25:1-6
>Job's response: Sarcasm—26:1-14

ACT 4: THE MONOLOGUES OF JOB—27:1-31:40

SCENE 1:
>Hopelessness of wicked—27:1-23

SCENE 2:
>True wisdom of God—28:1-28

SCENE 3:
>Job's past—29:1-25

SCENE 4:
>Job's present—30:1-31

SCENE 5:
>Job's claim of innocence—31:1-40

ACT 5: IN DEFENSE OF GOD—32:1-37:24

SCENE 1:
> Elihu tells Job to acknowledge God as
> always right—32:1-33:33

SCENE 2:
> He condemns Job's attitude—34:1-37

SCENE 3:
> He refutes Job's comment that being
> righteous is of no benefit—35:1-16

SCENE 4:
> He states God is good and His greatness
> is seen in nature—36:1-37:24

ACT 6: JOB MEETS GOD—38:1-42:9

SCENE 1:
> God reviews His creation—38:1-40:2
> Job relinquishes his challenge—40:3-5

SCENE 2:
> God charges Job with self-deification;
> describes two of His created beings—
> 40:6-41:34
> Job cries out in humility—42:1-6

SCENE 3:
> God's verdict in Job's favor; orders his
> friends to ask Job's forgiveness—
> 42:7-9

EPILOGUE—42:10-17

Job prays for his friends—42:10
Job's blessings and his death—42:11-17

MAJOR PLACES IN ORDER

The Land of Uz *(In all probability, located in northern Arabia, perhaps near the oasis of Medina or near Azraq in the Wadi Sirhan.)*

MAJOR PEOPLE IN ORDER

God, Satan, Job, Eliphaz, Bildad, Zophar, Elihu, God, Job

DATE

Job is probably the oldest book in the Bible. It demonstrates the patriarchal pattern, and is so old it does not reflect the Commandments, thus almost guaranteeing it is older than Moses. Some even put Job at the time of Abraham.

NOTES

THE "WISDOM" LITERATURE

There are three major divisions in the Hebrew Bible: *Law, Prophets,* and *Writings.* In the English Bible, we call the *"Writings"* the *"Books of Poetry."* These five books are:

- •Job
- •Psalms
- •Proverbs
- •Ecclesiastes
- •Song of Solomon

Israel's Books of Poetry all have different themes or purposes:

- •JOB: "Why Do The Righteous Suffer?"
- •PSALMS: The Song Book Of Israel
- •PROVERBS: A Study Of Godly Values
- •ECCLESIASTES: Godless Life-styles Evaluated
- •SONG OF SOLOMON: Human Love As A Picture Of Divine Love.

Of these books, the Psalms are the most important of the writings.

UNDERSTANDING HEBREW POETRY

Unlike English poetry, Hebrew poetry does not rhyme the end word of each line. Instead, this form of poetry is called *PARALLELISM.*

Their poetry does not play with words, but with thoughts.

It is not difficult to understand this and to gain a deep appreciation for their poetry!

There are only 4 types of "rhymes" to remember:

(Underline the scriptures below as we read them)

1. **SYNONYMOUS**
   The Second line repeats the idea of the first line:
   Psalm 3:1, 24:1, 49:1, 8:4, 19:1

2. **ANTITHETIC**
   The Second line contrasts the idea of the first line:
   Psalm 1:6, 90:6, 37:9, 1:6

3. **SYNTHETIC**
   The Second line develops the idea of the first line:
   Psalm 1:1, 19:7, 55:6, 95:3

4. **EMBLEMATIC**
   The Second line illustrates the idea of the first line:
   Psalm 42:1

5. **CLIMACTIC**
   The second line amplifies the first line:
   Psalm 55:12,13

NOTES:

BACKGROUND OF JOB:

SATAN AS DESCRIBED IN JOB:

SOURCES OF RELIGIOUS AUTHORITY IN JOB:

JOB'S *GO'EL:* Job 19:23-27

ABOUT SUFFERING:

OUTLINE OF PSALMS 1-72 (BOOKS 1 AND 2)

BOOK 1: PSALMS 1-41

The Godly Man Vs. The Ungodly Man—1
Messiah's Kingship and Kingdom—2
Trials of the Godly—3-7
Messiah's Sovereignty—8
The Godly and The Wicked One—9-15
Prophetic Vistas of Christ—16-24
Soul Exercise of the Godly—25-39
David's Experiences Foreshadow Christ's—40-41

BOOK 2: PSALMS 42-72

Through Tribulation to Kingdom Blessing—42-49
The Righteous God and His Penitent People—50-51
Israel's Time of Trouble—52-55
Trials of the Saints Before Blessing—56-60
Through Sufferings to Kingdom Blessing—61-68
Christ Rejected and Exalted—69-72

NOTES

THE USE OF ACROSTICS

Nine of the Psalms play with the alphabet, or are acrostic. They are:

9, 10, 25, 34, 37, 111, 112, 119, 145

The classic example of this is 119. Each stanza of 8 verses begins with a successive letter of the Hebrew alphabet, and each verse in a stanza begins with the same letter.

Of course, all this is lost in the translation of the Hebrew into English. *(In some English Bibles, Psalm 119 has captions showing the Hebrew alphabet used in the acrostics.)*

EDITORIAL TITLES

For all but thirty-four of the Psalms, there are editorial titles introducing them. In the Hebrew text, these titles are considered the first verse of the Psalm. In your English Bible, they are usually in italics and are printed above the first verse.

These titles include:
- Technical names designating the type of Psalm
- Musical terms
- Hymn tunes to be used
- Liturgical notes
- Historical information

AUTHORSHIP OF THE PSALMS

David—approximately 92
Moses—Psalm 90
Solomon—Psalm 72, 127
Heman the Ezrahite—Psalm 88
Ethan the Ezrahite—Psalm 89
Asaph—Psalm 50 and 73-83
Sons of Korah—Psalms 42, 44-49, 84, 85, 87,88

The oldest Psalm is written by Moses.

The youngest Psalm is 137, written in the Sixth Century B.C.

The final compiling of the Psalms was done in the time of Ezra and Nehemiah.

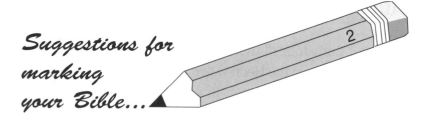

Suggestions for marking your Bible...

1. Copy the outline into your Bible.

2. Add headings to chapters in Psalms. It will help you become familiar with them! The following material can be transferred as chapter headings...

Types Of Psalms

Penitential: 6,32,38,51,102,130,143
Praise: 113-118
Imprecatory (Invokes evil on one's enemies):
   35,52,58,59,69,79,83,109,137,140
"Songs of Ascent": 120-134
Probably written by Hezekiah (2 Kings 20:1-11.)
   His sun dial reversed 15 degrees to signify God's promise of 15 additional years of life. It is believed he wrote these Psalms in gratefulness for the extra years of life God granted him.
Messianic Psalms: 2, 8, 16, 22-24,
   40-41, 45, 68-69, 72, 89, 96,
   98, 102, 110, 118, 132

4. Add any other notes from the explanations which you wish to preserve in your Bible.

Unit Twenty One
PSALMS 73-150
PROVERBS

OUTLINE OF PSALMS 73-150 (BOOKS 3, 4, AND 5)

BOOK 3: PSALMS 73-89—
THE HOLINESS OF THE LORD'S SANCTUARY

Why do the wicked prosper?—73

The Sanctuary desecrated—74

God intervenes for the sanctuary—75

Divine government set up—76

The troubled saint—77

God seen in Israel's history—78

Prayer for judgment on enemies—79

Cry for restoration of Israel—80

Israel's regathering—81

Pre-Kingdom judgment—82

Israel's enemies overthrown—83

Prayer Issuing in Kingdom glory—84-89

BOOK 4: PSALMS 90-106—WILDERNESS EXPERIENCES

From sinful wandering to redemption rest—90-93

Judgment; the glories of the coming Kingdom age—
94-100

The Righteous King in humiliation and glory—101-106

BOOK 5: PSALMS 107-150—PRAISES TO GOD

Israel's deliverances and praise to God—107-108

Christ in rejection, exaltation and coming glory—109-113

Past deliverances and future praise—114-117

Messiah and Word of God exalted—118-119

The Psalms of Ascent—120-134

Restored Israel worships—135-136

The exile's experiences—137

Praise to the Lord—138

Israel's Creator-Redeemer—139

Trials and troubles of God's people—140-143

Prayer for the Lord's power—144

The Messiah's glory and His Kingdom—145

The Grand Hallelujah Finale—146-150

A WALK THROUGH THE PSALMS—NOTES

PROVERBS

BOOK 1: PROVERBS OF SOLOMON—1-9

Introduction—1:1-6
Lessons in wisdom—1:7-4:27
Discussion of folly, the prelude to sin—5-7
An ode to wisdom—8-9

BOOK 2: VARIOUS SAYINGS OF SOLOMON—10-22:16

Contrast of the wise and foolish—10-15
Moral, ethical, and spiritual lessons—16-22:16

BOOK 3: WORDS OF THE WISE—22:17-24

The first series—22:17-24:22
The second series—24:23-34

BOOK 4: PROVERBS OF SOLOMON COPIED BY
HEZEKIAH'S COMMITTEE—25-29

Wise conduct—25-27
Other comments on conduct—28-29

BOOK 5: FINAL APPENDICES

The sayings of Agur—30
The sayings of Lemuel—31:1-9
The "Perfect Wife" acrostic—31:10-31
(Each verse begins with a letter of the Hebrew alphabet)

AUTHOR

1 Kings 4:32 attributes 3,000 proverbs to Solomon (there are 800 in Proverbs.) Most are his work.

DATE

About the tenth century B.C., during the lifetime of Solomon.

NOTES

You will notice "balanced antithesis" in these writings: the wise and the foolish, the good and the wicked, etc.

USING PROVERBS WITH THE FAMILY

The family holds a pivotal position in this book, just as it did in God's covenant with Israel on Sinai.

Because of this fact, the use of the book of Proverbs in raising children is important! As you read it, notice how it deals with moral and ethical problems, the use of money, the importance of good judgment, the value of spiritual viewpoints about secular things, etc. *There is literally no area of life that is not touched on in this book!*

Note also the number of chapters in Proverbs...*one for each day of the month.* Time yourself as you read a chapter aloud...it takes *just a few minutes.*

Many years ago, the Chinese evangelist Leland Wang shared how he had used this book for family devotions as his children were growing up. I heard this report of his when I was a college student.

As our children came along, we began to use Proverbs as the material for our daily devotions. Using a modern paraphrase, easy to understand, these truths were given to our three sons.

When our third son was entering his teen years, we went to Singapore as missionaries. Living outside his own culture was not an easy adjustment for him. For an entire year of our stay there, we used Proverbs *every night* for our family devotions. At the end of the meal, we took turns reading the chapters. On the twelfth month, I asked Randall to read *all* the chapters *every* night.

He became so well acquainted with the materials that he would make comments, with boyish humor, before reading for us—remarks such as, "Oh, boy! We're going to get the word about *prostitutes* again tonight!"

Those truths have carried him through life into adulthood. Many times, in many ways, I see him living by the standards of the book of Proverbs.

If you have children *(or grandchildren!),* give Proverbs a chance to influence them. You will be glad you helped to saturate their values with the wisdom of Solomon!

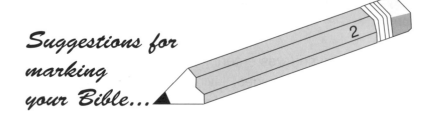

Suggestions for marking your Bible...

1. Copy the outline into your Bible.

2. Write beside Proverbs 1:7:

   "Fear" in Hebrew: "Reverence and Awe"

3. Write beside Proverbs 3:5-6:

   "Trust" in Hebrew: "Cling to"

4. Add any other notes from the explanations which you wish to preserve in your Bible.

Unit Twenty Two
ECCLESIASTES
SONG OF SOLOMON
ISAIAH 1-44

OUTLINE OF ECCLESIASTES

FIRST SERMON: 1:2-2:26
Premise: Effort and achievement futile—1:2-3
   Premise demonstrated—1:4-2:23
     •By life and history—1:4-11
     •By human wisdom and philosophy—1:12-18
     •By pleasure and wealth—2:1-11
     •By certainty of death—2:12-17
     •By the inequity of work—2:18-23
   Conclusion: contentment with God's providence—
     2:24-26

SECOND SERMON: 3:1-5:20
Premise: Reality of life and death—3:1-22
   Frustration and disappointment in life—4:1-16
   Conclusion: Self-seeking life is futile—5:1-20

THIRD SERMON: 6:1-8:17
Premise: Materialism is inadequate—6:1-12
   Wise counsel for living—7:1-8:11
   Conclusion: God's justice—8:12-17

FOURTH SERMON: 9:1-12:8
Premise: Death certain; life uncertain—9:1-18
   Premise demonstrated—10:1-20
   Conclusion: each man responsible for life—11:1-12:8

(Outline, continued...)

EPILOGUE: THE THEME PRESENTED
The cycles of life—12:9-12
The duties of life—12:13-14

TITLE

Ecclesiastes is a Greek word, which means "Assembly" or "Congregation." The Hebrew title is *Koheleth,* meaning *"the same,"* and thus translated *"The Preacher"*—i.e., "the one who assembles the congregation."

AUTHOR

Solomon (See 1:1 and 12)

DATE

Tenth Century B.C.

THEME

Solomon presents man seeking the meaning of life without God. In the final chapter, Solomon gives the solution (12:1,13,14).

The theme describes the futility of a value system based upon material possessions and ambitions. It points out that to seek happiness as one's primary goal is absurd.

OUTLINE OF SONG OF SOLOMON

Bride muses in the Bridegroom's palace—1:1-3:5
  She muses on her first love for Solomon—1:1-17
  The Bride's musings on the blossoming romance—
    2:1-3:5

Bride accepts the Bridegroom's invitation—3:6-5:1
  Solomon brings his Bride to Jerusalem—3:6-11
  The Bridegroom praises the Bride—4:1-15
  Anticipation of the joys of married love—4:16-5:1

Bride dreams of separation from the Bridegroom—5:2-6:3
  The Bride's second dream—5:2-8 (cf. 3:1-4)
  In praising him to others, she claims him as her
    own—5:9-6:3

*Bride and Bridegroom express ardent love for each
    other—6:4-8:14*
  He praises her loveliness—6:4-10
  Her experience in the nut orchard—6:11-13
  Mutual praise and devotion—7:1-8:14

TITLE
Taken from 1:1

AUTHOR
Solomon (see 1:1)

DATE
Tenth century B.C.

THEME

1. Literally, conjugal love
2. Allegorically, God's love for Israel
3. Allegorically, Christ's love for the Church
4. Typically, conjugal love as a type of (2) and (3). See Ephesians 5:22-33.

SETTING OF THE POEM

(From the pen of Dr. H. A. Ironside)

"King Solomon had a vineyard in the hill country of Ephraim, 50 miles N. of Jerusalem (8:11). He let it out to keepers (8:11), consisting of a mother, two sons (1:6), and two daughters: the Shulammite (6:13) and a little sister (8:8). The Shulammite was the 'Cinderella' of the family (1:5), naturally beautiful but unnoticed. Her brothers were likely half brothers (1:6). They made her work very hard tending the vineyards, so that she had little opportunity to care for her personal appearance (1:6). She pruned the vines and set traps for the little foxes (2:15). She also kept the flocks (1:8). Being out in the open so much, she had a deep tan (1:5).

"One day a handsome stranger came to the vineyard. It was Solomon disguised. He showed an interest in her, and she became embarrassed concerning her personal appearance (1:6). She took him for a shepherd and asked about his flocks (1:7). He answered evasively (1:8), but also spoke loving words to her (1:8-10), and promised rich gifts for the future (1:11). He won her heart and left with the promise that some day he would return.

"She dreamed of him at night and sometimes thought he was near (3:1). Finally, he did return in all his kingly splendor to make her his bride (3:6-7).

(continued on next page)

(Continued from preceding page)

"This prefigures Christ, who came first as Shepherd and won His Bride. Later He will return as King, and then will be consummated the marriage of the Lamb."

OUTLINE OF ISAIAH 1-44

The Setting: 1:1-31
    Judah's sinful condition—1:1-9
    God's judgment on Judah—1:10-31

Isaiah's Early Messages: 2:1-6:13
    Christ's Kingdom announced—2:1-5:30
    Isaiah's call—6:1-13

Isaiah's Messianic Messages: 7:1-12:6
    The sign of Emmanuel—7:1-25
    Deliverance foreshadowed—8:1-9:7
    Samaria will be invaded; Northern Kingdom will
        collapse—9:8-10:34
    The Throne of David restored in the Rule
        of the Messiah—11:1-12:6

The Oracles of Divine Judgment Against The Enemies of Israel: 13:1-23:18
    Fall of Babylon—13:1-14:27
    Fall of Philistia—14:28-32
    Fall of Moab—15:1-16:14
    Fall of Damascus and Samaria—17:1-14
    Fall and Conversion of Ethiopia—18:1-7
    Afflictions of Egypt—19:1-20:6
    Defeat of Babylon—21:1-10
    Defeat of Edom—21:11-12
    Destruction of Dedan and Kedar—21:13-17
    Fall of Jerusalem predicted—22:1-25
    Fall and Enslavement of Tyre—23:1-18

(Continued on next page)

(Continued from preceding page)

Messages on the Consummation of the Age: 24:1-27:13
> The universal judgment—24:1-23
> A song of praise for Jehovah—25:1-12
> A hymn of thanksgiving—26:1-21
> Punishment of oppressors; preservation of Israel—
> 27:1-13

Messages of Woe upon Israel: 28:1-35:10
> On Ephraim's drunks and Israel's scoffers—28:1-29
> On the hypocrites—29:1-24
> On the Egyptian alliance—30:1-31:9
> The final deliverance of Israel—32:1-33:24
> On the complete destruction of Israel's enemies—
> 34:1-17
> The glory of the redeemed of God—35:1-10

A Historical Interlude Concerning Hezekiah: 36:1-39:8
> The deliverance of Judah—36:1-37:38
> The healing of Hezekiah—38:1-39:8

Messages of Comfort: 40:1-66:24
> Comfort through trust in the Lord—40:1-11
> The Lord's majesty—40:12-31
> Israel's final restoration—41:1-20
> No hope apart from the Lord—41:21-29
> The Lord's Servant—42:1-16
> Israel's suffering: result of sin—42:17-25
> The Lord the only Redeemer—43:1-28
> God's redemption; idols are folly—44:1-28

AUTHOR:

Isaiah—*ONE* Isaiah!!!

THEME:

Salvation by faith (7:9, 28:16, 30:15)
God's holiness and holy living (6:1-8, 37:23)
Man's sins an offense (1:2-4, 29:13-17)
The certainty of judgment (chs. 1-35)
The assurance of redemption to a remnant
    (1:9, 19; 10:19-22; 46:3-4; 65:8-10)

DATE:

740 to 681 B.C.

NOTES:

MESSIANIC PREDICTIONS:
His incarnation—7:14, 9:6
His youth—7:15, 11:1, 53:2
His mild manner—42:2
His obedience—50:5
His message—61:1-2
His miracles—35:5-6
His sufferings—50:6
His rejections—53:1-3
His shame—53:4-6
His vicarious death—53:10
His ascension—52:13

Suggestions for marking your Bible...

1. Copy the outline into your Bible.

2. Write beside Ecclesiastes 12:3-8:

    "Allegorical description of a very old person"

3. Write beside Isaiah 7:14:

    "Virgin Birth predicted 742 years in advance!"

4. Add any other notes from the explanations which you wish to preserve in your Bible.

Unit Twenty Three
ISAIAH 45-66
JEREMIAH
OUTLINE OF ISAIAH 45-66

Messages of Comfort: 40:1-66:24
(Continued from last unit...)

A charge to Cyrus, not yet born—45:1-7
The Lord the Creator—45:8-13
An everlasting salvation for Israel—45:14-25
God's power vs. that of idols—46:1-13
Judgment on Babylon—47:1-15
Israel's unfaithfulness rebuked—48:1-22

Final deliverance through the Prince of Peace: 49:1-53:12
The Restorer of Israel—49:1-26
The Lord of Israel—50:1-11
The Judge of Israel—51:1-52:12
The Suffering Servant of Israel—52:13-53:12

Final promises to Israel from the God of Peace:
    54:1-57:21
The blessings for Israel and the Church—54:1-17
God's grace toward repentant sinners—55:1-13
Gentiles included in Israel's blessing—56:1-8
Israel's corrupt leaders condemned—56:9-57:21

Final details of the Program of Peace: 58:1-66:24
True and false worship compared—58:1-14
Israel's confession and God's deliverance—59:1-21
The prosperity and peace of the redeemed—
    60:1-63:6
Prayer; plea for revival to come—63:7-64:12
God's answer of mercy and deliverance—65:1-66:24

NOTES

ISAIAH 44:28
150 years before his birth, Isaiah spoke to Cyrus, a future king! Thus, his visions of future events included more than the birth and death of Christ. His leaps of prophetic vision carry him through time in an amazing manner. Critics find this irrational, and insist this passage must postdate the event. In doing so, they simply reveal their unbelief and cynicism against God's revelation.

ISAIAH 52:13-15
Note the "sandwiching" of the horror between reassurances that this suffering one WILL be victorious! These verses are the Prologue to the powerful chapter depicting our Lord's crucifixion.

ISAIAH 60ff.
It is important to note that these chapters are addressed to ISRAEL, not to the CHURCH! This misinterpretation results from the teaching that Israel has forfeited her election, and the church has replaced her in God's covenant relationships. (See 66:22)

ISAIAH 61:1-3
This is Isaiah's "Job Description" for the ministry of our Lord. He Himself read this passage aloud in Luke 4, remarking in v. 21: "This day is this scripture fulfilled in your ears." Now that WE have become "The body of Christ," He continues to do this work through us—whenever and wherever we become the authentic church.

ISAIAH 63:7
"Lovingkindness"—our old friend *chesed!*

ISAIAH 64:1-8

This deeply moving passage became the wail of the people of Wales, quoted with tears and prayer. It triggered the mighty Welsh Revival (about 1900 A.D.). Thousands of people were swept into the Kingdom of God at that time. One pastor from England embarked from the boat in Wales, walked up to a policeman and asked: "Can you tell me where I can find the revival?" The officer, choking with emotion, tapped his chest and said, *"Sir, it is in here!"*

OUTLINE OF JEREMIAH

Introduction—1:1-19

Prophetic Proclamation—2:1-33:26
 Divine judgment pronounced—2:1-29:32
        Prophecies about the coming captivity—2:1-20:18
        Messages illustrating the captivity—21:1-23:40
        Signs of the severity of the captivity—24:1-29:32
 The extension of Divine Favor—30:1-33:26
        Promised return of Israel and Judah—30:1-24
        The New Covenant—31:1-40
        Illustration of faith triumphant—32:1-44
        Promised Branch of Righteousness—33:1-26

The Historical Realization—34:1-39:18
 Zedekiah's revelation of the coming captivity—34:1-7
 Liberty for Hebrew slaves—34:8-22
 The lesson of the Recabites—35:1-19
 Jeremiah's scroll—36:1-32
 Jeremiah's Final Appeal—37:1-39:18
        Concerning the Babylonian invasion—37:1-21
        Concerning Zedekiah—38:1-28
        Concerning the fall of Jerusalem—39:1-18

Messages Of The Prophet—40:1-51:64
    Messages of hope—40:1-44:30
    Message of promise—45:1-5
    Messages of judgment—46:1-51:64
       To Egypt—46:1-28
       To Philistia—47:1-7
       To Moab—48:1-47
       To Ammon—49:1-6
       To Edom—49:7-22
       To Damascus—49:23-27
       To Kedar and Hazor—49:28-33
       To Elam—49:34-39
       To Babylon—50:1-51:64

Epilogue—52:1-34

AUTHOR

Jeremiah of Anathoth, a suburban city located 3 miles northe
of Jerusalem.

THEME

The judgment of God on Israel for constant rebellion. The
coming captivity is predicted by a prophet who *weeps* as
he strives to turn the people back to God.

DATE

Seventh century B.C. (See 2 Kings 21-25)

ABOUT THE BOOK OF JEREMIAH

Jeremiah lived during the reigns of 7 Kings of Judah:

    Manasseh—686-642 B.C.
    Amon—642-640 B.C.
    Josiah—640-609 B.C.
    Jehoahaz—609 B.C.
    Jehoiakim—609-597 B.C.
    Jehoiachin—597 B.C.
    Zedekiah—597-586 B.C.

It was under Jehoiakim in 605 B.C. that Jehovah told Jeremiah to write the prophecies of this book (36:1-2). So inflammatory were the writings that the king burned the scroll. Jeremiah reproduced its contents again! The final compilation of the book was made subsequent to the fall of Jerusalem and the death of the prophet.

The chronology of the book is confusing to the ordered mind of the Westerner. It is helpful to remember that Jeremiah is described as "The Weeping Prophet." Those who live in deep emotional sorrow are more regulated by their sobs than their minds. Jeremiah is as a man who looks this way and that, seeing with the visions of a prophet, and randomly recording what he sees and feels.

For your use, Jeremiah is a powerful book to use when reflecting on the meaning of true reform. You will find scores of passages which will tear at your heart and cause you to underline truths.

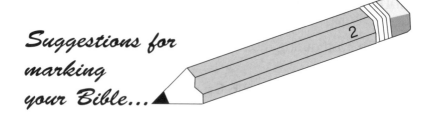

Suggestions for marking your Bible...

1. Copy the outline into your Bible.

2. Write beside Isaiah 43:25:

   Excludes human merit!

3. Write beside Jeremiah 31:31-34:

   Promise of a new Covenant: see Heb. 8:8-12

4. Add any other notes from the explanations which you wish to preserve in your Bible.

Unit Twenty Four
LAMENTATIONS
EZEKIEL
DANIEL
HOSEA

OUTLINE OF LAMENTATIONS

THE FAITHFUL GOD AND THE FALLEN CITY: 1:1-22
 The Suffering of Jerusalem—1:1-11
 A Cry for Sympathetic Understanding—1:12-22

THE SOVEREIGN GOD AND HIS SUFFERING PEOPLE:
 2:1-22
 The Mystery of Suffering—2:1-10
 God's Purpose and Power—2:11-17
 God's Judgment and Mercy—2:18-22

THE COMFORTING GOD AND HIS AFFLICTED PEOPLE:
 3:1-66
 A Personal Participation in Affliction—3:1-21
 A Corporate Anticipation of Hope—3:22-39
 A Corporate Admission of Guilt—3:40-54
 A Prayerful Affirmation of Assurance—3:55-66

THE COMPASSIONATE GOD AND HIS CORRUPTED PEOPLE:
 4:1-22
 A Description Of The Corruption—4:1-10
 The Judgment Of God Upon Them: Scattered Among
  The Nations—4:11-20
 Judgment Pronounced On Edom—4:21-22

THE ETERNAL GOD AND HIS PRAYING PEOPLE: 5:1-22
 An Occasion for Prayer—5:1-15
 A Prayer of Confession—5:16-18
 A Prayer of Confidence—5:19
 A Prayer of Inquiry—5:20
 A Prayer of Petition—5:21-22

AUTHOR

Jeremiah

THEME

An acrostic poem, built on the letters of the Hebrew alphabet. Each chapter has 22 verses except Chapter 3, which has 3 x 22=66.

DATE

Sixth Century B.C.

NOTES

Shows the sorrows which flooded Jerusalem when its destruction took place. Jeremiah affirms the rightness of the judgment. Chapter 3 is a beautiful promise, filled with a message of hope and deliverance.

Lamentations is read annually in Israel to remind the Jewish people of their deepest hour of grief, caused by their sin and guilt. It also reminds them of the future deliverance God has promised!

Saddest of all, it is the heart cry of a Godly man who was caught in the general judgment of a sinning nation. If it had not been for the "remnant" within Israel who had not bowed to worship Baal, this event would have happened years earlier. When it *did* happen, it swept the *devout*, along with the wicked, into captivity. Is this not always the result of sin? In a home with a rebellious family member, does not *all* the family suffer as a result? Consider Germany under Hitler: Godly people *also* suffered in the terrible judgment he brought down upon his nation. *Remember that this is one of the reasons why Godly people suffer.*

INTRODUCTION TO PROPHETIC SCRIPTURES

We have already learned that prophets appeared in Israel after the time of the Judges, as the Kings began to reign over the nation. Disobedient political leaders often found these men of God to be thorns beside their thrones!

But, for 200 years, these prophets were not writers of their prophecies. During that period, none of them made any mention of the Messiah or His Kingdom. *Why?*

The depraved conditions in Judah and Israel caused them to have no interest—*none*—in spiritual truths. Therefore, the prophets of that time *did not speak of future spiritual blessings.*

It's a terrible thing to live in a culture like that. In our world today, such cultures also exist. In the midst of them, the word of the Lord is hated. These are called "the resistant peoples" by church growth scholars. On the other hand, there *are* cultures where people have a thirst for God, and where the power of God is mighty. An example of such a nation in our generation is Korea.

Then, God began to cause his prophets in both Israel and Judah to write! This began about the eighth or ninth century B.C. It's important for you to understand the way they wrote. Their words were ominous!

They told of a withdrawal of Jehovah's presence, the ending of prophetic messages from Him, and a long delay in the establishing of the Messianic kingdom. *(See Amos 8:11-12 and Lamentations 2:9.)* Even more significant, they began to write words for *future generations.*

In stairsteps, Israel and Judah would deteriorate and go into captivity. Remember that Israel fell to the Assyrians in 722 B.C., never to return to their land again in any national capacity. One hundred and forty years later, Judah was carried away into Babylon.

Seventy years later, Judah would see a remnant return to the land, but not to establish the *nation* of Israel. With the exception of one very brief time in the Interbiblical Period, Israel as a nation would not be established again until the "end times." We have seen that happen in our own generation! For this reason alone, we may be sure we are living in an age very close to the time when Christ will return to establish the Messianic reign.

THE PROPHET'S TWO-FOLD MISSION

The prophet's writings sometimes spoke about activities in the *present* which also applied to events in *the distant future.* Their messages revolved around three points:

1. God's blessings to his covenant people if they would be faithful to Him.
2. Coming judgment for unfaithfulness.
3. His promise of grace to them when they would repent.

Each prophet will speak in a slightly different way, the result of his own context, but all will refer to:

1. A day of judgment is coming.
2. It will bring true repentance to God's chosen race.
3. This repentance will prepare the way for the coming of the Messianic kingdom.
4. While these judgments chiefly affect Israel, they will also involve all the Gentile nations of the whole earth.

5. The tribes of Israel will be regathered.
6. A remnant, purified by discipline, will form the nucleus of the reconstituted Israel, among whom Jehovah will again dwell with spiritual and temporal blessings.
7. This reconstituted Israel will be the beginning of the Messianic Kingdom, which will extend over the whole earth and encompass all nations and tribes.

IS THE PRESENT NATION OF ISRAEL THIS "RECONSTITUTED ISRAEL?"

Absolutely not! The present nation has no sensitivity to its relationship to Jehovah, although within it are strongly committed religious sects who preserve the traditions of Judaism. The prophets of the Old Testament see a remnant within Israel who will *follow the Messiah*—Jesus Christ—and be totally under His Lordship.

Therefore, what we are viewing today is a *political Israel,* not the *spiritual Israel* which is prophesied. Today's scene is only the preparation for that which is to come!

WHY DID JEWISH PROPHETS ADDRESS THE GENTILES?

As we enter the study of the Prophets, we will see some of them "do a 360 degree rotation" as they send their cries of "woe, woe" into the nations surrounding Israel. As the hands of a clock move across the dial, they will face each compass point, look at the wickedness in Gentile nations, and speak God's word of judgment upon them.

Since many of these nations no longer exist, why did the Holy Spirit cause these words to be recorded for us to read? One quick answer would be to say that their predictions about these nations were accurately fulfilled, thus confirming our faith in the inspiration of the Bible.

There is a more important reason. God will "sprinkle" the Jew among the Gentile nations. While names may change (example: "Moab" is now "Jordan"), others will continue: Syria and Egypt, for example. Wherever Jews are found, whatever nation they are within, they continue to have a sacred character! In their day of their restoration and the judgment of the nations, one question God will always ask will be, *"How did this Gentile nation regard my chosen people? How did they treat them?"*

Yes, there *will* be a day of reckoning for Nazi Germany and their ovens, for Russian persecution today of the Jew, *and for me and for you if we hate the Jew who lives beside us!*

HOW OUR HEARTS SHOULD BLEED IN LOVE FOR THE PRECIOUS JEWISH COMMUNITY TODAY!

Have you had much dialogue with Jews who live near you? Blindness to God's Messiah continues among most of them. *"Having ears to hear, they will not hear."*

Further, the Jew today is often not a religious person. Only a small percentage of them actually practice one of the three forms of current Judaism (Reformed, Conservative, Orthodox). Some forms of Judaism actually reject the existence of a personal God, and are totally humanistic.

Yet, the "remnant of faith" in our generation grows among them! More and more are receiving Jesus as their Messiah, rejoicing in their *spiritual* heritage. They are often heavily persecuted by fellow Jews whose loyalty is only to their *cultural* heritage.

Remember that there is a *blessing* promised to those who love and respect God's chosen people, and a *judgment* upon those who do not. A father may *discipline* his own disobedient child—but he will not tolerate others who *hate* that disobedient child. *Israel is a child still loved!*

HOW MANY MILES DO THESE MOUNTAIN RANGES EXTEND IN THIS PICTURE?

They seemingly extend for *miles*...perhaps a hundred or more! In reality, the entire mountain range extends no more than the thickness of the ink on this sheet of paper.

Note that we can't see what might be on the *backside* of each mountain range. It is hidden from view. In one of the valleys there might be a lovely lake, or a city teeming with people.

THIS IS THE WAY THE PROPHETS VIEWED THE MESSAGES GIVEN THEM BY THE HOLY SPIRIT!

They wrote for their own day, for the future, and for both Jews and Gentiles. Some of what they wrote was understood by them, *but a great deal of it was not!* When the vision and inspiration of the Holy Spirit came upon them, they often saw, in one glance, events "close," events "later on," and events "far off." It was all in "one picture," and impossible for them to interpret chronologically. Peter tells us that this mystified them! In fact, after they had written prophecy, they tried to understand it:

(continued on next page)

Concerning this salvation, the prophets, who spoke of the grace that was to come to you, searched intently and with the greatest care, trying to find out the time and circumstances to which the Spirit of Christ in them was pointing when he predicted the sufferings of Christ and the glories that would follow. It was revealed to them that they were not serving themselves but you, when they spoke of the things that have now been told you by those who have preached the gospel to you, by the Holy Spirit sent from heaven. Even angels long to look into these things.
—1 PETER 1:10-12

THE SIGNIFICANT RANGES IN THEIR VISIONS...

1. The things which would take place within the coming century or so.
2. Details about the coming Messiah's birth, life, and death—to occur centuries later.
3. Details about the coming Messianic Age, when the Kingdom Reign would occur.

In the valley between (2) and (3) above, the time of the Church Age was unseen, hidden from view!

There is no vision given to the Old Testament prophets about that period in history when the Church would exist. This period, in which we now live, was not a part of what God showed these men. The reason is important: *they saw only that which related to Israel, not to the gentiles.*
They wrote without awareness of the time frames mingling within their prophecies.

In some instances, they would see a vision of that which was impending, jump to the far-off Messianic age, and perhaps then jump to the time of the Messiah's coming! This mixture of time frames is called the "scissors effect" in prophecy, and we will study several examples of it.

OUTLINE OF EZEKIEL

THE PROPHETIC CALL OF EZEKIEL—1:1-3:27

THE PROPHETIC MESSAGES CONCERNING JUDAH AND
JERUSALEM—4:1-24:27
    The Destruction of Judah and Jerusalem—4:1-7:27
    The Pollution of the Temple—8:1-11:25
    Judgments on Jerusalem—12:1-19:14
    Judgments on Judah—20:1-24:27

THE PROPHETIC MESSAGES CONCERNING FOREIGN
 NATIONS—25:1-32:32

THE PROPHETIC MESSAGE CONCERNING THE RESTORED
 ISRAEL—33:1-39:29

THE PROPHETIC VISIONS OF THE RESTORED
 COMMUNITY—40:1-48:35
    The New Temple—40:1-43:27
    The New Priesthood—44:1-46:24
    The New Boundaries—47:1-48:35

AUTHOR

EZEKIEL ("God Strengthens")

THEME

JUDGMENT

DATE

591-586 B.C.

NOTES

A COMPARISON OF THREE PROPHETS...

Jeremiah: "The Prophet of the Father"
Isaiah: "The Prophet of the Son"
Ezekiel: "The Prophet of the Spirit"

The responsibility of each individual before God is stressed by Ezekiel.

NOTE 2:3-5: What a solemn assignment!

NOTE 8:1-4: Ezekiel is sitting in his house in Tel Abib when he is taken to Jerusalem in a vision, then returned to his house. He makes prophecies about the final fate of King Zedekiah, *5 years in advance.*

NOTE CHAPTER 20: Study the passages where God explains, *"I acted for the sake of my name..." (v. 9, 14, 22, 44).* In this chapter, God rehearses His dealings with Israel. Read also 36:21-27—powerful!

NOTE 22:30-31: Without an intercessor, the judgment had to come!

NOTE 33:30-33: There's no business like "show" business—no business at all!

NOTE 34:4ff.: What an accusation against those who are called to shepherd the sheep...and what an awesome thing it is to be a shepherd of God's people in any age...

NOTE 37:24-28: The renewal of the covenant by God and Israel, restated. It has *never* been cancelled!

EZEKIEL 38—AN AMAZING PROPHECY,SPEAKING OF EVENTS TAKING PLACE *IN OUR OWN GENERATION...*

Write the following explanations in your Bible:

VERSE 1:
- Gog: "A powerful ruler"
- Land of Magog: The land of the Scythians, north of the Caucasian mountains—Russia!
- Rosh: Ancient term for Russia
- Meshech: Ancient name for the city of Moscow
- Tubal: Ancient name for modern Tobolsk

VERSE 5:
- Persia: Modern Iran
- Cush: Modern Iraq
- Put: Modern Central Europe

VERSE 6:
- Gomer: Modern Germany, the Crimea, and Turkey
- Beth-Togarmah: Armenia and Afghanistan
- "From the far North:" Russia

VERSE 8:
This speaks directly of Israel's restoration to the land, accomplished in 1948 for the very first time in history!

VERSE 10:
The scheming by nations that is going on now...control the oil, and you will control the world! We now see the unfolding: Russia will move through Afghanistan, gathering forces from other nations, continuing through Iran and Iraq, and entering Israel with her armies. Read verses 11 and 12 to get the details...

VERSE 13:

- Sheba and Dedan: The ancient great trade centers in Arabia—where there now is OIL!
- Tarshish: Arabia. (Are the "merchants" members of OPEC?)

THE STORY UNFOLDS FURTHER:
BEGIN READING IN V. 14...

God says Russia will come into Israel "in the last days." Note that the "great earthquake" is the activity of *God* acting against Russia.

Does verse 20 describe a massive atomic blast? *(We can only wonder...)*

War of immense proportions is described in these closing verses. We have seen Israel enter the land, and we have seen Russia enter Afghanistan. We may be very near to the time when this begins to unfold!

THE OIL IN ISRAEL WILL GIVE A REASON FOR ALL THIS TO TAKE PLACE!

A Houstonian named Andrew C. Sorrelle, Jr., found oil *exactly* where the Bible said it would be *(see Deut. 33:24)*, where Asher would dip (bathe) his foot in oil. He drilled in this spot for no other reason than his belief that the Bible told the truth.

Sorrelle found, at 24,000 feet, a vast bed of oil...in all likelihood, the same oil bed that is being drilled at 5,000 feet in Saudi Arabia and elsewhere in the Arab world. This recent find, which may just be the largest oil field in the world, gives good reason for the events of these verses. *Stay tuned to your newscasts for more about Ezekiel 38...*

CHAPTER 40:

The Temple envisioned by Ezekiel is shown on page 1284 of the NIV Study Bible. It does not match the temples built by Solomon, Zerubbabel, or Herod. *It has not yet been constructed in the history of the world.* But it will be...in the Kingdom age!

CHAPTER 43:

The glory of God returns to the Temple. The altar is reconsecrated, and sacrifices are reconstituted.

ABOUT BLOOD SACRIFICES IN THE FUTURE TEMPLE...

Those who reject the clear teaching in the scripture about the thousand year reign of Christ usually ask, "Do you *really* believe that in the future Temple there will be the bloody sacrifices reinstituted? *That's absurd!* Did not Christ's sacrifice of Himself remove the need for animal sacrifices?"

Throughout the Old Testament, the use of animal sacrifices was only **symbolical** *of THE LAMB OF GOD THAT WOULD REMOVE THE SINS OF THE WORLD. Even as the observance of the Lord's Supper in this church age commemorates Jesus' death, in the Millennial Age, the age of Ezekiel's Temple, there will be similar commemorative ceremonies looking back to the past.. Read Revelation 5:11-14: thanksgiving for the atonement will remain throughout eternity. Thus, the commemorative act of the sacrifices are also appropriate.*

CHAPTERS 47-48:

A new Holy Land is also described. Note the boundaries of it. It extends through a great deal of territory now in the hands of the Arabs, *including Syria!*

OUTLINE OF DANIEL

GOD'S PROVIDENCE DURING THE EXILE—1:1-6:28
    The historical setting—1:1-7
    The purity of Daniel and his friends—1:8-21
    The dream of Nebuchadnezzar—2:1-49
    The image of gold and the furnace of fire—3:1-30
    Nebuchadnezzar's insanity—4:1-37
    Belshazzar and the Fall of Babylon—5:1-31
    Darius the Mede and the den of lions—6:1-28
GOD'S PURPOSE IN HISTORY—7:1-12:13
    Daniel's vision of 4 World Empires—7:1-28
    The rise and fall of Alexander the Great and Antiochus
        Epiphanes—8:1-27
    Daniel's understanding of Jeremiah—9:1-19
    The 70 Weeks of God's purpose for Israel—9:20-27
    A Theophany—10:1-21
    Prophecy of the conflicts of the Ptolemies and
        Seleucids—11:1-35
    The activity of the Antichrist—11:36-45
    A chronology of the Seventieth Week—12:1-13

AUTHOR

DANIEL (A contemporary of Jeremiah and Ezekiel)

THEME

A. The providence of God among His people, even in
     exile.
B. Visions of future events.

DATE

535 B.C.

APOCALYPTIC LITERATURE

The word *apocalypse* means *"unveiling."* Daniel is the only Old Testament book which is classified as "apocalyptic." Revelation is the only New Testament book written in this form.

An apocalyptic book is an unveiling of secret purposes of God, truths not otherwise known. The way these events are revealed is primarily by visions filled with images and symbols. In Daniel, the terms "vision" and "visions" appear a total of 32 times. This style of literature is written as prose, but it is packed with images and symbols. As a result, it may look like poetry.

The significance of Daniel is that it gives detailed information about Gentile nations. So accurate were his predictions about the emerging of kingdoms following his own day that skeptical Bible scholars 75 years ago insisted that Daniel was probably written after the time of Christ, and forged to look like it was written in 530 B.C. Their cynicism was shattered with the discovery of the Dead Sea Scrolls, which included an early copy of Daniel.

When Alexander the Great conquered the area occupied by Israel, the prediction of his own life and reign were read to him from Daniel. So impressed was he that he gave many special privileges to the Jews!

The diagrams on the following pages, adapted from those created by the gifted Irving L. Jensen, will help you understand the meaning of the dreams and visions in this book.

THE PROPHECIES OF DANIEL

NATION and DATE	CHAPTER TWO	CHAPTER SEVEN	CHAPTER EIGHT
BABYLON 606-539 B. C.	HEAD Gold	LION Nebuchad-nezzar	
MEDES and PERSIANS 539-331 B.C.	CHEST AND ARMS Silver	BEAR Persia Cyrus	TWO HORNED RAM Darius II
GREECE 331-323 B. C.	STOMACH AND THIGHS Brass	LEOPARD Alexander the Great	ONE HORNED GOAT Alexander
ROME 322 B.C. to 476 A.D.	LEGS AND FEET Iron and Clay	MONSTER Historical: Caesars; Prophetical: Antichrist	TWO LITTLE HORNED KINGS Antiochus Epiphanes
YET FUTURE ERA	GREAT STONE Jesus Christ	EVERLASTING KINGDOM Jesus Christ	REVIVED ROMAN EMPIRE Antichrist

CHAPTER 11—KINGS
Verses 1-20: Alexander and his predecessors
Verses 21-15: Antiochus Epiphanes (Syrian) 175-164 B. C.
Verses 36-45: Antichrist

CHAPTER NINE
THE SEVENTY SEVENS

THE SEVEN WEEKS
49 Years (7 times 7)
445-396 B.C.
The walls of Jerusalem to be rebuilt in troubled times

THE SIXTY-TWO WEEKS
434 Years (62 times 7)
396 B.C.—32 A.D.

THE ONE WEEK
Seven Years (7 times 1)
From the Rapture (taking away of the church)
  to the Battle of Armageddon
The activity of the Antichrist
The return of the Lord Jesus Christ

There is a gap between the sixty-ninth and seventieth weeks. During that time the period we are now living in is taking place. It is the "Church Age," and will come to an end when the church is taken away.

No one knows for sure when the action will start, but at some point God will start the clock running again.

That clock stopped at Calvary and starts with the Rapture of the church. Events of our own day give us every reason to believe we are on the verge of the end of this period.

(See 1 Thessalonians 4:13-18)

OUTLINE OF HOSEA

INTRODUCTION: 1:1

UNFAITHFULNESS, REJECTION, AND
RESTORATION OF ISRAEL...
...ILLUSTRATED BY HOSEA'S MARRIAGE: 1:2-3:5
    Symbolized by Gomer's 3 children—1:2-9
    Promised restoration—1:10-2:1
    Condemnation of Israel's unfaithfulness—2:2-7
    Announcement of Israel's punishment—2:8-13
    Promise of God's restoration of Israel—2:14-23
    Symbolized by Hosea's restoration of Gomer—3:1-5

UNFAITHFULNESS, REJECTION, AND
RESTORATION OF ISRAEL...
...ILLUSTRATED BY HOSEA'S MESSAGES: 4:1-14:9
    God's controversy with Israel—4:1-19
    Warning to priests, the people, and the king—5:1-7
    Announcement of Israel's judgment—5:8-15
    Call to repentance—6:1-3
    Gods' concern for inner love, not rituals—6:4-11
    Israel's inner iniquity and outer rebellion—7:1-16
    Announcement of Israel's Judgment—8:1-14
    Rejection and exile—9:1-17
    Israel's idolatry and wickedness—10:1-15
    God's sorrow like that of a father for a child—11:1-11
    Wicked Israel contrasted with Jacob—11:12-12:14
    Certainty of Israel's destruction—13:1-16
    Israel's restoration dependent upon repentance—
       14:1-9

AUTHOR

Hosea's ministry overlapped that of Isaiah and Micah in Judah, and Amos in Israel. The period of his prophetic activity is dated according to the reigns of these kings in Judah:

- Uzziah
- Jotham
- Ahaz
- Hezekiah

In Israel, the kings were:

- Jeroboam II
- Zachariah
- Shallum
- Menahem
- Pekahiah
- Pekah
- Hoshea

THEME

God's redeeming love for Israel is depicted through the way Hosea treats his wife, a common whore and bearer of illegitimate children.

DATE

755-725 B. C.

Suggestions for marking your Bible...

1. Copy the outline into your Bible.

2. Write beside Ezekiel 36:26-27:

   Clearest statement of N.7. conversion found in O.7.

3. Write beside Hosea 11:8-9:

   The God of Mercy does exist in the Old Testament!

4. Add any other notes from the explanations which you wish to preserve in your Bible.

Unit Twenty Five

JOEL
AMOS
OBADIAH
JONAH

OUTLINE OF JOEL

The locust plague in Judah—1:1-12
Joel's warning and intercession—1:13-20
Call to repentance and fasting—2:1-17
God's response and promise—2:18-27
The outpouring of God's spirit—2:28-32
Judgment on the nations—3:1-21

AUTHOR

JOEL

THEME

Repentance

DATE

About 835 B.C.

NOTES

Israel has not yet been taken into captivity when Joel writes. A locust plague has covered the land (ch. 1). Joel says it is because of Israel's sin (v.5). He calls for a season of repentance and prayer.

PROPHECIES OF THE FUTURE: CHAPTERS 2-3

Joel gives us a picture of the coming invasion of Israel, probably in two phases:

The Russian invasion (Ezekiel 38-39)
The final invasion at the end of the Tribulation, led by the Antichrist (Revelation 16:13-16; 19:11-21)

This is to take place in the Valley of Jehoshaphat (3:2, 9-14). The results will be the salvation of Israel (3:15-21). It is then that God's Spirit will be poured out upon all flesh—see 2:28-32. All needs will be provided for, and nature will be transformed. Christ Himself is seen as reigning in Zion (3:21).

ABOUT MOUNT ZION...

Surrounding Jerusalem are "mounts," or heights. The one at the southwest corner of the ancient city is called "Mount Zion." It was once within the walls of Jerusalem. It is there David was buried, and it is to this place our Lord will come to reign.

PETER'S USE OF JOEL IN HIS SERMON

In Acts 2:16-21, Peter quoted from this passage in his sermon delivered on the day of Pentecost. He did not indicate that Pentecost was the *fulfillment* of Joel's prophecy, but rather *an example* of it. He said, "This is *like* that which was spoken of by the prophet Joel..." Be careful to make a note of that distinction in the margin of your Bible.

OUTLINE OF AMOS

Judgments on Israel's neighbors—1:1-2
Damascus—1:3-5
Gaza—1:6-8
Tyrus—1:9-10
Edom—1:11-12
Ammon—1:13-15
Moab—2:1-3
Judah—2:4-5
Judgment on Israel—2:6-16
The lion roars—3:1-8
The condemnation of Samaria—3:9-15
The depravity of Israel—4:1-3
God's punishments have not reformed Israel—4:4-13
A call to repentance—5:1-27
The judgment on Israel—6:1-14
The grasshoppers—7:1-3
The fire—7:4-6
The plumb line—7:7-9
Amos and Amaziah—7:10-17
The basket of summer fruit—8:1-3
The imminent judgment—8:4-14
The Lord's judgments inescapable—9:1-10
The future restoration of Israel—9:11-15

AUTHOR

AMOS ("The Lord Upholds")

THEME

Certainty of judgment on Israel

DATE

760 B.C.

NOTES

Amos is a rugged, blunt prophet. He is a "pincher of sycamore fruit," a task requiring the bruising of the fruit on the trees to make it ripen, and a herdsman. His name means "burden."

Get the picture: at the annual gathering of Israel for a "religious" festival (really not religious at all!), Amos strides into the carnival-like atmosphere. He is wearing skins, and his eyes are flashing with indignation. He strides to a high promontory which overlooks the priests fawning over the rich families, the fine foods, and the public officials. He releases his words with power and without fear.

He tells the priests they are panderers. He calls the wives of the rich "fat cows of Bashan," the fattest cows of all, and warns the rich they will pay for their greed. He rips apart the hypocritical priests, and does not spare the king or the other government officials.

He begins with Syria, and pronounces judgment upon all the territories surrounding Israel, includes Judah, and then touches on his own nation. He says God has tried everything to bring them to repentance, and now will judge them severely.

He presents five visions: The Locust Plague, The Great Fire, The Plumb Line, The Basket of Summer Fruit, and The Lord at the Altar. In 9:11-15, he sees the restoration of David's Tabernacle during the glorious millennium. James quotes from Amos at the Jerusalem Council (Acts 15:14-17), refusing to vote to circumcise saved Gentiles.

OUTLINE OF OBADIAH

Natural security for Edom—1:1-9
Judah's misfortunes—1:10-14
Edom's fate—1:15-16
Israel's ultimate triumph—1:17-21

AUTHOR

OBADIAH ("Servant of the Lord")

THEME

The judgment of Edom for its treatment of Jerusalem.

DATE

586-539 B.C.

NOTES

Obadiah is the shortest and smallest Old Testament book. All we know of the author is the meaning of his name: "The servant of the Lord."

The single theme of this book is the destruction of Edom for its treachery toward Judah. There are four instances when Edom helped plunder Jerusalem and Judah:
1. During Joram's reign: 2 Chronicles 21:8, 16, 17 with Amos 1:6.
2. During Amaziah's reign: 2 Chronicles 25:11, 12, 23, 24.
3. During Ahaz' reign: 2 Chronicles 28:16-21.
4. During Zedekiah's reign: 2 Chronicles 36:11-21 with Psalm 137:7.

PETRA was found in 1812. *It has **never** been built upon since the time of its destruction, as Obadiah predicted!*

OUTLINE OF JONAH

Jonah commissioned—1:1-2
Jonah flees—1:3
The storm at sea—1:4-17
Jonah's prayer and God's answer—2:1-10
Jonah's second commission—3:1-4
Nineveh repents—3:5-10
Jonah's displeasure—4:1-3
God's lesson to Jonah—4:4-11

AUTHOR

JONAH

THEME

God's mercy to Gentile nations through the preaching of repentance.

DATE

About 745 B.C.

NOTES

The significance of this book is related to its use in Matthew 12:38-41, where it is specifically stated that Jonah's entombment in the belly of the great fish was a prediction of the death and resurrection of Christ.

In 2:1-8, it is obvious that Jonah *actually died*. See v. 2, 6, and 7. In doing so, he validated the *actual death of Jesus*. While some suggest he was simply at the *point* of death, there is no reason to so interpret these verses except for a skepticism of God's power.

MORE ABOUT JONAH...

To get this book into perspective, recognize that Nineveh was, in Jonah's day, the center of world power. It was the capital of Assyria at its height. It fell in 612 B. C. The ruins of Nineveh are surrounded by a rectangle of walls nearly eight miles in circumference.

The Assyrians were vicious and heartless invaders of territories. Jonah had no reason to appreciate God's compassion for this city. Destroyed, Jonah's generation would have been freed from the hostile activities of its powerful rulers. Jonah wanted Nineveh *destroyed!*

Once again, we are impacted by the compassion of God in the Old Testament setting. For the sake of the innocents who lived there, God was willing to withhold his judgment if repentance could be created. He *Himself* initiated the call to repentance by sending Jonah to them.

God has never been willing that men should perish. Regardless of the viciousness and wickedness of their hearts, He does not easily give up on people. The end of Nineveh is prophesied by Zephaniah and Nahum.

Interesting comparisons exist between Jonah as a type of Jesus. Both were dead for three days and nights. But there is another comparison: the coming of Jonah to call Nineveh to repentance, and the coming of Jesus to call the Jews to repentance. The people of Nineveh, according to Jesus, will rise up at the last day to *condemn* the generation of Jesus, who rejected His call to repentance (Matthew 12:41, Luke 11:30, 32).

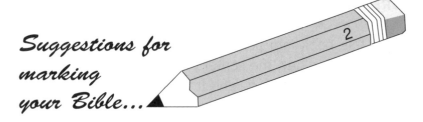

Suggestions for
marking
your Bible...

1. Copy the outlines into your Bible.

2. Write beside Joel 2:13-14:

   One of most powerful expressions
   of repentance in the Bible.

3. Write beside Amos 9:11-15:

   The hope here refers
   to the Millennium.

4. Add any other notes from the explanations which you wish to preserve in your Bible.

Unit Twenty Six

MICAH
NAHUM
HABAKKUK
ZEPHANIAH

HAGGAI
ZECHARIAH
MALACHI

THE WRITING PROPHETS
IN THE PERIOD OF KINGDOM CHAOS

AUTHOR	YEARS SERVED	DATES	DESTINATION
OBADIAH	10	850-840	EDOM
JONAH	35	785-750	NINEVEH
NAHUM	30	650-620	NINEVEH
AMOS	7	760-753	ISRAEL
HOSEA	60	760-700	ISRAEL
JOEL	7	841-834	JUDAH
ISAIAH	58	739-681	JUDAH
MICAH	35	735-700	JUDAH
ZEPHANIAH	20	640-620	JUDAH
HABAKKUK	3	609-606	JUDAH
JEREMIAH	32	627-575	JUDAH
LAMENTATIONS	—	586	JUDAH

OUTLINE OF MICAH

Judgment on Samaria and Jerusalem—1:1-16
Woe to the oppressor of the poor—2:1-11
Promise to the remnant—2:12-13
Judgment on Israel's leaders—3:1-4
Judgment on the prophets—3:5-12
Swords into plowshares—4:1-13
The Deliverer, Who will come from Bethlehem—5:1-15
The Lord's contention with Israel—6:1-5
The requirements of the Lord—6:6-16
The moral sins of Israel—7:1-7
God's concern for His people—7:8-20

AUTHOR

Micah is a prophet of the Southern Kingdom, Judah.
He was a contemporary of Amos, Hosea, Isaiah, and
Jonah. He lived about 20 miles southwest of Jerusalem.

THEME

See 6:8: God expects His people "to do justly, and
love mercy." Micah sees beyond current events to the
incarnation of Christ and the blessings of the millennial
Kingdom.

DATE

740-686 B.C.

KING	DATE	CONDITION
UZZIAH (AZARIAH)	767-740 B.C.	Nation prospered; Assyria was weak, non-threatening.
AHAZ	745-739 B.C.	Tiglath-Pileser III revived Assyria. Both Damascus and Israel were controlled by him. Ahaz was contacted by Israel, asked to join in a rebellion against Assyria. Instead, Ahaz informed the Assyrians of the plot. He became totally dependent upon them. He even introduced Assyrian worship to Jerusalem.
	732 B.C.	Assyrians began the deportation of Israel (N. Kingdom).
HEZEKIAH	701 B.C.	Tried to secede from Assyria. Judah was overrun by its enemies. (2 Kings 19:34-37)

KEY VERSES

4:1-4— Millennium. Jerusalem the capitol, Gentiles there, (v.2). Peace. No abolishment of property rights (v.4).

4:10— Not fulfilled for over a century.

5:2— See Matthew 2:5; 5:3—See Isaiah 7:14.

6:8— Underline verse; 7:18-20—Covenant is intact!

OUTLINE OF NAHUM

God's wrath concerning Nineveh—1:1-15
The siege and destruction of Nineveh—2:1-13
The overthrow of Nineveh—3:1-19

AUTHOR

NAHUM

THEME

Nineveh's doom. The Assyrian capitol will be destroyed because of the inhumanities of their army (2:12) and the vice in the city (3:4). 1:2-10 speaks generally of God's wrath.

DATE

About 663 B.C. (Nineveh fell in 612.)

NOTES

Excavations of Nineveh began in 1845 and corroborate the predictions of Nahum.

1:9—Literally fulfilled. Since 612 B.C., Nineveh has never been rebuilt.

1:12—The Assyrian slogan (see King James Version) *"Quiet And Likewise Many"* is referred to here. It meant they were so united they made the sound of only one voice when they spoke!

2:6—Nineveh fell because the flooding rivers eroded the defenses of the city.

WORTH MEMORIZING: 1:7

OUTLINE OF HABAKKUK

Why does God permit injustice?—1:1-4

God uses the Chaldeans to punish Judah—1:5-11

Why does God use the wicked for His judgment?—1:12-17

The just live by faith—2:1-4

The unrighteous are judged—2:5-20

The prayer of Habakkuk—3:1-19

AUTHOR

HABAKKUK

THEME

How can a holy God use the wicked Chaldeans (Babylonians) to chastise His children? God responds by saying His way is always best; Habakkuk must be concerned instead about his own righteousness and live by faith (2:4).

DATE

609-605 B.C.

NOTES

Chapter 3 is unrivalled in literature!

OUTLINE OF ZEPHANIAH

The day of the Lord's wrath—1:1-18
The scope of divine judgment—2:1-15
Jerusalem's sin and redemption—3:1-8
Ultimate supremacy of Israel—3:9-20

AUTHOR

1:1 traces Zephaniah's lineage back four generations to King Hezekiah. Zephaniah was a prophet of Judah, the Southern Kingdom. He was a contemporary of Jeremiah.

THEME

The coming of the Day of the Lord

DATE

626-625 B.C.

NOTES

Zephaniah was the great-great-grandson of King Hezekiah and, therefore, of royal blood. He was also kin to Josiah, under whose godly reign he prophesied.

Zephaniah was used of God to prepare for the great revival of 621 B.C. It was at that time the law of Moses was rediscovered during the repair of the temple. The record of this event is found in 2 Chronicles 34-35.

OUTLINE OF HAGGAI

First Message: Rebuke—1:1-15
Second Message: Encouragement—2:1-9
Third Message: Promise—2:10-19
Fourth Message: Prophecy—2:20-23

AUTHOR

Haggai (cf. Ezra 5:1, 6:14)

THEME

Despite all the odds against them, God will guarantee the peace and prosperity of Jerusalem if the people will be faithful to Him.

DATE

520 B.C.

NOTES

Haggai is a "Post-Exile Prophet." Judah has returned to Jerusalem. The walls and houses are rubble. The Temple is rubbish and ashes. There is drought in the land. In 536 B.C. the Temple foundations are laid.

Judah's enemies politically succeed in stopping the work for 16 years. The people become lethargic, worshipping in the unfinished Temple structure. Haggai's four messages are intended to inspire them and to resume the construction.

OUTLINE OF ZECHARIAH

Three Messages To Those Rebuilding the Temple...

- *First Message: Call for National Repentance—1:1-6*

- *Second Message: Eight Visions concerning Israel's comfort—1:7-6:15*

1. The Angel of JHWH and the horsemen—1:7-17
2. The 4 horns and 4 craftsmen—1:18-21
3. The man with the measuring line—2:1-13
4. Vision of Joshua the High Priest—3:1-10
5. The golden lamp stand and 2 olive trees—4:1-14
6. Vision of flying scroll—5:1-4
7. The woman in the ephah—5:5-11
8. Vision of 4 chariots—6:1-8

Climax of visions: Joshua is crowned—6:9-15

- *Third Message: Fasts will become feasts—7:1-8:23*

Two Messages Concerning the Messiah...

- *Initial rejection of Messiah—9:1-11:17*
  Triumphant arrival of Messiah—9:1-9
  Announcement of Messiah's Kingdom—9:10-10:12
  Israel's rejection of the Good Shepherd—11:1-4
  Israel's acceptance of the worthless shepherd—11:5-17
- *Final establishment of Messiah's Kingdom—12:1-14:21*
  The triumph and conversion of Israel—12:1-13:6
  The enthronement of Israel's rejected King—13:7-14:21

AUTHOR

Zechariah

THEME

The rebuilding of the Temple is bound up with God's purpose to establish the Messianic Kingdom. Eight visions are given, each speaking directly to the contemporary situation but also pointing toward the ultimate fulfillment of prophecy related to the coming of the Messiah.

DATE

520-519 and 480 B.C.

NOTES

Zechariah means "Jehovah Remembers." He was of priestly descent. Josephus (a historian following Jesus' generation) tells us he was killed in the Temple, a martyr for his faith in God.

He was born in Babylon, but wrote in Israel. His writings resemble those of Daniel, and remind us of Revelation. His book contains more Messianic passages than any other Minor Prophet: see 3:8, 13:7, 9:9, 11:12-13, 12:10, and 14:3-8.

His visions apparently were all received during the same night. The close connection between his prophecies and those of Revelation make this book, along with Daniel, a very special book for those interested in prophecy.

This significant prophecy sees many details related to both the first coming and the second coming of Christ. From the betrayal of Jesus, to the settling of Israel in the land, the visions this man saw could not have occurred apart from the divine inspiration of God's Spirit.

OUTLINE OF MALACHI

Six Messages of the Prophet

Introduction—1:1

The Six Messages:
1. God's love for Israel reaffirmed—1:2-5
2. Priestly corruptions denounced—1:6-2:9
3. Proliferation of divorce and mixed marriages
    denounced—2:10-16
4. Announcement of a coming day of judgment—
    2:17-3:5
5. Rebuke for the neglect of tithes
    and offerings—3:6-12
6. Vindication of the Godly remnant—3:13-4:3

Concluding Exhortations—4:4-6

AUTHOR

Malachi

THEME

Only a century after the judgment of God fell upon Israel, they have once again forgotten their walk before Him. Their moral degeneracy causes Malachi to indict and warn them of the consequences.

DATE
433-430 B.C.

MALACHI'S FINAL WORDS...

The last of the prophets, Malachi is a miniature of the entire Old Testament. Among his great themes is this summary:

1. ISRAEL SELECTED BY GOD: 1:2; 2:4-6, 10

2. ISRAEL TRANSGRESSED AGAINST GOD: 1:6; 2:11, 17

3. THE MESSIAH IS MANIFESTED: 3:1, 4:2

4. THE TRIBULATION UPON THE NATIONS: 4:1

5. THE FINAL PURIFICATION OF ISRAEL: 3:2-4 and 12; 3:16-18; 4:2-6

The prophecies of Daniel's 70 weeks conclude in 396 B.C., the date of Malachi's ministry.

Malachi answers the *"Seven Stupid Questions"* the Israelites address to God:

1. *In what way have You loved us?—1:2*
2. *In what way have we despised Your name?—1:6*
3. *In what way have we polluted You?—1:7*
4. *In what way have we wearied You?—2:17*
5. *In what way shall we return?—3:7*
6. *How have we robbed You?—3:8*
7. *What have we spoken so much against You?—3:13*

Using these questions as a basis for your study, underline the answers God gives through His prophet. You will learn much about the ways of God by doing so!

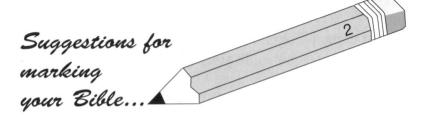

Suggestions for marking your Bible...

1. Copy the outline into your Bible.

2. Write beside Zechariah 9:9-10:

> *One of the clearest*
> *Messianic prophecies*
> *in O.T.*

3. Write beside Malachi 3:8-10:

> *This exhortation speaks*
> *to the Church, too!*

4. Add any other notes from the explanations which you wish to preserve in your Bible.

Unit Twenty Seven
THE INTERBIBLICAL PERIOD
THE SYNOPTIC GOSPELS

THE INTERBIBLICAL PERIOD

I. THE HISTORICAL SETTING

On the following 4 pages are charts taken from the New Testament Time Line (© Moody Press) which show the history of this important period of time.

II. THE SEPTUAGINT

The Hebrew Old Testament was translated into Greek about 250 B.C. The name means "Seventy," the approximate number of men who translated the Torah into Greek. (Sometimes you will see it referred to as "LXX"—Latin for 70.) Ptolemy II Philadelphus reigned over Egypt from 285-247. He developed the largest collection of books in the world (over 500,000), and commissioned the translation.

Thus, Jews from one end of the Greek empire to the other were able to read their sacred writings in the language of the streets—Greek. For those who had lost the ability to read their mother language, this was a great boon. A great portion of the quotations from the Old Testament found in the New Testament are from the LXX. You will find that they vary slightly from the actual quotation in your Old Testament. The reason is because your Old Testament is a direct translation from Hebrew to English, while the LXX is Hebrew to Greek to English.

THE INTERBIBLICAL PERIOD—PART 1

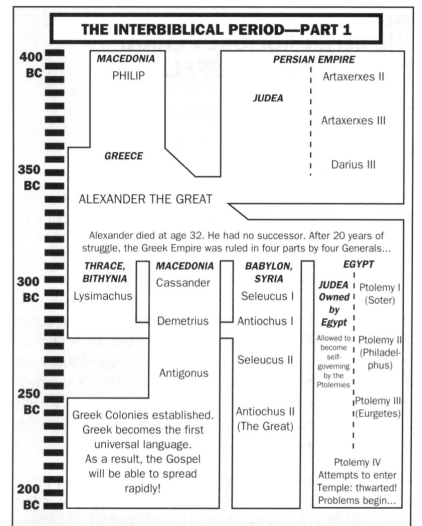

400 BC	*MACEDONIA* PHILIP	*PERSIAN EMPIRE* Artaxerxes II
	JUDEA	
		Artaxerxes III
350 BC	*GREECE*	Darius III
	ALEXANDER THE GREAT	

Alexander died at age 32. He had no successor. After 20 years of struggle, the Greek Empire was ruled in four parts by four Generals...

THRACE, BITHYNIA	*MACEDONIA*	*BABYLON, SYRIA*	*EGYPT*
300 BC Lysimachus	Cassander	Seleucus I	*JUDEA Owned by Egypt* Ptolemy I (Soter)
	Demetrius	Antiochus I	
		Seleucus II	Allowed to become self-governing by the Ptolemies — Ptolemy II (Philadelphus)
	Antigonus		
250 BC		Antiochus II (The Great)	Ptolemy III (Eurgetes)
200 BC	Greek Colonies established. Greek becomes the first universal language. As a result, the Gospel will be able to spread rapidly!		Ptolemy IV Attempts to enter Temple: thwarted! Problems begin...

After Alexander's death, the Greek Empire emerged as two sub-empires:
• **The empire of the SELEUCIDS, covering the northern sector of the Mediterranean and eastward all the way to Babylonia.**
• **The empire of the PTOLEMIES, covering Egypt, Arabia, and the area of Palestine. The Greek rulers took names of "Pharaohs" for themselves. Thus, "Ptolemy II" became the name for General Philadelphus. Primarily because of the impact of Daniel's prophecies about Alexander the Great, Judea was given special freedom. However, when Ptolemy IV tried to personally enter the sacred Temple, things quickly deteriorated for Judea, and severe persecution took place.**

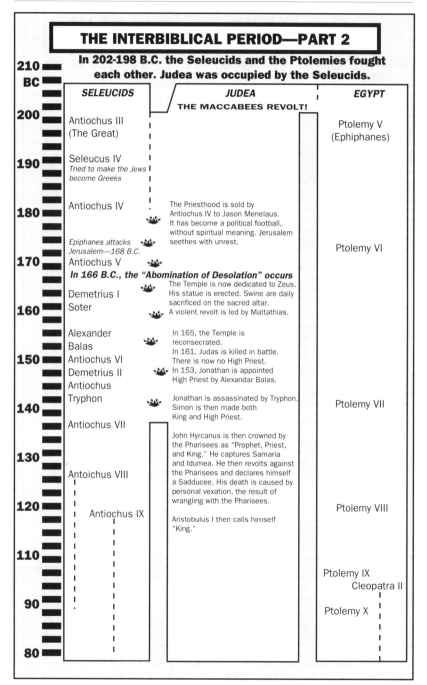

THE INTERBIBLICAL PERIOD—PART 2

In 202-198 B.C. the Seleucids and the Ptolemies fought each other. Judea was occupied by the Seleucids.

	SELEUCIDS	JUDEA	EGYPT
		THE MACCABEES REVOLT!	
210 BC			
200	Antiochus III (The Great)		Ptolemy V (Ephiphanes)
190	Seleucus IV *Tried to make the Jews become Greeks*		
180	Antiochus IV	The Priesthood is sold by Antiochus IV to Jason Menelaus. It has become a political football, without spiritual meaning. Jerusalem seethes with unrest.	
170	*Epiphanes attacks Jerusalem—168 B.C.* Antiochus V		Ptolemy VI
	In 166 B.C., the "Abomination of Desolation" occurs	The Temple is now dedicated to Zeus. His statue is erected. Swine are daily sacrificed on the sacred altar. A violent revolt is led by Mattathias.	
160	Demetrius I Soter		
150	Alexander Balas Antiochus VI Demetrius II Antiochus	In 165, the Temple is reconsecrated. In 161, Judas is killed in battle. There is now no High Priest. In 153, Jonathan is appointed High Priest by Alexandar Balas.	
140	Tryphon Antiochus VII	Jonathan is assassinated by Tryphon. Simon is then made both King and High Priest.	Ptolemy VII
130	Antoichus VIII	John Hyrcanus is then crowned by the Pharisees as "Prophet, Priest, and King." He captures Samaria and Idumea. He then revolts against the Pharisees and declares himself a Sadducee. His death is caused by personal vexation, the result of wrangling with the Pharisees.	
120	Antiochus IX	Aristobulus I then calls himself "King."	Ptolemy VIII
110			
			Ptolemy IX Cleopatra II
90			Ptolemy X
80			

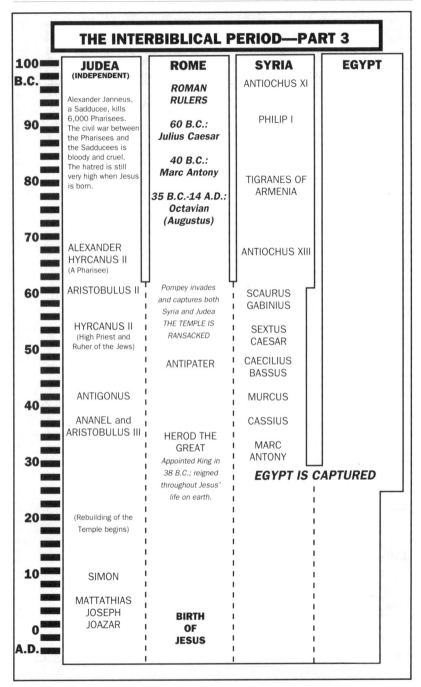

THE INTERBIBLICAL PERIOD—PART 3

	JUDEA (INDEPENDENT)	ROME	SYRIA	EGYPT
100 B.C.		**ROMAN RULERS**	ANTIOCHUS XI	**EGYPT**
90	Alexander Janneus, a Sadducee, kills 6,000 Pharisees. The civil war between the Pharisees and the Sadducees is bloody and cruel. The hatred is still very high when Jesus is born.	**60 B.C.: Julius Caesar**	PHILIP I	
80		**40 B.C.: Marc Antony**	TIGRANES OF ARMENIA	
		35 B.C.-14 A.D.: Octavian (Augustus)		
70	ALEXANDER HYRCANUS II (A Pharisee)		ANTIOCHUS XIII	
60	ARISTOBULUS II	*Pompey invades and captures both Syria and Judea*	SCAURUS GABINIUS	
50	HYRCANUS II (High Priest and Ruher of the Jews)	*THE TEMPLE IS RANSACKED*	SEXTUS CAESAR	
		ANTIPATER	CAECILIUS BASSUS	
40	ANTIGONUS		MURCUS	
	ANANEL and ARISTOBULUS III		CASSIUS	
30		HEROD THE GREAT *Appointed King in 38 B.C.; reigned throughout Jesus' life on earth.*	MARC ANTONY	
			EGYPT IS CAPTURED	
20	(Rebuilding of the Temple begins)			
10	SIMON			
	MATTATHIAS JOSEPH JOAZAR	**BIRTH OF JESUS**		
0 A.D.				

THE INTERBIBLICAL PERIOD—PART 4

THE LIFE OF OUR LORD JESUS CHRIST

BC				
4	BIRTH	TEMPLE HIGH PRIESTS:	DEATH OF HEROD THE GREAT	
3				
2				
1		JESUS	HEROD ANTIPAS	HEROD PHILIP
AD			Tetrarch of Galilee and Perea	Tetrarch of Batania, Trachonitis, Auranitis
1				
2				
3				
4				
5				
6		JOAZAR		
7				
8				
9	AGE 12 JESUS VISITS THE TEMPLE	ANNAS		
10				
11				
12	JESUS GROWS TO MANHOOD IN NAZARETH	ISHMAEL ELEAZAR SIMON		
13				
14				
15				
16				
17				
18		JOSEPH		
19				
20				
21				
22				
23		CAIAPHAS (To 36 AD)		
24				

Your study of the life of Jesus will be much enlarged if you will take a little time to get the facts in mind which are presented in the tables on pages 238-241.

As you read the New Testament, take a few moments to look up the backgrounds of the people mentioned, using your Zondervan Pictorial Bible Encyclopedia. If you will take a little time to do this, the significance of what is being explained will be multiplied tenfold!

HIS PUBLIC MINISTRY (29-30)

CRUCIFIXION (33)

OLD TESTAMENT APOCRYPHA
"The Outside Writings"

1 ESDRAS
Another version of parts of Chronicles, Ezra, and Nehemiah.

2 ESDRAS
Written after the Romans destroyed Jerusalem in A. D. 70. Style is Apocalyptic.

TOBIT
A short story. Tobit arranges a marriage in God's will for his son.

JUDITH
A resourceful Jewess delivers her people.

ADDITIONS TO ESTHER
Interesting additions to part of the book.

WISDOM OF SOLOMON
A book of theology.

ECCLESIASTICUS
Wise sayings (like Proverbs).

BARUCH
Supposedly written by Jeremiah's scribe, in captivity.

A LETTER OF JEREMIAH
A sermon on idolatry, supposedly by Jeremiah.

(Continued on next page)

242

ADDITIONS TO DANIEL:

Song of the Three
A prayer of praise by the young men in the fiery furnace.

Daniel and Susanna
A courtroom drama.

Daniel, Bel, and the Dragon
Wise Daniel exposes idolatry in Babylon.

PRAYER OF MANASSEH
Supposedly by a King of Judah in captivity.

1 MACCABEES
Epic history of a successful Jewish revolt.

2 MACCABEES
A second account of the revolt.

IN ADDITION, THERE ARE "APOCALYPTIC" BOOKS WHICH WERE ADDED...for example, **1 ENOCH** and **THE BOOK OF THE JUBILEES.**

None of these writings have ever been accepted as a part of the Canon *("rule")* of the Scriptures. Because they were included in the LXX (Septuagint), they were translated by Jerome and made a part of the Catholic Bible. Protestant Reformers firmly rejected them; therefore, they are not found in Protestant versions (exception: New English Bible).

The best way to convince yourself they are *not* inspired and do not belong in your Bible is to read them! They are "religious fiction."

WHILE WE'RE ON THE SUBJECT...

Have you ever picked up a magazine and read an ad telling you to order the "Lost Books of the Bible?" Such spurious writings are called *"pseudepigrapha"* (*Pseude* = false; *Grapha* = writings).

What you buy are not "lost books," but some of the many writings which were fabricated to *look* like Bible books. Most of them were written about the second century A.D., probably by enterprising writers who preyed on the devout. Some of these are quite impressive at first reading! (Such enterprisers sell them today to the gullible public. After all, there's no copyright on them!)

However, unless you are a collector of oddities, save your money. There is not a *possibility* there are any "lost books." The Holy Spirit of God is in charge of the Scriptures, and He has not permitted the loss of any writing we need.

At the same time, there is not a *possibility* that any of the existing Bible books should be eliminated. Martin Luther did not like the book of James, calling it "a right strawy epistle." His inability to reconcile faith and works within it said more about his personal deficiencies in theology than the value of the book. Nevertheless, he left the book intact when he translated the Bible into German.

Our Bible is, indeed, "a perfect treasury of truth!"

(Suggestion: in your Bible Encyclopedia, read the section on the Canon of the Scriptures.)

THE SYNOPTIC GOSPELS

"Synoptic" *(meaning "synopsis")* Gospels are those which tell the story of Jesus *chronologically*. The first three Gospel accounts are chronological: Matthew, Mark, Luke.

John's Gospel is totally different! It is not written to tell the story of Jesus' life, but rather to reveal miracles performed by Him which prove His divinity. Thus, John records "SIGNS," or "MIRACLES," in the life of Jesus.

Matthew, Mark, and Luke, therefore have a special relationship to each other. Note their emphases:

MATTHEW: BEHOLD YOUR KING
The genealogy proves Jesus had a legal right to be King of the Jews through His "legal" father, Joseph.

MARK: BEHOLD THE SERVANT
There is no genealogy: who cares about the lineage of a servant? Christ is portrayed in a totally different perspective; therefore, there are special details about His life not related by Matthew's account.

LUKE: BEHOLD THE MAN
Written by a physician, the genealogy flows through Mary back to David, then to Abraham, then to Adam! It is proving a different point than the one recorded in Matthew. Again, there are special details about His life not included by either Matthew and Mark.

HAVE YOU EVER HEARD OF A "HARMONY OF THE GOSPELS?"

It's a great tool for Bible study! It combines, in parallel columns, the chronology of Christ's life. Get one soon.

As you enter your study of the Gospels, you will do well to remember the facts given on this page and the one which follows.

It would be a good idea to write this outline in a blank page in your Bible...perhaps on one of the flyleafs inside the back cover.

COMPARISON OF THE FOUR GOSPELS				
	MATTHEW	**MARK**	**LUKE**	**JOHN**
PORTRAIT OF JESUS	The Prophesied King	The Obedient Servant	The Perfect Man	The Divine Son
PROMINENT WORDS	"Fulfilled"	"Straightway"	"Son Of Man"	"Believe"
CULTURES OF THE ORIGINAL READERS	Jews (Jesus, Son of Abraham)	Romans (Action, no genealogy)	Greeks (Jesus, Son of Adam)	Church (Jesus, Son of God)
OUTLOOK AND STYLE OF THE WRITERS	TEACHER	PREACHER	HISTORIAN	THEOLOGIAN
OUT-STANDING SECTIONS	SERMONS	MIRACLES	PARABLES	DOCTRINES
PROMINENT IDEAS	LAW	POWER	GRACE	GLORY
BROAD DIVISION	"SYNOPTIC GOSPELS" Stresses the humanity of Christ, from the outward, earthly side.			"FOURTH GOSPEL" Stresses His Deity.

PORTRAITS OF CHRIST IN THE GOSPELS

PORTRAITS	MATTHEW	MARK	LUKE	JOHN
REVELATION 4, EZEKIEL 1	FIRST CREATURE: LION-LIKE	SECOND CREATURE: OX-LIKE	THIRD CREATURE: MAN-LIKE	FOURTH CREATURE: EAGLE-LIKE

THE GENEALOGICAL RECORDS

MATTHEW 1:1-17
Written from the view of Christ's right to be King.
Traces the regal line of David through Solomon.
Leads to Joseph, the legal stepfather of Jesus.

LUKE 3:23-28
Written from the view of Christ's perfect humanity.
Traces the physical line of David through another son,
　　Nathan.
Leads to Mary, the physical mother of Jesus.

BEHOLD, THE...

KING _____

SERVANT _____

MAN _____

GOD _____

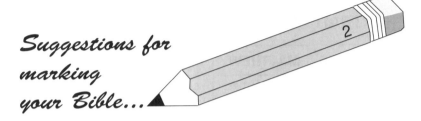

Suggestions for marking your Bible...

1. Copy the outline into your Bible.

2. Write beside MATTHEW, MARK, LUKE, and JOHN chapter headings the following:

    (Matthew): Behold The King
    (Mark): Behold The Servant
    (Luke): Behold The Man
    (John): Behold Your God!

3. Write beside Matthew 1:1:

    The Book of the Generation of...the same phrase used for the outline in Genesis! As Genesis traced the First Adam, so Matthew will trace the lineage of the Second Adam.

4. Add any other notes from the explanations which you wish to preserve in your Bible.

Unit Twenty Eight
THE GOSPEL OF MATTHEW

OUTLINE OF MATTHEW

I. THE BIRTH OF THE KING
    The Genealogy of the King—1:1-17
    The Incarnation—1:18-25
    The Visit of the Magi—2:1-12
    The Flight to Egypt—2:13-23
II. THE GALILEAN MINISTRY OF THE KING
    The Forerunner of Jesus—3:1-12
    The Baptism of Jesus—3:13-17
    The Temptation of Jesus—4:1-11
    The Initial Ministry of Jesus—4:12-25
    The Sermon on the Mount—5:1-7:29
    The Miracles of Authentication—8:1-9:38
    The Mission of the Twelve—10:1-42
    The Question of John the Baptist—11:1-19
    Warnings—11:20-12:50
    The Parables of the Kingdom—13:1-58
    The Death of John the Baptist—14:1-12
    The Miracles of Providence—14:13-36
    Conflicts with Religious Authorities—15:1-16:12
    The Confession of Peter—16:13-28
    The Transfiguration—17:1-13
    The Continuing Ministry in Galilee—17:14-18:35
III. THE JUDEAN MINISTRY OF THE KING
    Questions Concerning the Family—19:1-15
    The Approach of the Rich Young Ruler—19:16-30
    The Parable of the Vineyard Workers—20:1-19
    The Request of Zebedee's Wife—20:20-29
    The Healing of Two Blind Men—20:30-34

IV. THE LAST DAYS IN JUDEA
- The Triumphal Entry—21:1-11
- The Cleansing of the Temple—21:12-22
- The Questions of Authority—21:23-46
- The Questions of Theology—22:1-46
- Prophetic Woes—23:1-39
- The Olivet Discourse—24:1-25:46
- The Passover and Last Supper—26:1-35
- The Garden of Gethsemane—26:36-46
- The Betrayal and Trial—26:47-27:45
- The Scourging and Crucifixion—27:46-66

V. THE CONCLUDING EVENTS
- The Resurrection—28:1-15
- The Commission—28:16-20

AUTHOR

Matthew, the Apostle. Papias, who lived in 130 A.D., mentioned that Matthew compiled the "sayings of Jesus" in "the Hebrew speech," i.e., Aramaic.

DATE

Probably 50-53 A.D. Those who accept the theory that Matthew used Mark to write his Gospel would say 45-70 A.D.

THEME

Matthew presents Jesus as the Messiah, who fulfilled the promises of the Old Testament. He wrote for Jews. He presents the mission of Jesus as bringing the kingdom of God to mankind in His person, words, and deeds.

NOTES

Matthew alone, of the 4 Gospels, mentions the Church.

He is also the only one who calls Jesus the King of the twelve tribes of Israel (19:28).

He also is the only writer who includes nine proof verses from the Old Testament which would be especially appealing to Jewish readers: 1:22-23; 2:15, 17-18, 23; 4:14-16; 8:17; 12:17-21; 13:35; 27:9-10.

Their purpose is to prove that Jesus *is* the promised kingly Son whose coming has brought God's Kingdom against the kingdom of Satan in this age.

THE GENEALOGY IN CHAPTER 1

It is taken from the LXX (Septuagint Version) record of 1 Chronicles 1-3, transliterated from Hebrew into Greek. His divisions point to Abraham as the beginning, David as the high point, the Captivity as the low point, and Jesus' coming as the final point.

As mentioned earlier, the legal rather than the biological descent of Jesus is traced from David to Joseph. Through Joseph, his legal father, Jesus has *legal* rights to the throne of Israel. Through Mary, he has *blood* rights to it (see Luke's differing genealogy).

1:18-25: Matthew and Luke affirm the virgin birth of Jesus. A rejection of the virgin birth usually proceeds from, or ends in, the rejection of the supernatural nature of Christ.

251

GENERAL OUTLINE OF THE NEW TESTAMENT

HISTORY

GOSPELS
Matthew
Mark
Luke
John

ACTS OF THE APOSTLES

EPISTLES

PAULINE
JOURNEY EPISTLES
Galatians
1 and 2 Thessalonians
1 and 2 Corinthians
Romans
PRISON EPISTLES
Philemon
Colossians
Ephesians
Philippians
PASTORAL EPISTLES
1 Timothy
Titus
2 Timothy

GENERAL

HEBREW-CHRISTIAN
Hebrews
James
OTHER
1 and 2 Peter
1, 2, and 3 John
Jude

VISIONS
Revelation (The Apocalypse)

THE KINGDOM OF GOD

Note: because of their reverence for the name of God, the Jews rather referred to that which was closer to Him... "heaven." Thus, in Matthew, the term "Kingdom of Heaven" is used instead. The term refers to the "Kingdom of God."

The word "Kingdom" means literally, *"Rule, Reign."* In scripture, the Kingdom is viewed in five aspects:

1. A Kingdom introduced by Jesus, its King and Head. See Mark 1:14,15.
2. A Kingdom rejected by Israel, and now restricted to those who are committed to its principles. Those who are so committed compose the church, the body of Christ. To "testify the gospel of the grace of God" is the equivalent of "preaching the Kingdom of God." See Acts 20:24,25.
3. In Matthew 13, the visible Kingdom includes all who profess to belong to Christ—some truly, some falsely. The wheat and tares grow together until the final judgment, when they are separated.
4. There is a future aspect to the Kingdom, reference when we pray *"Thy Kingdom come..."* The government of Christ will be brought in power over all the earth. This Kingdom will include the risen "church of the first-born ones," described in Hebrews 12. But it will also consist of Israel as a converted people, along with the converted Gentiles throughout the earth.
5. In 1 Corinthians 15:24, we discover this Kingdom of Christ will be delivered up to God the Father. An eternal Kingdom will be established, which will never end.

POWERFUL CHAPTERS YOU WILL WANT TO STUDY IN DEPTH IN THE DAYS TO COME...

CHAPTERS 5-7: THE SERMON ON THE MOUNT

These chapters contain the only section of scripture in which our Lord summarized His entire teaching. It contains the Beatitudes and many significant truths. One brilliant attorney committed the entire passage to memory as a means of filling his heart with the truths of Christ...an excellent idea!

CHAPTER 13, ETC: THE PARABLES

Sprinkled through Jesus' teachings are the illustrations taken from common things, which illustrate the Kingdom of God. A special study of them will open many insights for you!

CHAPTER 16: FOUNDING OF THE CHURCH

Note the church is not founded on Peter, but upon the *insight* Peter verbalized: *"You are the Christ, the SON OF THE LIVING GOD."* This is the truth that Jesus said He would build His church upon. One human, frail and capable of denying His Lord, is not the "rock" which is the foundation for the church. There is *another* Man who is the "foundation which no man can lay"—Jesus!

*HAS IT BEEN SETTLED IN YOUR MIND AND HEART THAT JESUS IS NOT **LIKE** GOD, BUT THAT **HE IS GOD**?*

It is amazing to discover how many people have never truly understood this basic truth. All who are a part of the true Church acknowledge this: Romans 10:9-15.

CHAPTER 24-25: WORDS ABOUT THE FUTURE

In 24:3, the disciples ask him three questions:
1. When will the Temple be destroyed (see v. 1 and 2)?
2. What will be the sign of Your coming?
3. What will be the sign of the end of the age?

In 24:1-14, He outlines the events between His departure and His coming, which will come with the end of the age.

In 24:15-28, He outlines the culminating events in the city of Jerusalem at the time of His coming.

In 24:29-31, He describes the actual event of His second coming.

The judgment of the nations, fitting Old Testament prophecies, is given in 25:31-46. This does not occur at the end of the world (see Revelation 20), but rather at the end of this present age, when Jesus comes to set up His earthly Kingdom with Israel as its center.

CHAPTERS 26-27: THE DEATH OF OUR LORD

In these chapters, He offered Himself as the "Lamb of God," to take away the sin of all men.

CHAPTER 28: THE TRIUMPH OF THE MESSIAH
Two great facts are recorded: His resurrection from the dead, and the "Great Commission" given in 28:18-20. *If you should memorize only one scripture beyond John 3:16 in your entire life, let that scripture be Matthew 28:18-20!*

Suggestions for marking your Bible...

1. Copy the outline into your Bible.

2. Write beside Matthew 28:18-20:

    The Great Commission applies to MY life!

3. Write beside Matthew 5:1:

    The Sermon on the Mount Full summary of Jesus teachings

4. Add any other notes from the explanations which you wish to preserve in your Bible.

Unit Twenty Nine
THE GOSPEL OF MARK

OUTLINE OF MARK

INTRODUCTION—1:1-8

I. THE PREPARATION FOR CHRIST'S MINISTRY
    The Baptism of Jesus—1:9-11
    The Temptation of Jesus—1:12-13
II. THE BEGINNING OF CHRIST'S MINISTRY
    The Early Ministry in Galilee—1:14-15
    The Call of the First Disciples—1:16-20
III. THE HEALING MINISTRY OF CHRIST
    The Demoniac Healed—1:21-28
    Peter's Mother-In-Law Healed—1:29-31
    A Multitude Healed—1:32-34
    A Brief Tour of Galilee—1:35-39
    The Leper Healed—1:40-45
    The Paralytic Healed—2:1-12
IV. OPPOSITION TO THE ENLARGED MINISTRY
    The Charge: A Friend of Sinners—2:13-17
    Jesus' Answer to His Critics—2:18-3:6
    The Pressure From the Multitude—3:7-12
    The Appointment of the Twelve—3:13-19
    Increased Opposition—3:20-30
    Relationships in the Kingdom of God—3:31-35
    Lessons on Discipleship—4:1-25
    Kingdom Parables—4:26-34
    Jesus Works Miracles—4:35-5:43
    Jesus' Visit to Nazareth—6:1-6
    The Sending Out of the Twelve—6:7-13
    The Martyrdom of John the Baptist—6:14-29

V. THE TRAINING MINISTRY OF CHRIST
    Jesus Seeks A Quiet Place—6:30-52
    Ministry in Gennesaret and Galilee—6:53-7:23
    The Twelve Trained in Tyre and Sidon—7:24-30
    The Twelve Trained in Decapolis—7:31-8:26
    The Twelve Trained in Caesarea Philippi—8:27-9:29
    The Journey Through Galilee—9:30-50
    Enroute to Jerusalem—10:1-52
VI. THE REDEMPTIVE MINISTRY OF CHRIST
    The Presentation of the Messiah—11:1-11
    A Demonstration of Messiah's Authority—11:12-19
    Questioning the King—11:20-12:40
    A Lesson in Christian Giving—12:41-44
    Eschatological Teachings—13:1-37
    Increased Persecution—14:1-11
    Final Hours with the Twelve—14:12-52
    Trial and Crucifixion of Jesus—14:53-15:47
    Resurrection of Jesus—16:1-20

AUTHOR

John Mark, son of Mary and cousin of Barnabas, is the author. His mother Mary was evidently a woman of prominence and wealth. His attempts at missionary service with Paul did not work out well (Acts 13:13), but later he became closely associated with him, according to the historian Papias (140 A.D.).

DATE

Probably 55 A.D.

THEME

The Servanthood of Jesus Christ, the Son of God.

NOTES

As Matthew wrote for the Jews, Mark wrote for the Gentiles. Evidences of this are:

1. He omits practically all Old Testament references, except in 1:1-2 and as Jesus quotes from it.
2. He omits a genealogy.
3. All allusions to His birth and infancy are eliminated.
4. Mark feels a necessity to explain Jewish terms, which he would skip over if he had been writing for Jewish readers (5:41; 7:34; 7:1-4).

What Gentiles? A large host of scholars have concluded this book was probably written in Rome. It was directed to the *Romans*, the citizens of the ruling power. Thus, it has an evangelistic motive.

Jesus is presented as being in direct conflict with all their value systems! He is described as a slave—a common servant. Romans believed the greatest was the one who sat at the head of the table; Jesus taught the exact opposite.

Omitted are the following passages:

- The Sermon on the Mount
- Jesus' charge to the twelve
- His discourses on the Second Coming

(For more on this theme of servanthood, see the article which follows in this Unit. This is one of the most important themes in the Bible, and certainly is the key to the Christian life.)

A WORD PECULIAR TO MARK

The word "STRAIGHTWAY" is used about 40 times in this book. It reveals to the Roman Gentiles the energy, the thrust, in the Gospel. Most important, it is the sign of a servant who reveals unquestioning obedience—without hesitation—to the will of the Master. The use of the word places side by side two thoughts: the energy and power of Jesus, the Christ; and His humility and patience.

1:14-15: MORE ON "THE KINGDOM OF GOD"

KINGDOM: *"Basileia,"* "Reign, Rule"

Seven Things To Remember About The Kingdom:

1. God owns and possesses all things.
2. God is the only King of Israel. In the Old Testament, we saw Him as King, and there was a "Theocracy." He only *tolerated* the desire of the Israelites to have human kings. His permission proved to them the foolishness of their choice.
3. God is reestablishing His throne once again over Israel. The Theocracy is thus reestablished!
4. Jesus comes, with every right to the Throne, and offers Himself. He is rejected.
5. Jewish rejection opened the way for Gentiles to be included in the Kingdom. This is a "mystery," the Church. Christ reigns in the hearts of subjects who have experienced the New Birth and become members of His Body.
6. This "hidden" nature of the Kingdom, within the hearts of men, is only temporary. Jesus shall return, usher in the Kingdom, and reign on the throne of David for a thousand years (Rev. 20:4-6).

260

7. This reign of Christ will be replaced at the end of His thousand year reign by God's eternal reign. He will turn over the Kingdom to the Father.
   (1 Cor. 15:24-26, 28; 2 Tim. 4:18; Rev. 22:3,5).

In Mark, two facts are continuous: God ushers in the Kingdom, and Jesus is His King!

NOTES ABOUT THE PARABLES

Every one of these parables relates to the Kingdom of God. You will enjoy "digging out" the truths for yourself. This is where your library of study books will come in handy!

THE SOWER, SEED AND SOIL—Matthew 13

THE GOOD SAMARITAN—Luke 10:30-37

THE RICH FOOL—Luke 12:16-21

THE LOST SHEEP, COIN, AND SON—Luke 15:3-32

LAZARUS AND THE RICH MAN—Luke 16:19-31

THE BUDDING OF THE FIG TREE—Matthew 24:32-35

THE TEN VIRGINS—Matthew 25:1-13

SEPARATING OF THE SHEEP AND GOATS—
    Matthew 25:31-46

MARK'S EMPHASIS ON SERVANTHOOD

One of the most overwhelming studies you can do on your own is to research all the passages where Jesus speaks of servanthood. This is an excellent way to learn the value of using your exhaustive Concordance.

Look up all the verses in which the word "Servant" appears. Note the number of times in the Old Testament God speaks of His relationship with *"Abraham, my servant..." "Moses, my servant..."*

In Mark, the life of Jesus is portrayed as One who has come to be the "servant of all." He runs totally counter to all the structures of men in teaching that the greatest among us is the one who serves, not the one who sits at the head of the table.

His disciples did not comprehend what He was teaching. They expected Him to establish a political kingdom, perhaps like the one established during the Interbiblical Period. He was seen by them to be a Moses, who would set His people free. They argued among themselves about who would be the greatest among them when He handed out offices in His kingdom.

You have not even *started* to grasp the teaching of Jesus until you have grasped the meaning of the Kingdom and the importance of being a *servant*. This is at the very heart of Christ's truth.

Mark 9:35 is a classic statement which summarizes His teaching. God's value system runs exactly counter to that of man. To comprehend this, take notes during the lecture on this Unit, using the following diagrams...

TWO WAYS OF RELATING TO GOD

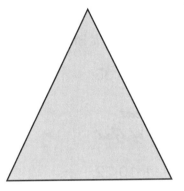

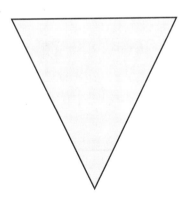

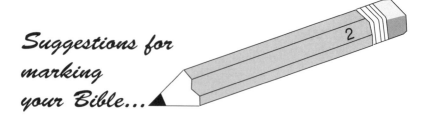

Suggestions for marking your Bible...

1. Copy the outline into your Bible.

2. Write beside Mark 10:35:

   *The way to be great
   in the Kingdom of God*

3. Write beside Mark 10:22:

   *Greek is <u>stugnasa</u>,
   meaning shocked, appalled*

4. Add any other notes from the explanations which you wish to preserve in your Bible.

Unit Thirty
THE GOSPEL OF LUKE

OUTLINE OF LUKE

INTRODUCTION—1:1-4

I. THE INFANCY AND EARLY YEARS OF JESUS
     Annunciation of the Birth of John the Baptist—1:5-25
     Annunciation of the Birth of Jesus—1:26-38
     Visit of Mary to Elizabeth—1:39-56
     Birth of John the Baptist—1:57-80
     Birth of Jesus—2:1-20
     Circumcision and presentation of Jesus in
        the Temple—2:21-40
     Jesus' boyhood—2:41-52

II. THE BEGINNING OF JESUS' MINISTRY
     John the Baptist's ministry—3:1-20
     Baptism of Jesus—3:21-22
     Genealogy of Jesus—3:23-38
     Jesus' temptation in the wilderness—4:1-13

III. JESUS, THE AGENT OF GOD'S SALVATION
     The rejection at Nazareth—4:14-30
     The dawning of the new age—4:31-44
     The first Disciples—5:1-11
     The struggle between the new and old—5:12-6:11
     The new community of Disciples—6:12-49
     Reaching out to others—7:1-8:3
     The itinerary of Jesus' ministry—8:4-56
     An assignment for the Disciples—9:1-17

(continued on next page)

(Continued from previous page)

Peter's great confession—9:18-21

Jesus foretells His death—9:22-27

The Transfiguration—9:28-36

The future of the Disciples—9:37-50

IV. THE SAVIOR PROCEEDS TOWARD THE CROSS

The meaning of discipleship—9:51-11:13

Israel's rejection of the Savior—11:14-13:17

Teaching about the Kingdom—13:18-14:35

Recovering the lost—15:1-32

Teaching the duties of discipleship—16:1-17:19

Watching for the Kingdom—17:20-18:34

Jericho, the last stop on the road—18:35-19:27

V. JESUS IN JERUSALEM

The enthusiasm of the crowds—19:28-38

Jesus points out the failures of Judaism—19:39-21:4

Warnings about the future—21:5-36

Summary of His days in Jerusalem—21:37-38

VI. THE DEATH AND RESURRECTION OF JESUS

Preparing for the cross—22:1-53

The trials of Jesus—22:54-23:25

The crucifixion—23:26-56

His resurrection and ascension—24:1-53

AUTHOR

Luke, a physician, was the companion of Paul on his trips. From historical writings we are told he was a native of Antioch, he wrote his gospel in Achaia, and he died unmarried and childless in Boetia at the age of 84. He appears to be a "second-generation" Christian. However, he had closely associated with eyewitnesses of the beginning of Christianity. This group included Mary, Jesus' mother. With the skill of a diagnostician, he gathered the details of the life of our Lord. He was highly educated. This is revealed in the quality of Greek he used and his almost poetic ability to write prose. It is practically certain he was a Gentile, probably a Greek. This is surmised from Col. 4:10-14, where Paul divides six of his helpers into two groups. The first three are "of the circumcision" (Jews); Luke is among the second three, who are Gentiles.

DATE

58-63 A.D.

THEME

The Son of Man among men.

LENGTH OF BOOK

Mark is the shortest of the Gospels; Luke is the longest, and the most detailed of the four Gospels.

THE "SON OF MAN"

God refers to Ezekiel more than 90 times as the "Son of man." It referred to his humanity and frailty, as compared with God's power and deity. In Daniel 7:13 and 8:17, it is given a totally new meaning: it becomes the title for the person who will receive the kingdom from the "Ancient of Days," and who will offer it to the saints.

Jesus assigned the term to Himself often. In doing so, He referred not only to His humanity, but also to His role as the One who *would* offer the kingdom to the saints.

WRITTEN FOR GENTILES

Luke explained Jewish customs and localities. He traced the genealogy back to Adam. He used reigns of Roman emperors to date Jesus' birth and John's preaching. He substituted Greek terms for Hebrew words. He often quoted Old Testament passages which include Gentiles in the promises of God. He presented Jesus universally for every man on the earth!

SPECIAL SECTION

9:51-18:14 is a section containing many parables not otherwise recorded.

JESUS' JOB DESCRIPTION

Luke 4:18-19, recorded by Isaiah 742 years earlier, is the "job description" of our Lord. Because He has come to dwell in YOU when you are born again, it is also YOUR job description, if He is to minister through you!

CHRONOLOGY: THE MINISTRY OF CHRIST

I. THE YEARS OF PREPARATION (About 30)

Birth at Bethlehem (January-March, 4 B.C.)

Boyhood at Nazareth

To Jerusalem for Passover, age 12

II. THE YEAR OF INAUGURATION

(13 Months)

THE BEGINNING

    Baptism by John

    Temptation in the wilderness

    First miracle at Cana

EARLY JUDEAN MINISTRY (8 Months)

    First Passover of Jesus' ministry

    Cleansing of Temple

    Public preaching

SAMARIA (A Few Days)

    Woman at the well

RETURN TO GALILEE (2 Months)

    Healing of the nobleman's son

    Rejection at Nazareth

    Move to Capernaum

III. THE YEAR OF POPULARITY (14 Months)

EARLIER GALILEAN MINISTRY (4 Months)

    Ministry near Sea of Galilee

    Calling of Disciples

    Second Passover

    Sermon on the Mount

LATER GALILEAN MINISTRY (10 Months)

    Raised widow's son

    Stilled the storm

    Raised daughter of Jairus to life

    Second rejection at Nazareth

    Sent out 12 disciples

    Feeding of 5,000

    Third Passover

IV. THE YEAR OF OPPOSITION

(12 Months)

PERIOD OF RETIREMENTS (6 Months)

    In Tyre and Sidon

    In Decapolis

    To the North—Transfiguration

LATER JUDEAN MINISTRY (3 Months)

    Feast of Tabernacles

    Mary and Martha

    Feast of Dedication

PEREAN MINISTRY (3 Months)

    Parables along the way

    Raising Lazarus from the dead

    Prediction of death

PASSION WEEK

    The final passover

    Resurrection (About A. D. 30)

ASCENSION (40 Days Later)

269

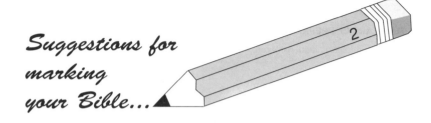

Suggestions for marking your Bible...

1. Copy the outline into your Bible.

2. Write beside Luke 1:1:

   Theophilus: "Lover of God"
   Luke's content: "exact truth"
   Luke's form: "consecutive order"

3. Write beside Luke 9:51:

   From here to end of
   chapter 18—60% of
   material is found only in Luke

4. Add any other notes from the explanations which you wish to preserve in your Bible.

Unit Thirty One
THE GOSPEL OF JOHN

OUTLINE OF JOHN

I.   JESUS–THE WORD OF GOD,
        INCARNATE AND REVEALED
     The Prologue—1:1-18
     A Week of Witness and Revelation—1:19-2:11
          Day 1—v. 19
          Day 2—v. 29
          Day 3—v. 35
          Day 4—v. 40
          Day 5—v. 43
          Day 6—2:1(3 days after first disciples followed
          Him)
     The first "Sign"—2:1-11

II. THE NEW TEMPLE; THE NEW BIRTH;
        THE NEW WORSHIP
     The cleansing of the Temple—2:12-25
     "Beholding His signs"—2:23
     The interview with Nicodemus—3:1-21
     John the Baptist's final witness to Jesus—3:22-36
     The woman of Samaria—4:1-42
     The healing of the Nobleman's son—4:43-53
     The second "Sign"—4:54

III. THE UNBELIEF OF ISRAEL
     Bridge verse—5:1
     The disabled man at Bethesda—5:2-47
     The third "Sign"
     The feeding of the 5,000—6:1-15
     The fourth "Sign"
     Walking on the Water—6:16-21

271

IV. JESUS, THE APOSTLE OF GOD; THE GIVER OF SIGHT; THE SHEPHERD OF THE SHEEP

The Feast of Tabernacles—7:1-13
Jesus the Apostle of God—7:14-52
Jesus and the woman taken in adultery—7:53-8:11
Jesus the Light of the World—8:12-30
Christian freedom—8:31-59
The man born blind—9:1-41
The fifth "Sign"
Jesus the Good Shepherd—10:1-21

V. JESUS, THE GIVER OF ETERNAL LIFE

The Festival of Dedication—10:22-42
The raising of Lazarus—11:1-57
The sixth "Sign"
The supper at Bethany—12:1-8
The triumphal entry and the final rejection—12:9-50

VI. THE UPPER ROOM

The washing of feet—13:1-17
The traitor—13:18-35
The Disciple's questions—13:36-14:31
The allegory of the vine and the branches—15:1-16
Persecution—15:17-25
The work of the Advocate—15:26-16:15
The "Little While"—16:16-33
The prayer of the Great High Priest—17:1-26

VII. THE ARREST, TRIALS, AND CRUCIFIXION OF JESUS

The arrest of Jesus—18:1-11
The trial before the High Priest—18:12-27
The trial before Pilate—18:28-19:16
The crucifixion—19:17-37
The burial—19:38-42

VIII. THE RESURRECTION APPEARANCES
The seventh "Sign"
    To Mary Magdalene—20:1-10
    To Mary—20:11-18
    To the Disciples—20:19-23
    To Thomas— 20:24-29

IX. THE PURPOSE OF THE EVANGELIST—20:30,31

X. THE EPILOGUE—21:1-23

XI. THE CONCLUSION—21:24, 25

AUTHOR

"The disciple whom Jesus loved" is the author (see 21:20, 23-24). John thus described Himself out of modesty. He was a son of Zebedee (21:2) and Salome (John 19:25, Mark 15:40, Matthew 27:56). His brother was James, and they were the "Sons of Thunder"—fishermen from Galilee. He lived to be a hundred, and according to Galatians 2:9 he became a leader of the Jerusalem church. He wrote five books of the New Testament: the Gospel of John, 1, 2, 3 John, and Revelation.

DATE

About 85 A.D., while John was ministering at Ephesus. Ten years later, about 95 A.D., he wrote Revelation.

THEME

Behold your God!

NOTES

John explains in 20:30-31 why he is writing his account. It was primarily to bring unbelievers (Jew and Gentile) to a saving faith.

John focuses on Jesus' ministry around Judea. While the Synoptic Gospels mention only one Passover, John records three, possibly four of them (2:13, 5:1, 6:4, 11:55).

John also extensively covers the first year of Jesus' ministry. He also gives lengthy coverage of the last months of His life. Interestingly, *one verse,* 7:1, then covers six months of His specialized ministry.

KEY WORDS

- *Believe*—98 times
- *World*—78 times
- *Jew*—71 times
- *Know*—55 times
- *Glorify*—42 times
- *My Father*—35 times

The Private Ministry of Jesus is beautifully recorded by John, beginning with 12:36. It includes chapters 14, 15, 16, 17, 18, 19, 20, and 21. *All these chapters cover only a few days of His life.*

274

SPECIAL THINGS ABOUT JOHN'S GOSPEL...

The Witness of His Deity

In 1:1-14, John gives his witness that Jesus was not just a great teacher: He was God! In his powerful book, *Mere Christianity,* C. S. Lewis reminds us that Jesus claimed to be God. As he points out, what can you do with a man who walks up to you and says,

> "*I and the Father are one.*"
> "*If you have seen me, you have seen the Father.*"
> "*Before Abraham was, I am.*"

What response can be made to such comments? He suggests that the one thing you *cannot do* is to call Him a "great teacher." Either he is...

> *A Liar,* and knows He is lying...
> *A Lunatic,* as crazy as one who claims to be an egg...
> *...Or He is exactly who He claims to be!*

John doesn't have any doubts about Jesus being God. His powerful opening verses do not appear in the other Gospels. He is careful to point out that *Jesus alone* is the source of spiritual life within each person.

The Testimony of John the Baptist

In 1:15-18, the testimony of this witness is clear. Jesus pre-existed, and He was God. In verse 29, the significance of His sacrificial death is presented.

The important point of this Gospel is made over and over...*JESUS IS GOD!* John, writing a little later than the first three writers of the Gospels, is already feeling the first wave of unbelief which begins to buffet the church. He is speaking to *all* generations when he stresses this point.

Special Section...

LEARNING TO USE YOUR HARMONY OF THE GOSPELS

One of the finest tools you will use as a Bible student will be the Harmony of the Words and Works of Jesus Christ. This volume is carefully prepared to coordinate all the details of the life of Christ, stressed in different ways in the other Gospels.

Remember the four themes of the writers:
- Matthew—*Behold The King*
- Mark—*Behold The Servant*
- Luke—*Behold The Man*
- John—*Behold Your God*

As a result of these differing emphases, there are some details of our Lord's life which may be mentioned *only once, by only one writer.* There are other details which are mentioned by all four writers, but with different information about the same event. Thus, to truly digest the details of the life of our Lord, it is good to spend some extended time in the Harmony.

In this section, you will be given the opportunity to use your Harmony. These practical questions will show you why this volume is significant to your personal growth as a Christian.

Using your Harmony, answer the questions on the following pages...

Special Section...
HOW YOUR HARMONY IS ARRANGED...
Note: this material assumes you have your own personal copy of <u>Harmony of the Words and works of Jesus Christ</u>
(J. Dwight Pentecost; Zondervan, 1981).

PAGE 3:
This page provides the parallel accounts of Matthew and Luke, registering the genealogies of Jesus.

QUESTION:
Why only Matthew and Luke? Why are there not columns for the genealogies in Mark and John?

PAGES 4-5:
Now we have records *only* from *Luke!* These have been put into the Harmony at this point because they fit chronologically. The reason there are *not* columns of text here is because *Luke is the only writer to share this information.*

PAGE 7:
Note that a segment of Matthew is inserted. *Again, Matthew is the only one to share this information.*

PAGE 12:
On this page, there are three columns to show the parallel accounts of Matthew, Mark, and Luke. At the bottom of the page, there are only *two* columns, sharing details recorded by only Matthew and Luke.
PAGE 62:
Here we find *all four Gospels* relating material.

Special Section...

THE MAPS IN THE BACK OF THE HARMONY...

The maps inserted showing the Herodian Kingdoms and the Road System in Roman Palestine really help you to understand the reasons for many of the comments made in the Gospels.

Also note the rivers and valleys on the maps. It's really helpful to "see" the geography as you read the story of Jesus' earthly ministry.

Note the small size of Jerusalem in the day of Jesus. Actually, it covered less than 30 acres! Many times we feel that Jerusalem was a massive city; in reality, it probably did not have a population much larger than 35,000—*including the suburbs.* "Upper" and "Lower" cities reflect the topography of the area. The Kidron Valley is far below the wall you see. It's a *sharp* drop down from that wall to the valley, and then another *sharp* rise up to the place called Gethsemane. Descending down and then up again, the task force sent to arrest Jesus would clearly be visible as they laboriously made the journey to Him.

THE ACCOUNTS OF JESUS' CRUCIFIXION

PAGES 141-142:
The accounts of the three writers vary in length. Note the differences in emphasis made among them. John simply notes the fact that Jesus was in the garden, while Matthew focuses on His prayer and the attitudes of the disciples during this time. Note this will be typical of all the accounts which follow: each writer focuses on details important to his emphasis.

Special Section...

As you read through the accounts sharing the details of the death of our Lord, you will gain a special appreciation for the value of a Harmony. Each separate account reemphasizes important details which all four writers did not wish to exclude. At the same time, by reading the parallel accounts, a richer awareness of the complete details is provided for you.

Note on page 149 that John goes into much detail about the trial before Pilate. This is in keeping with John's special emphasis. Here the deity of Christ is *reaffirmed* for us: *"My kingdom is not of this world. If it were, my servants would fight to prevent my arrest by the Jews. But now my kingdom is from another place."* The conversation which follows these words confirms the truth that Jesus is King of Kings!

PAGE 156:
Note that under "Accompanying Signs", it is only Matthew who records the fact that from the tombs came the bodies of many holy people who had died and who were raised to life. Were it not for his account, this would not be known to us.
PAGE 157:
The details about the burial of Jesus are a special focus of John. He is giving all this information to confirm that He was *really* dead. God has gone to the world of the dead, we shall discover, to preach peace to those who are its captives.

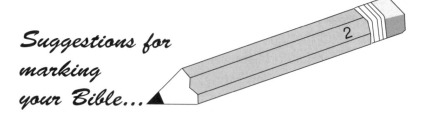

Suggestions for marking your Bible...

1. Copy the outline into your Bible.

2. Write beside John 20:30-31:

    Key to the book

3. Write beside John 9:4:

    Written by Samuel Johnson in Greek across the face of his watch before he began his famous dictionary of the English language.

4. Add any other notes from the explanations which you wish to preserve in your Bible.

Unit Thirty Two
THE BOOK OF ACTS
PART 1: CHAPTERS 1-13

OUTLINE OF ACTS 1-13

PROLOGUE: 1:1-3

PART I: THE BIRTH OF THE BODY
> The Ascension—1:4-11
> The birth of Christ's new body—1:12-2:4
>> The place—1:12-13a
>> The persons—1:13b-14
> Judas' replacement in the body—1:15-26
> The Coming of Christ into the new body—2:1-4

PART II: THE ACTIVITY OF THE BODY
> Jerusalem reacts to the new body—2:5-13
> Peter explains the body's presence—2:14-36
> The body increases—2:37-41
> The body's life-style, Part 1—2:42-47
> Healing of the lame beggar—3:1-10
> Peter's second explanation—3:11-26
> Peter and John arrested—4:1-3
> The body increases again!—4:4
> Peter and John face the Council—4:5-22
> The body's life style, Part 2—4:23-37
> The purification of the body—5:1-11
> The body's life style, Part 3—5:12-16
> Imprisonment and deliverance of the apostles—
>> 5:17-32
> Gamaliel's advice—5:33-41
> The body's life style, Part 4—5:42-6:7

(continued from previous page)

The ministry and arrest of Stephen, a member of the
Body—6:8-7:1

Stephen's indictment of Jews—7:2-53

The Body suffers martyrdom—7:54-60

The Body scattered *(The "Diaspora")*—8:1-4

PART III: THE BODY SPREADS FROM JERUSALEM TO
SAMARIA

Philip evangelizes in Samaria—8:5-8

Simon the Sorcerer introduced—8:9-14

The Body established in Samaria—8:15-17 and 25

Simon rebuked—8:18-24

Ethiopian eunuch included in the Body—8:26-40

PART IV: THE BODY DEVELOPS A MISSIONARY STRATEGY

Conversion of Saul—9:1-19

Saul witnesses—9:20-22

Assassination of Paul thwarted—9:23-25

Paul meets the Apostles—9:26-27

Second assassination of Paul attempted—9:28-30

The Body's life-style, Part 5—9:31

Peter at Lydda—9:32-35

The Body sees a dead member restored to life—
9:36-43

PART V: THE BODY STRUGGLES WITH THE ENTRY OF
GENTILES

Cornelius converted through Peter's reluctant ministry
—10:1-48

Peter faces the anger of the Jerusalem church
—11:1-18

Further spread of the body among Gentiles
— 11:19-21

Barnabas in Antioch; Paul brought from Tarsus
—11:22-26

Prophecy of Agabus; support sent to Judean
Christians through Paul and Barnabas—11:27-30

Another martyrdom; Peter arrested—12:1-4

The Body's life-style, Part 7—12:5

Peter's deliverance—12:6—11

The Body's surprise at answered prayer—12:12-17

The death of Herod—12:18-23

PART VI: THE BODY REACHES TO THE UTTERMOST
PARTS

Antioch (not Jerusalem) becomes the sending body
—12:24-13:3

Paul's First Missionary Journey

Cyprus: Conflict with Elymas; conversion of Sergius
Paulus—13:4-12

Antioch in Pisidia: Paul preaches in the Synagogue
—13:13-41

Conflict with the Jews; Paul turns to Gentiles
—13:42-49

Persecution; team moves to Iconium—13:50-52

AUTHOR

Without question, Dr. Luke! See 1:1. He was a companion of Paul in some of his journeys. Thus, much of this account is his personal observation of Paul's ministry. *Note: the "Luke-Acts" materials were originally combined into one book.*

Much attention has been called to the "We" Passages in the book—where Luke says, "We" did this or that... (Can you find them? Using your full-sized Concordance, it's easy! Or, look in 16:10-17; 20:5-21:18; 27:1-28:16.)

DATE

Luke undoubtedly wrote Acts while Paul was at the end of his 2-year imprisonment there. A.D. 61 is a proper date. He could not have written earlier than that, for the record of the imprisonment is in 28:30. It was not later than that date, because Luke does not record the Jewish War of 66-70, with the holocaust of Jerusalem's destruction. He does not mention Nero's anti-Christian policy, following the great fire of Rome (A.D. 64), nor Paul's time in the execution cell at Rome from which he wrote 2 Timothy, his "dying letter." Paul was executed shortly before Nero's suicide on June 8, 68 A.D.

THEME

Acts was NOT written (as was Romans) to furnish a system of doctrine for the church. Those who build doctrines from it create many errors to ensnare the "little children" in the church. Beware of people who "prove" a doctrinal point from Acts which is not validated with clear teaching in the doctrinal sections.

Acts was written to show the gospel of the Resurrected Christ at work. Luke obviously connected it to Luke to extend our knowledge of how the Church developed, and how it became the new body of Christ, replacing the body in which Jesus lived while on earth.

Particularly, the Greek word *AKOLUTOS* (translated "unhindered") reveals a major theme of the book. The way the gospel broke out of Judaism, struggling to be free of the bonds of Jewish traditions which made it unpalatable to "all nations" (Matthew 28:18ff), is a major theme.

NOTES

THE "UNHINDERED" THEME

Meditate on the "unhindering" of the Gospel in this book! The early church began within the eggshell of Judaism. Centuries of self-righteous thinking made the Apostles reject the idea that the Gentiles should be a part of God's activity. Peter's struggle over the conversion of Cornelius and his vision of unclean animals (chapter 10) is a crucial issue. You will note that there is a subtle switch in the leadership of the Jerusalem church after this: James replaces Peter!

As you read the chapters of Acts, you see the "breakout" taking place. Tradition has never been a friend to the Gospel. The struggle goes on today. Those who want to preserve the "status quo" often seem to be like the Pharisees of Jesus' day, who saw Him do miracles and claimed He did it by the power of Satan. We are still trying to "break out" of hinderances, aren't we?

THE FORMING OF THE CHURCH

A careful study of Acts indicates that the Holy Spirit fell on each new segment of the Body. First, the Jews received the Holy Spirit in Jerusalem (2:4). Next, the half-Jews, called Samaritans, received Him (8:14-17). Then Gentiles received the Spirit (10:44-46, 15:7-9).

Of great importance is the passage in Acts 8:16. Ray Stedman writes in *Birth of the Body,*

Both outwardly and inwardly these Samaritan believers were demonstrating the presence of the Holy Spirit in their lives. They were regenerate. They had been baptized in water as a testimony to that...what the account specifically says is that the Holy Spirit had not yet fallen upon them...These Christians had not yet been baptized by the Spirit into one body. They were still separate, individual, regenerated Christians–just as the Apostles themselves had been before the Day of Pentecost. On that day they were baptized into a body and made members of one another...What the Christians in Samaria had not yet received, then, was this baptism into one body and the gifts of the Holy Spirit. (Page 138)

Applying our statement that we are not to build doctrines from the Book of Acts, we turn instead to 1 Corinthians 12:13, where Paul is teaching doctrine. Here we have the key passage about the Baptism by the Holy Spirit:

*"For by one Spirit we were all baptized **into one body,** whether Jews or Greeks, whether slaves or free, and we were all made to drink of one Spirit."*

This is the only baptism described in the New Testament, apart from water baptism, which is a public act done after (never before!) we are born again. It is not a "baptism IN the Holy Spirit;" it is a "baptism BY the Holy Spirit." The Holy Spirit does not baptize us into Himself, but rather into the Body of Christ, the Church. Thus, the work of the Holy Spirit is to plunge us into Christ, making us a part of His present Body on the earth.

There are no "Lone Ranger" Christians!

THE LIFESTYLE OF THE EARLY CHURCH

Acts 2:42-46 reveals they moved from house to house, breaking bread, sharing, and praying. Their essential life was in small groups, not huge meetings. You see, there was no area in Jerusalem, *including the Temple itself,* which could house the 5,000 men (be sure to add on the 5,000 women!) mentioned in Acts 4:4.

With 30,000 people living in about 6,000 dwellings in Jerusalem, there were probably 1,500 of those dwellings used for the nightly gatherings of the Body. No wonder the cell groups had such an impact! Based upon this knowledge, our church has established cell groups which follow the pattern in Acts 2:42-46. They are God's natural way of evangelism—the living Body of Christ penetrating neighborhoods with love and truth.

Cell Group Churches around the world have taken very seriously the scripture in Ephesians 4 that says, "If you're a true Christian, you're also a *minister!*" Being equipped for your ministry involves learning about your Bible—but it also means you must learn about the *power of Christ* flowing through you into a world where Satan's power exists.

TONGUES SPEAKING IN THE BOOK OF ACTS

1. Spirit-directed, simultaneous translation into known languages (2:6-11).
2. Term in Greek *never* means *"unknown"* tongues.
3. Their message: *"The mighty deeds of God."*
4. Their motive: 1 Corinthians 14:20-22. This is precisely what happened in Acts. Their use of tongues in this case was to bring a warning to *unbelieving Jews.*
5. Not a *proof* of having been baptized by the Holy Spirit, but rather the *result* of it.
6. Used as a witness, a warning to unbelieving Jews. The history of this use of tongues, according to 1 Corinthians 14:20-22, is rooted in Deuteronomy 28:49, Isaiah 28:11-19, and Jeremiah 5:15-19. It was a warning to Jews who had rejected their Messiah that there was judgment by God, involving invasion of the land by foreign armies.
7. Jerusalem was destroyed in 70 A.D. in a horrible massacre. The prophecy given by these tongues was fulfilled. "Men of strange tongues" came as a Roman army of judgment, and conquered their land.

*Can...do...people authentically speak in tongues today in their prayer times? Of course! Paul claimed he spoke in tongues (a personal activity—see 1 Corinthians 14) more than all. Let's get some sanity about this issue which has, unfortunately and unnecessarily, divided the Body of Christ! Why have we made such a fuss over the least of all the gifts? Why not be thankful for the activity of God in our world? Why such suspicion over just one of the gifts, when we ignore the terrible lack of many of the others within the Body of Christ? Tongues are the least of all the gifts. What about the rest of them? If tongues are invalid today, why is the gift of wise speech, or putting deepest knowledge into words, still seen as valid? Because some segments of the Christian community have "wild fire," are we to reject the fire that **is** authentic (see Matthew 3:11)? How can the work of God be done without His power being manifested?*

THE BOOK OF ACTS AND THE POWER OF GOD

In our own day, we have substituted the power of man for the power of God! The work of the church often goes on without expecting the power of God and certainly not *appropriating* it.

One large church sponsored "the feeding of the 5,000" in their city. Women in the church cooked chicken all week long. Newspaper ads invited everyone to come and eat free. Men stood around the perimeter of the church grounds, carefully counting all who came to eat. With joy, the congregation sang the doxology at their next church service, rejoicing that at least 5,000 had been fed.

The only problem was that no one had broken a basket of loaves and fishes into enough particles to feed all these people.

Typically, the church activities of today use nothing but the human abilities of its pastors and members. When one reads the book of Acts, there is an *obvious* discrepancy between the activity of God among these early Christians and His activity among us today.

To further complicate matters, numerous charlatans prey upon the desire of people to experience the miraculous, faking clairvoyant "words from the Lord," unreal "healings," etc. They only affirm the point: we lack the *reality* of God's power among us in today's church.

Pure Christianity will always reveal the power and the presence of God in its activity. Dead religious rites do not. "Wildfire" activities which deceive the gullible do not. *There **is** a form of church life which manifests the true work of God. Don't settle for anything else! God's power **is** manifested in our age. People **are** authentically healed and freed from strongholds. The power encounters of the New Testament take place DAILY in our world.*

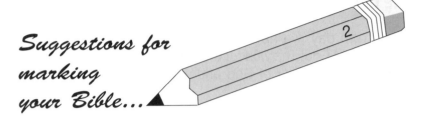

Suggestions for marking your Bible...

1. Copy the outline into your Bible.

2. Write beside Acts 28:31:

   Unhindered—
   Greek: Akolutos—
   Theme of Acts. Book
   shows how Gospel broke
   out of Judaism to reach
   all men.

3. Write beside Acts 4:4:
   (Or, put an asterisk beside it and write this on the bottom of the page as a footnote...)

   "Men"—Jewish. Add
   the women on a 1:1
   ratio (conservative!)
   equals 10,000 people. Total
   population of Jerusalem
   was only 30,000!

4. Add any other notes from the explanations which you wish to preserve in your Bible.

Unit Thirty Three
THE BOOK OF ACTS
PART 2: CHAPTERS 14-28

OUTLINE

PART VI *(CONTINUED):*
THE BODY REACHES TO THE UTTERMOST PARTS

Paul's First Missionary Journey
    Iconium:
        Mixed response—14:1-7
    Lycaonia, Lystra, Derbe:
        Lame man healed—14:8-10
        Barnabas and Paul mistaken for gods—14:11-14
        A model for witnessing to pagans—14:15-18
        Paul stoned, left for dead—14:19-20
    Derbe:
        Many converts—14:21
    Lystra, Iconium, Antioch:
        Elders appointed—14:22-23
    Missionaries return to base—14:24-28

Furlough Report: Further Unhindering of the Gospel
    A Council called—15:1-21
    Council's Report distributed to churches—15:22-34
    Paul and Barnabas split over John Mark—15:35-38
    Two missionary teams sent in place of
        one—15:39-41

Paul's Second Missionary Journey
    Derbe and Lystra:
        Timothy selected and circumcised—16:1-3
        Discipling activity—16:4-5
    Waiting for Spirit's directions—16:6-12

Macedonia:
> Conversion of Lydia—16:13-15
> Healing of a slave-girl; persecution—16:16-23
> Paul and Silas released from prison;
>> Jailer converted—16:24-34
>
> Paul demands his rights as Roman citizen
>> —16:35-40

Thessalonica:
> Pattern repeated: converts and controversy
>> —17:1-9

Berea:
> Pattern repeated: Paul departs, leaving Silas
>> and Timothy—17:10-15

Athens:
> Paul's strategy among educated pagans
>> —17:16-34

Corinth:
> Aquila and Priscilla, "Tentmakers"—18:1-4
> Paul's "unhindering" step to Gentiles—18:5-11
> Paul before Gallio—18:12-17
> Paul's vow of the Nazarite—18:18-23
> Apollos corrected—18:24-28

Paul's Third Missionary Journey
> Ephesus:
>> A Body of Christ is born—19:1-7
>> The Body's presence starts a riot—19:8-41
>
> Macedonia and Greece:
>> A period of moving about—20:1-5
>
> Troas:
>> Paul's long preaching and Eutychus—20:6-12
>
> Miletus:
>> Account of journey—20:13-16
>> Meeting with Ephesian elders—20:17-38
>
> Tyre:
>> Account of journey—21:1-3
>> Holy Spirit forbids Paul to go to Jerusalem
>>> —21:4-6

Ptolemais and Caesarea:
    Holy Spirit again warns Paul—21:7-14
Jerusalem:
    The party arrives—21:15-16

PART VII: PAUL'S IMPRISONMENTS AND TRIBULATIONS

Paul an embarrassment to Jerusalem leaders; he
    takes a Jewish vow to become palatable
    —21:17-26
Paul seized in the Temple—21:27-30
Paul rescued and arrested by Roman soldiers
    —21:31-40
Paul fearlessly addressed crowd—22:1-21
Paul incites riot; he asserts rights as Roman citizen
    —22:22-29
Paul brought before Sanhedrin—22:30-23:5
Paul appeals to Pharisees—23:6-10
A word from the Holy Spirit—23:11
Conspiracy to kill Paul—23:12-22
Paul removed by night to Caesarea—23:23-35
Paul before Felix, the governor—24:1-9
Paul's defense—24:10-23
Felix adjourns the case—24:24-26
Two years at Caesarea—24:27
Paul before the new governor, Festus—25:1-9
Paul appeals his case to Caesar—25:10-12
Festus rehearses case to King Agrippa—25:13-22
Agrippa prepares to hear Paul—25:23-27
Paul's defense before Agrippa—26:1-23
Personal appeal to Agrippa—26:24-32

PART VIII: PAUL'S JOURNEY TO ROME

Paul sent to Rome—27:1-13
Caught in a storm—27:14-20
Paul's strong leadership—27:21-38
The ship sinks; all escape—27:39-44
Mileta (Malta): miracle of viper's bite—28:1-6
Father of Publius healed—28:7-10
Paul arrives in Rome—28:11-16
Paul witnesses to the Jews in Rome—28:17-24
Paul turns to the Gentiles—28:25-29
Paul under house arrest in Rome—28:30-31

NOTES

PAUL'S DISOBEDIENCE

Scripture never "covers up" the foibles in the lives of Godly men! We have seen the weaknesses in Abraham, Jacob, Moses, and others. Now we see the human side of Paul as well. His planned ministry was cut short by a determination to go back to Jerusalem. In 21:4, the Holy Spirit warns Paul *not* to go there!

In earlier times, Paul has been careful to hear the instructions of the Holy Spirit. He previously diverted his trip, you recall, to obediently go to Macedonia. This time, however, he stubbornly continues toward Jerusalem.

More than once, the Spirit warns him not to do it. *What is causing this man to function in this way?* Two answers come quickly from scripture: the first one is that his burden for the salvation of Israel was deeper than life itself to him. Carefully begin reading at Romans 9:1 to catch his heavy heart!

He had raised funds throughout the Gentile churches in Asia for the poor Christians in Jerusalem (Romans 15:25-28). He felt this might open the hearts of the Jewish believers there to understand the good news of God's grace. (They were legalistic to the core!)

Paul's message had everywhere stirred up anger among the orthodox Jews. He had Jewish enemies all over his mission fields. Yet, he desired to have the endorsement of the Christian Jews in Jerusalem. This second reason for going to Jerusalem—to receive affirmation from those who had not appreciated his ministry—perhaps was a bit of the "flesh" in Paul which had not been crucified. On the other hand, perhaps it was a deep yearning for a more pure Christian teaching among the leaders there.

When he arrived in Jerusalem, his presence was an embarrassment to the church leaders. They felt he could only cause them trouble. It is very significant that this brief stop in Jerusalem is the only place where absolutely nothing of spiritual value came from his activity.

In 21:13, Paul agonizes as he says, *"I am ready not only to be bound, but also to die at Jerusalem for the name of the Lord Jesus!"*

Who can fault the zeal of this man's heart? Although his planned trip to Jerusalem was not in God's *perfect* will for his life, it fell within God's *permissive* will for him. (Does he not do the same for us today—allowing us to learn from our mistakes?)

At any rate, this decision of Paul cut short his desire to minister the Gospel in Spain. It would limit other missionary trips, too. His next stop would be Rome...*and death by beheading.*

"AKOLUTOS"
IN THE BOOK OF ACTS. . .

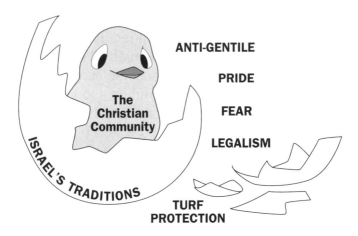

ANTI-GENTILE

PRIDE

The
Christian
Community

FEAR

LEGALISM

ISRAEL'S TRADITIONS

TURF
PROTECTION

NOTES

THE JERUSALEM COUNCIL

In Acts 15:1-35, Paul plays a role in trying to settle some of the conflicts which arose between the Gentiles and the Jews within the Body of Christ. Jerusalem leaders were demanding that all Gentile converts be circumcised—a rite of Judaism, not of Christianity.

A significant struggle took place in this Council, with both public (4,5) and private (6) sessions held. A second public session followed (7-21), leading to a decision: Gentiles do not have to be circumcised, but do have to abstain from pollutions of idols, fornication, and from things strangled and from eating blood.

Formal letters were drafted and sent to all local churches, telling them of the decision of the Jerusalem Council. Thus, a part of the "akolutos" process was dealt with, and the "unhindering" of the gospel accomplished to some degree.

LATER COUNCILS

This gathering of key men to struggle with key issues set a pattern. The history of the church from then until now is the record of scores and scores of such councils. They would deal with heresies, doctrinal disagreements, etc., in the centuries to follow. Even today, when Christians cannot see eye to eye, it is wise for them to follow the teaching of Jesus and "take it to the church."

It was at a Council held many generations later that the "canon" of Bible books would be prayerfully established, and the endorsement of scriptures which obviously had the marks of inspiration upon them would be given.

THE MISSIONARY JOURNEYS OF PAUL

FIRST	SECOND	THIRD	TO ROME
TEAM Paul Barnabas John Mark	*TEAM* Paul Silas Timothy *(At Lystra)* Luke *(at Troas)* Aquila and Priscilla *(Corinth to Ephesus)*	*TEAM* Paul Timothy Erastus Gaius Aristarchus Luke	*TEAM* Paul Luke Epaphroditus Aristarchus *(Centurion)*
STOPS	**STOPS**	**STOPS**	**STOPS**
Antioch in Pisidia Iconium Lystra Antioch in Syria *(Home Base)*	Lystra Troas Philippi Thessalonica Berea Athens Corinth Ephesus Antioch, Syria *(Home Base)*	Ephesus Troas Island of Miletus Tyre Caesarea Jerusalem *(Imprisoned)*	Caesarea *...Before Felix* *...Before Festus* *...Before Agrippa* Myra Lasea, Crete *(Fair Havens)* Mediteranean Sea *...Shipwrecked* Island of Melita Rome

As you read through the letters of Paul, consider the additional names of those he has with him at the time of writing each letter, and the many names of people he greets or refers to who live in each location. Paul had many contacts! He left his life all over his world, impacting many cities and regions.

THE TWENTY-NINTH CHAPTER OF ACTS

Someone has said that Acts should be called "The Acts of the Holy Spirit," not "The Acts of the Apostles." The continuation of the ministry of the Spirit has never slowed down!

In every generation, in every area of earth, the presence of God's loving Spirit has been calling men to Him. This generation is no exception. However, there is one significant difference in our day...*the population explosion.*

In 1900, there were *two* billion people on earth. It took the history of man to create that many people, all alive at once. Look what has happened since then:

- In 1929, there were *three* billion people.

- In 1974, there were *four* billion people.

- In 1986, the *five* billion figure was passed.

- In 2000, the figure will pass *six* billion, perhaps closer to *seven* billion.

But—Christians are not making converts as fast as the world is being populated! *To preserve the same ratio of believers to unbelievers we have today, in the year 2000, it will require every believer in the world to evangelize four persons per year.*

Dear reader, have you ever recognized the urgent responsibility *you* must assume to reach unbelievers in *your* personal "world" for Christ?

If *you* do not bring them to Jesus, do you think someone will come to do it *for you?*

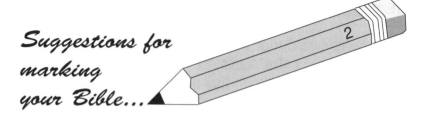

Suggestions for marking your Bible...

1. Copy the outline into your Bible.

2. Write beside Acts 15:20:

   > *The sacredness of the blood is because it is the source of life and the source of forgiveness for sin. Sanctity of blood remains for the Gentiles, too!*

3. Write beside Acts 16:27:
   (Or put an asterisk beside it and write on the bottom of the page as a footnote...)

   > *In Roman law, if a prisoner escaped, the guard who was responsible for the prisoner was required to serve the sentence, even if it meant death.*

4. Add any other notes from the explanations which you now wish to preserve in your Bible.

Unit Thirty Four
THE BOOK OF ROMANS

OUTLINE

NOTE: For this precious book, you will be given the major headings, but NOT the references showing the beginning and ending of each section. Dig it out for yourself, and grow another level in your Bible study. (Estimated time to do so: one hour or less!)

PROLOGUE: 1:1-17
    Salutation: _____
    Personal Testimony: _____
    Theme Introduced: _____

DOCTRINAL SECTION: 1:18-11:36
    God's Holiness in condemning sin: 1:18-3:20
        The guilt of mankind: _____
        The revelation of God to all men: _____
        The steps of rebellion against His
            revelation:_____
        To judge others is to condemn self: _____
        God is no respecter of persons: _____
        The Jew and the law: _____
        What advantage has the Jew?: _____
        There is none righteous: _____
    God's Grace in justifying sinners: 3:21-5:21
        Righteousness through faith: _____
        Abraham's justification: _____
        The promise realized through faith: _____
        Results of justification: _____
        Sin through Adam; salvation through Christ:_____

God's Power in sanctifying believers: 6:1-8:39
    Freedom from sin's power: _____
    Christians are under grace, the Spirit's "law:"
    _____

    The law and sin: _____
    The problem of indwelling sin: _____
    The struggle of two natures: _____
    Life in the Spirit: _____
    More than conquerors: _____
God's Sovereignty in saving Jew and Gentile—
    9:1-11:36
    The Jew and the Gospel: _____
    Zeal but no righteousness: _____
    Righteousness is by faith in Christ: _____
    The remnant of Israel: _____
    Salvation has come to the Gentiles: _____
    The Gentiles are warned: _____
    The restoration of Israel: _____
    The almighty God: _____

PRACTICAL SECTION: 12:1-15:13
    God's Glory, the object of service: _____
    Consecration of Christians: _____
    Practical Christian Service: _____
    Honor authority: _____
    Walk in love: _____
    Conduct and the weaker brother: _____
    Christ, the only Judge: _____
    Unity in Christ: _____
    The Gospel to the Gentiles: _____

EPILOGUE: 15:14-16:27
    Personal notes: _____
    Benediction and Doxology: _____

AUTHOR

Paul, written during his third missionary journey.

DATE

56 A.D., 11 years before his death by beheading in Rome. James Stalker in *The Life Of St. Paul* writes,

> **Paul was condemned and delivered over to the executioner. He was led out of the city with a crowd of the lowest rabble at his heels. The fatal spot was reached; he knelt beside the block; the headsman's axe gleamed in the sun and fell; and the head of the apostle of the world rolled down in the dust. So sin did its uttermost and its worst. Yet how poor and empty was its triumph!...ten thousand times ten thousand welcomed him in the same hour at the gates of the city which is really eternal. Even on earth Paul could not die...in ten thousand churches every Sabbath ...his eloquent lips still teach that gospel of which he was never ashamed. (p. 143)**

THEME

GOD'S SALVATION FOR SINNERS

THE LETTERS OF PAUL

SITUATION	LETTERS WRITTEN DURING THIS PERIOD
FIRST MISSIONARY TRIP	NONE
FIRST FURLOUGH	GALATIANS
SECOND MISSIONARY TRIP	1 THESSALONIANS 2 THESSALONIANS
THIRD MISSIONARY TRIP	1 CORINTHIANS 2 CORINTHIANS ROMANS HEBREWS (?)
FIRST IMPRISONMENT	EPHESIANS COLOSSIANS PHILEMON PHILIPPIANS
RELEASE	1 TIMOTHY TITUS
FINAL IMPRISONMENT	2 TIMOTHY

If you would like more information about the life of Paul, see the extensive article in the ZONDERVAN PICTORIAL ENCYCLOPEDIA...

PAUL'S CONTRAST OF ADAM AND CHRIST

ADAM	CHRIST
BROUGHT SIN AND DEATH INTO THE WORLD	BROUGHT RIGHTEOUSNESS AND ETERNAL LIFE INTO THE WORLD
REASON: Desired to be like God	REASON: God's desire for men to be reconciled
RESULTS: Condemnation— Upon himself Upon all men Eternal judgment upon all men	RESULTS: Justification— immediate, imputed. Eternal life for all who believe
THE LAW GIVEN TO REVEAL THE DEPRAVITY OF MAN'S HEART	GRACE GIVEN TO REVEAL THE LIMITLESS LOVE OF GOD FOR MAN
THE IMPACT OF ADAM'S ACT: Spread to all who would ever be born from his seed	THE IMPACT OF JESUS' ACT: Made salvation available to all who would ever confess "Jesus is Lord!"

NOTES

THE BOOK OF ROMANS, SUMMARIZED...

The writer of Romans neatly summarizes this book in Galatians 3:22-29. It's an interesting passage to read after you have digested this book.

DO ALL MEN HAVE AN EQUAL OPPORTUNITY TO KNOW GOD?

Yes! According to Paul (1:18ff), God has revealed all of his character and attributes through the creation He made. Indeed, the very *purpose* of creation is to reveal Him! Thus, all men in all generations have had equal access to the truth that there is a God.

HAVE ALL MEN EQUALLY REJECTED THAT KNOWLEDGE?

Yes! Paul says (1:21ff) men have equally recognized God's presence, and have *all* rejected the obvious call to become His servants. Having "eliminated" God from their thinking, they began to create manufactured gods of their own (v.23).

WHY DID GOD "GIVE THEM UP?"

Because *they* gave *Him* up! The staircase of depravity is revealed for us (1:24ff), and we see the degrading of the dignity and worth of man taking place.

WHO WILL WITNESS AGAINST EACH MAN?

According to 2:1-16, each individual's *conscience* will testify that the knowledge of God was deliberately scorned!

WITHOUT EXCUSE!

That's what Paul's conclusion is! The Jew had the Law to remind him how short he fell from God's righteousness. The Gentile had the Law written in his heart, even though he had never read it with his eyes. Therefore, *all men everywhere are without excuse.*

TESTIMONIES FROM TWO WHO EXPERIENCED JUSTIFICATION CENTURIES EARLIER...

Abraham (4:1ff) was saved by faith. His faith caused righteousness to be "imputed" to him. ("Imputed" is to add something to someone's account.) Paul indicates Abraham was saved *before* circumcision, not *after* it! (Compare Genesis 15:6 with 17:24.)

David (4:6ff) was forgiven by God's "imputing" righteousness without works (4:6). No sin offering in the Levitical system could forgive, or cover, the sins of adultery and murder—both of which David committed! By throwing himself upon the mercy of God, he bypassed the law and became the subject of God's grace.

JUSTIFICATION SUMMARIZED...

In 5:1-21, we are told that we have peace with God through Jesus Christ. ***Note that there is no other way for man to have peace with God! It is not offered by any world religion. It is not available by living a good life. It is not available by joining a church. It is not available by being active in a church. It is only available through the activity of Jesus Christ!*** Has that truth clearly lodged in your heart and your mind?

PEACE WITH GOD!

In chapter 5, Paul begins verse 1 with the pronoun "we." He is now writing to those who are believers, and will discuss details about our Christian walk.

This is not a small fact for you to digest!

There are those who seek to make chapter 7 a reference to *unbelievers,* and not to *believers.* This violates the very integrity of Paul's letter. Back here in chapter 5, he begins to discuss details of the Christian walk for us. From now on, this book discusses our life in Christ.

FIND AND UNDERLINE CHAPTER FIVE'S "MUCH MORE'S"

As you do so, your heart will sing worship songs to your God! It's one of the beautiful self-studies in this great book of Romans.

THE MEANING OF BAPTISM...

In 6:1, we discover that baptism is a means of identification of the believer with the death, burial, and resurrection of our Lord. Note that it *does not bring salvation—the blood of Christ does that—but it does bring witness to that salvation.*

KING SIN AND KING JESUS AND YOUR THRONE ROOM

In 6:12ff, we are told that we have one throne and two masters...the old "King Sin," which reigned freely for so long, and the new "King Jesus," now come to be Lord. This passage deserves careful study and meditation. Note that you are not *free* from the presence of that old nature. That comes later...at His coming or at your death.

IT'S TIME NOW TO SET YOU FREE TO COMPLETE THE STUDY OF ROMANS ON YOUR OWN!

In chapter 7, the war between the two natures is described. In chapter 8, the liberty that is ours in Christ is outlined. Then, in chapters 9-11, Paul deals with the Jew. In chapter 12, he speaks to us again, and tells us a little bit about the spiritual gifts which God has given to those in the church, the body of Christ. Beginning in chapter 13, he presents clear teaching about ethical issues we will face in our daily walk. Chapters 14 and 15 present a very important discussion about the responsibility of the "stronger" Christian toward the "weaker" one. Chapter 16 is not a chapter to "skip" because of all the names and the local greetings. In fact, it has much meat in it.

HIGH DRAMA IN ROMANS 16:15...

In 95 A.D., Rome was shocked when its two most out—standing citizens were condemned for becoming Christians. Flavius Clemens was the Consul of Rome; he was put to death for his faith. His wife, Domatilla, was of royal blood, a niece of the Emperor Domitian. She was, therefore, spared—but banished to the island of Pontia, where she lived her life in isolation. Their two sons were both in line as heirs to the throne of Rome!

How did the Gospel penetrate their chambers, and enter their hearts?

History tells us their chamber-slave was...

NEREUS!

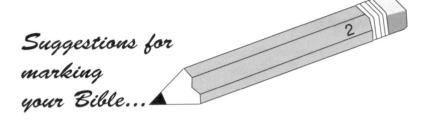

Suggestions for marking your Bible...

1. Copy the outline into your Bible.

2. Write beside Romans 1:16-17:

   Key verses of Romans

3. Write beside 16:11:

   "household"—such persons so designated were slaves of the person named. A large number of the names in this chapter refer to slaves who were believers.

4. Add any other notes from the explanations which you now wish to preserve in your Bible.

Unit Thirty Five
1 CORINTHIANS
2 CORINTHIANS

OUTLINE OF 1 CORINTHIANS

INTRODUCTION
Opening statement—1:1-9

DISORDERS REPORTED TO PAUL
Division at Corinth—1:10-4:21
Church Discipline—5:1-13
Judicial Entanglements—6:1-8
Immorality—6:9-20

PROBLEMS RAISED BY THE CORINTHIANS
Marriage—7:1-40
Meat Offered to Idols—8:1-10:33

MORE DISORDERS REPORTED TO PAUL
The Woman's Position and Covering—11:1-16
Factions Within The Church—11:17-19
Abuses related to the Lord's Supper—11:23-34
The use of spiritual gifts—12:1-31

THE EXCELLENCE OF LOVE—13:1-13

THE IMPORTANCE OF EDIFICATION
Prophecy a Superior Gift—14:1-11
Purpose of Cell Groups: Edification—14:12-19
Instructions to the Church—14:20-40

THE RESURRECTION OF CHRIST—15:1-58

THE OFFERING
The collection for the saints—16:1-4
Personal plans—16:5-12

CONCLUSION
Exhortations—16:13-24

2 CORINTHIANS

INTRODUCTION
    Salutation—1:1-2
    Paul's affliction—1:3-14

THE CHANGE OF PLAN
An explanation of the change of plan, Part 1—1:15-2:13
    The Christian Ministry—2:14-6:10
    Led in triumph—2:14-17
    Ministry of the New Covenant—3:1-18
    Encouragement in difficulty—4:1-5:10
    The motive and the message—5:11-21
    Appeal to the Corinthians—6:1-7:4
An explanation of the change of plan, Part 2—7:5-16

THE OFFERING FOR THE JERUSALEM CHURCH
    Presentation of need—8:1-8
    Christ the example—8:9
    Message on stewardship—8:10-24
    God loves a cheerful giver—9:1-15

PAUL'S DEFENSE OF HIS AUTHORITY
    Spiritual warfare—10:1-6
    Painful rebuke—10:7-15
    Paul's suffering as an Apostle—10:16-33
    Paul's "thorn in the flesh"—12:1-10
    Paul's Apostleship demonstrated—12:11-13
    A third visit planned—12:14-18
    Paul seeks repentance from the Corinthians—
        12:19-21

CONCLUSION
    Paul speaks of his coming; warns of sin—13:1-10
    Benediction—13:11-14

AUTHOR

Paul, as validated by 1:1 in each book.

DATE

1 Corinthians

Paul wrote this letter between 54 A.D. and before the Spring of 57 A.D. 2 Corinthians was written 6 months later. In 50 A.D., Paul reached Corinth on his second missionary journey, staying 18 months (Acts 18:1-8). The first letter Paul wrote them has been lost (5:9). In 5:9-11, Paul heard they had misunderstood some things he had said, and that there were divisions in the church (1:11). He had received three questions from them (7:1), and wrote the letter known as First Corinthians to answer them. At the time, Paul was in Ephesus (16:8), near the end of a three-year stay there (Acts 20:31), and before his departure for Macedonia (16:5, Acts 20:1).

2 Corinthians

After writing 1 Corinthians, Paul visited Corinth (13:1), which was a painful experience involving discipline (2:1-6). Paul then wrote "The Sorrowful Letter" (2:4), which is lost.

Titus carried this letter to Corinth, bringing good news to Paul when they regrouped in Macedonia (7:6-8). In relief, Paul wrote 2 Corinthians in October of 57 A.D., following the Macedonian and Jewish civil new year, which began in September (8:10).

THEME

1 Corinthians—Various problems in the church, some moral, some doctrinal. The book is a treasure house of doctrinal teaching on practical subjects.

2 Corinthians—Paul had been criticized by some at Corinth for not visiting as promised. He explains why his plans changed, describing his ministry. He discusses the collection for the saints at Jerusalem. He defends his authority because some had opposed him in the church there.

NOTES

THE CITY OF CORINTH

Located on an isthmus. Ships were unloaded on each side of the isthmus, goods transported across it, and reloaded on other ships. Meanwhile, sailors revelled in Corinth, filled with prostitutes who served the Goddess Aphrodite. A wild and wicked city!

THE CORINTHIAN LETTERS

Much speculation about these letters, based on internal evidence, has been written. How many letters were there, and how were they written? Here is one view:
(From *The Criswell Study Bible:*)

- FIRST LETTER—Lost (1 Corinthians 5:9)
- SECOND LETTER—1 Corinthians
- THIRD LETTER— Called "The Painful Letter;" Lost
      (See 2 Corinthians 2:4)
- FOURTH LETTER—2 Corinthians

314

IMPORTANT THEMES IN THESE LETTERS

Carnality

Stewardship

The Lord's Supper

The Gifts of the Spirit

The Resurrection of the Dead

Marriage

Church Order

The Kingdom of Christ

Why God Permits Weaknesses

The Ministry of the Spirit

Adiaphora (Doubtful Things)

Christian Liberty

THE CORINTHIAN CHURCH

Paul seemingly had nothing but headaches with this group of believers! To describe them, the one word *"carnal"* is used. The Greek word is *sarkikos*. As you pronounce it, it is a gutteral sounding word, isn't it? The word originated from the description of a bird of prey finding and eating the rotted flesh of a dead animal!

If you will scan the book of 1 Corinthians, the shocking problems of this church will become visible. Incest, pride, factions, class divisions, immorality, doctrinal errors, and more are revealed! In addition to all else, these Christians had taken spiritual powers (called "gifts") and misused them. Their pride had caused them to use their gifts as private toys.

SOME HELP WITH "SPIRITUAL GIFTS" IN THE BIBLE

TWO TYPES:
- SIGN GIFTS
  - Miracles
  - Healings
  - Tongues
  - Interpretation
- SERVICE GIFTS
  - Different levels:
  - 1. Basic Gifts
    - a. Serving
    - b. Giving
  - 2. Ministry Gifts
    - a. Faith
    - b. Helping Others In Distress
    - c. Discerning True and False Spirits
  - 3. Equipping Gifts
    - a. Prophecy (Forth-telling, not "Fore-telling")
    - b. Teaching
    - c. Putting Deepest Knowledge Into Words
    - d. Paraclete (Counselor)
    - e. Wisdom

Our gifts are *given* to us. Most important of all, gifts are not for private enjoyment, but are rather spiritual capacities to be poured out in service. Therefore, if we are not *serving*, there is no reason to expect we will have *any* use of our gifts. They are not to be *stored up*, but *poured out*. Hebrews 5:12-14, along with Hebrews 6:11-12, indicate that our gifts may not develop at all because of carnal immaturity and spiritual sluggishness. According to 1 Corinthians 14, the primary purpose of gifts is for the edification of others in the Body. Thus, unless and until the church is a "Basic Christian Community" of 8-15 people (a "cell group"), gifts cannot be effectively used. (See my book *Where Do We Go From Here?*)

THREE TYPES OF PEOPLE: 1 CORINTHIANS 2:14-3:3

There are three Greek words used in this section to describe three types of persons:

PSUKIKOS PEOPLE

The word *PSUKIKOS* is found in 2:14, translated "the man without the Spirit" in the NIV. Other translations simply call this person the "Natural" man. Here is described a person who is spiritually dead, rejecting truth about God. Note the person is deaf. This person has a *heart problem,* hates God, avoids Him, and is "far away" from interest in spiritual things.

SARKIKOS PEOPLE

The word *SARKIKOS* is found in 3:1, translated "worldly," or "men of flesh." This person is a believer, but living a disobedient, self-directed existence. Where the *PSUKIKOS* person *rejects*, the *SARKIKOS* person *rebels* against Christ's Lordship. They have a *value problem,* and use God for their own ends. They are uncomfortable to be too intimate with Christ. Like the Hebrew people in Moses' day, they feel most comfortable when someone else gets close to God and comes to tell them about it. These are Christians who live in the bondage of sin, and fight an inner war between their own desires and those of their rightful Lord and Master.

PNEUMATIKOS PEOPLE

The word *PNEUMATIKOS* occurs in 2:15, and is translated "spiritual." These persons receive the word of God, are alive, open, listening, and used by God.

SPIRITUAL GIFTS ARE GOING TO BE FOUND AMONG *PNEUMATIKOS* PEOPLE!

They do not belong to unbelievers. They are given only to those who are the children of God.

They will have no value or worth to those who are "carnal," who are God's disobedient children. What would *they* do with them? *They would use them for personal enjoyment!* They are not given for this purpose, but for the activity of God flowing through those who desire to do His will in all things.

Thus, spiritual gifts—while latently endowed in all believers at the time of conversion—will not be significant until the "battle within" is settled, and the believer is ready to engage in God's battles!

Every single Christian is to receive and use spiritual gifts as a part of life in the cell group. Gifts will vary with the ministry to be performed. Christ will provide that spiritual power which is required for His work to be done.

You are not to wait until you "feel" a gift coming on you. A gift is to be *exercised,* not *felt.* When you face a situation where you know Christ wants to use you, with boldness expect the gift to be present to do His work. For example, if someone needs healing, there is no reason why you cannot pray for this to be done. Let your gift of faith be strong enough to expect the healing to take place. After all, you know it doesn't depend on *you* or *your* power, but *His*—so step out in faith and pray for the healing. **God always gives His best to those who trust Him most!**

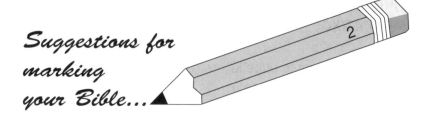

Suggestions for marking your Bible...

1. Copy the outline into your Bible.

2. Write beside 1 Corinthians 13:1:

   The Greatest Thing In The World: Love!

3. Write beside 2 Corinthians 9:8:

   God's Economy—Circulation of what He entrusts to us!

4. Add any other notes from the explanations which you now wish to preserve in your Bible.

Unit Thirty Six
THE BOOK OF GALATIANS

OUTLINE OF GALATIANS: "PASSPORT TO FREEDOM"

PROLOGUE
>   Opening statement—1:1-4

GALATIAN PROBLEM DEFINED
>   Paul labels them deserters—1:6a
>   False gospel defined—1:5b-7
>   Curse on heretic preachers and adherents—1:8-10

PAUL DEFENDS HIS APOSTLESHIP
>   Authority divinely received—1:11-12
>   Pharisaic background chronicled—1:13-14
>   Paul's commission—1:15-16a
>   Taught by the Spirit—1:16b-17a
>   Early missionary history—1:17b-24

JERUSALEM APOSTLES APPROVE PAUL'S MESSAGE
>   Divine Revelation—2:1-2
>   Titus not compelled to be circumcised—2:3-5
>   Paul directed to the Gentiles—2:6-10

PAUL REBUKES PETER
>   Peter's problem reviewed—2:11-14a
>   Peter openly criticized—2:14b-15
>   Paul champions faith—2:16-21

GRACE VS. THE LAW
Appeals to their experience—3:1-5
Appeals to Abraham's experience—3:6-7
Abrahamic prophecy—3:8-9
The curse of the Law—3:10-13
The promise of the Spirit—3:14-16
The Law vs. the Covenant—3:17-23
The Law as a tutor—3:24-25
Spiritual seed of the covenant—3:26-29

THE FULNESS OF TIME *(KAIROS)*
Heirs, yet slaves—4:1-4
Adoption as sons—4:5-7
Regression to slavery—4:8-11

PERSUASIONS AGAINST BONDAGE
Appeals to their initial faith—4:12-16
Denounces Judaistic intentions—4:17-18
States his perplexity—4:19-20
Allegorical: Ishmael and Isaac—4:21-27
Allegory explanations—4:28-31

JUSTIFICATION BY FAITH
The Law a slave yoke—5:1
They cannot have both!—5:2-3
Choice: Law or grace—5:4
Faith through the Spirit—5:5
Faith through love—5:6
A curse on Judaistic legalism—5:7-12

FREEDOM NOT A LICENSE TO SIN
Rather serve one another—5:13
Love your neighbour—5:14
Consume not one another—5:15

WALKING IN THE SPIRIT
> Precludes walking in the flesh—5:16
> The Spirit/flesh wars—5:17,18
> The deeds of the flesh—5:19-21
> The fruit of the Spirit—5:22,23
> Believers crucifying the flesh—5:24-26

HELPING THE SINNING MEMBER
> Restoring in gentleness—6:1
> Bearing one another's burdens—6:2
> Objective self-examinations—6:3,4
> Bearing and sharing burdens—6:5,6

SOWING AND REAPING
> God is not mocked—6:7a
> We reap what we sow—6:7b, 8
> Steadfast laboring—6:9,10

CONCLUSION
> Written in Paul's own hand—6:11
> Final blast at Judaizers—6:12-15
> Exhortation to walk as new creatures—6:16-18

AUTHOR

Paul, as validated by 1:1 and other personal references.

DATE

Approximately 48 A.D.; certainly before the Jerusalem conference in 49 A.D. (Acts 15), which supported Paul's position as detailed in this book.

THEME

Almost immediately behind Paul's missionary journey to the Galatians had come Judaizers attempting to undermine both Paul's apostleship and his message of Christian freedom.

Paul writes this biting, yet compassionate letter to defend his apostleship (as divinely received) and to attack the very foundation of the Judaizers' legalistic, bondage doctrine. Clearly he offered the Galatians and Christendom, for all time, a simple alternative: Law, or Christ. There could be no mixture, no compromise. Either live under the Law and obey every edict (which is impossible), or live under the grace of God through His son, Jesus Christ. The principle is:

"No Jesus, No Grace!"

Historically, he shows that the Law was not opposed to Christianity, but was a preparation for the Gospel. It kept the Jews under guardianship until "the fullness of time." However, that "fullness" had arrived in the person of Jesus, and every person was now confronted with that fact.

NOTES

GALATIA

The term "Galatia" was one used both geographically and politically. In this letter, it is most likely referring to South Galatia, the area covered in Paul's first missionary journey (47-48 A.D.). This territory would have included Lycaonia, Phrygia, and a portion of Pisidia, in which existed Antioch, Iconium, Lystra, and Derbe.

The Galatians were originally a torrent of barbaric peoples who poured into and across Asia Minor in the Third Century B. C. They were tough, aggressive, and extremely volatile. In no time they conquered the province, levying tribute on local kings and cities. Caesar Augustus conquered the province and it became a part of the Roman Empire.

These people had little traditional religion. They apparently adopted the superstitions and pagan mythologies of the Greeks. Paul introduced the Gospel to this people and, true to their historic nature, they readily accepted the faith. Shortly thereafter, Jerusalem Judaizers followed Paul. They preached a false doctrine, which the Galatians again accepted readily. This prompted Paul's amazement and perplexion (see 3:1).

SETTING

Push had come to shove!

In the fifteen years since Jesus ascended, a fundamental issue had arisen. It threatened to permanently alter the form and content of Christianity:

Would the church be a separate entity, or exist as a sect within Judaism?

The early Christians, mostly Jewish converts, were beginning to approach church doctrinal matters through Jewish traditionalist perspectives. True, Jesus was the Messiah. True, he came to establish His church.

Judaism was the religion from which Christianity and Christ Himself came. Both had been established by Jehovah. Could it be possible that a *combination,* a mixture of both, would be in order? Let Christ be the deity to be mixed with Judaistic worship. *Why not* mix a little freedom and a little Law? The welcome mat would thus be spread before the Gentiles by Israel—but it would be a *conditional* welcome.

Circumcision and legal observation of existing Jewish feast days would be required. After all, were not all the Apostles circumcised, and Paul, too? Was there any Christian law *against* celebrating certain special Jewish occasions?

Into this issue stepped an uncompromising, brilliantly logical Paul. He saw only too clearly what Jesus had warned His disciples about, time and time again: "A little leaven leavens the whole lump." *No easier could new wine be poured into old wineskins than could Jesus' new teachings be poured into the old wineskins of Judaism.*

The doctrinal question was LIBERTY versus BONDAGE. The underlying issue was the structure and content of the Christian faith. Paul knew this as did no one else around him! He wrote this crucial letter not only to discredit the Judaizers, but also to set forth once and for all time what the Christian faith *was*, and what it *was not!*

Today's church struggles with much the same issue. Tradition within the church has smothered the "new wine" of God's Spirit. Many who love the systems of "churchianity" are seeking to pour new wine in the old wineskins of churches which are rigid in their commitment to existing structures. *Old wineskins never have held new wine!*

IMPACT

Almost immediately following this letter, the Jerusalem Council convened to ratify Paul's message. They decreed that Gentiles were not to be forced to become partial Jews. Peter was to later say that Paul wrote scripture.

The Judaizers never forgave Paul. He had dealt them a death blow from which they never recovered.

Ironically, years later, the issue of works was to again raise its legalistic head. Again and again the church would wrestle with this problem. Fifteen centuries later, Martin Luther wrote his commentary on Galatians as a battering ram against the Catholic Church. Today, over nineteen centuries later, the battle still goes on. It is hard for man to accept the fact that NOTHING he accomplishes or does can give him "merit" to deserve special treatment by God.

KEY WORDS IN THIS LETTER

(CAN YOU FIND AND UNDERLINE EACH ONE?)

- LAW—31 times

- FLESH—18 times

- SPIRIT—15 times

- FAITH—22 times

- BONDAGE, or related words—11 times

THE KEY WORD OF THE ENTIRE LETTER

It is *liberty,* used eleven times. This word is used more in this one letter than in all his other letters combined!

THE NATURE OF THE BOOK

As you read through this document, notice that there is not a single word of praise, commendation, or thanksgiving.

There is not a single request for prayer. There is no mention of their standing in Christ, as in Ephesians. Paul is upset! He has absolutely no tolerance for legalism, and he shows it in this writing.

MARTIN LUTHER'S FAVORITE BOOK

In 1517, Luther was fighting the legalistic system of the church. This book of Galatians became his favorite volume in the entire Bible. His *Commentary on Galatians* remains to this day as the best treatise in print.

Luther realized that not *only* is a sinner *saved* by grace through faith, but that a saved sinner also *lives by grace!* Grace is not only the way we are saved; it is also our way of life from that time forward.

WHAT WAS...
PAUL'S SECRET?

Suggestions for marking your Bible...

1. Copy the outline into your Bible.

2. Write beside Galatians 2:20:

    Paul's "great secret"—
    Christ in me!

3. Write beside Galatians 6:14:

    In that cross I receive
    all God has for me!

4. Add any other notes from the explanations which you now wish to preserve in your Bible.

Unit Thirty Seven
THE BOOK OF EPHESIANS

OUTLINE OF EPHESIANS: "HIS VERY OWN"

PROLOGUE: 1:1-2

PART 1: STANDING...
   ...As His CHILDREN
      Father chooses, adopts, will accept—1:3-6
      Son purchases, enlightens, will inherit—1:7-12
      Spirit saves, seals, will claim—1:13,14

(PRAYER: 1:15-21)

   ...As His BODY
      Christ the Head—1:22a
      Church the body—1:22b-23
      Quickened by the grace of God—2:1-10
      Made one by the blood of Christ—2:11-17
      Given access by the one Spirit—2:18-19

   ...As His BUILDING
      The foundation—2:20
      Built together—2:21-22
      The household of God—3:1-13

   ...As His MYSTERY OF THE AGES
      The temple in the Lord—3:6

   ...As He REMOVES ALL PARTITIONS
      Paul's assignment to the Gentiles—3:7-10
      Done according to an eternal plan—3:11-13

(PRAYER: 3:14-21)

PART 2: WALKING...

...Worthily as a BODY

One Body (inward), with stature of Christ—4:1-16

New Man (outward), with fruit of Spirit—4:17-32

In love (upward), imitators of God—5:1-20

...Heavenward as a FAMILY

Wives and husbands—5:21-33

Children and parents—6:1-4

Servants (slaves) and masters—6:5-9

PART 3: WARRING...

...Finally, FACING THE FOE

Strength (inward) in Christ—6:10

Armor (outward) of God—6:11-17

Petition (upward) in the Spirit—6:18-20

EPILOGUE—6:21-24

AUTHOR

Paul, as validated by 1:1, 3:1, etc.

DATE

This is one of Paul's "Prison Epistles," along with PHILIPPIANS, COLOSSIANS, and PHILEMON. The date of the letter would be about 60-61 A.D., written from Rome. His time in prison permitted him the time to develop the meticulous outline of this powerful letter.

THEME

Our position in Christ and our responsibilities in Christian living.

NOTES

- *ROMANS* is God's message to the NATURAL man.
- *1, 2 CORINTHIANS, GALATIANS* are God's messages to the CARNAL man.
- *EPHESIANS, PHILIPPIANS, and COLOSSIANS* are messages from God to the SPIRITUAL man.

DESTINATION OF LETTER

"...at Ephesus" is omitted in some manuscripts. It has long been believed this was a circular letter, addressed to the churches of Asia Minor as a whole, and circulated from church to church. Each church would insert its own name in the salutation as it was read locally. Since Ephesus was the chief city in Asia Minor, it is not unusual that other manuscript copies would bear the name of this city.

SEVEN SIGNIFICANT WORDS IN EPHESIANS

GRACE
Occurs 13 times. The key word in the book. (Can you find and underline each time the word is used?)

SPIRITUAL
Also occurs 13 times. It speaks of the sphere of life in which we are living.

HEAVENLIES

Occurs 5 times (1:3, 20; 2:6; 3:10; 6:12). It is a plural noun in the Greek.

"Places" is not in the original: it is *"In the Heavenlies."* It references the "fourth dimension" of life. In these realms called the *Heavenlies* dwells every spiritual blessing. There, Christ is seated at God's right hand. Christians are seated there with Him. Angelic beings are there, learning the wisdom of God from the Church. It is also there that Christians war against spiritual hosts of wickedness!

MYSTERY

Occurs 5 times (1:9; 3:3, 4, 9; 5:32). It is a crucial word in Paul's writings. It refers not to something "mysterious," but rather a secret God reserved until it was time to reveal it. That time has now come. The mystery concerns the church and God's eternal purposes centering in her.

BODY

Occurs 8 times. It refers to the fact that we who are the "church" are *the literal body of Christ* on this earth! *In* this fact is found our position in Christ (ch. 1-3), and *from* this fact flow the duties of Christian living (ch. 4-6).

WALK

Also occurs 8 times. If the BODY is what we are, WALK is what we must do—and always in a manner worthy of Him who is the Head.

IN

Occurs 93 times in English, 89 times in Greek. It is the most used word in the book! It parallels John 15. Our life is *IN* Christ, *IN* union with Him, to be lived *IN* the unity that this relationship implies.

THE MANY "THREES" OF EPHESIANS

- Father, Son, Holy Spirit
- Past, Present, Future
- Natural, Carnal, Spiritual

Watchman Nee's Classic Outline...
SIT—WALK—STAND

In his lovely commentary on this book, Nee points out that in the first three chapters of this book there is absolutely *nothing* for the believer to do! He is "seated" with Christ in the heavenlies. Our position is beautifully described.

First, we were selected before the foundation of the world, predestined to be chosen in Christ. *Note this selection was made before we merited it by performing some good deed!*

Next, we were given an inheritance in Christ, and provided with the indwelling Holy Spirit as the "down payment" on it.

Then, God seated Christ at His right hand in the heavenly places, putting all things under His control. He then gave His Son a *new body...the church.* If you are a Christian, you are a part of the body of Christ. He lives in you, and your reason for being alive is to be a container for Him!

Paul then reminds us what "life in the tomb" was like for us, when previously we were dead in trespasses and sins. It seems the stark contrast between what we *are* and what we *were* is provided as a setting for the next great truth: we, too, along with Christ, are seated in the heavenly places.

In 2:10, we are described as His workmanship, with a special reason for our existence: the Godly activity He prepared for us before our existence.

Again, he contrasts what we *were* as *PSUKIKOS* people with what we are as *PNEUMATIKOS* people. Paul is hammering home the point that we have been brought near by the blood of Christ, not by some deed of our own.

Then, Paul adds another thought. Christ is our peace, and He has united both Jews and Gentiles into "one body" through the cross. There is no separation between us any more. We are all built together into a dwelling of God in the Spirit. That "dwelling" is a body—Christ's body—the church.

PAUL'S MYSTERY...

In Galatians, we were introduced to Paul's great secret— Christ is IN us, the hope of a glory which is still to come. Now, he adds to his *secret* a *mystery*. He points out in 3:5 this was a hidden truth until God revealed it to him. That marvelous mystery is that Gentiles are fellow-heirs, along with Jews, of the inheritance Christ purchased for mankind on the cross.

Chapter 3 ends with one of the most beautiful prayers in the Bible—one many Christians have memorized.

CHAPTERS 4 AND 5: "*WALK*"

The fourth chapter begins with Paul's reminder that he is writing to us as a "prisoner" of the Lord. Actually, you remember he wrote this while in Rome, incarcerated by the government. He discusses the *walk* of the believer. No longer "seated," the activity of Christ's body on earth is outlined.

This chapter points out the *unity* which should exist among the members of the Body of Christ. Underline the number of times the word "one" appears.

As a human body knows no competition or struggle among its members, so should the body of Christ flow with oneness and directed actions. As the bones of the hand perform different functions for the body than the bones of the foot, even so have each of us been given our "gifts" to operate effectively within the Body of Christ.

Remember...these "gifts" have *nothing to do* with physical "talents." They are the spiritual powers which exist within us *for no better reason than that Christ Himself dwells in us, and we are His body. He fills all things, including us, and he gives these gifts to men by giving Himself to dwell within them.*

GIFTED MEN GIVEN TO EQUIP THE GIFTED...

In our generation, the role of "prophets," "evangelists," and "pastor-teachers" has been severely distorted. We see the "prophet" as a special person who is to be *heard*. We see the "evangelist" as a special person who is to be *heard*. We view the "Pastor-teacher" as a special person who is to be *heard,* and who is to marry, bury, counsel, etc.

Perhaps no passage reveals the drift of the church in this generation as does 4:11ff! The significance of these offices within the church is made very clear: their job assignment is *"to prepare God's people for works of service..."* This is not understood or practiced by the church as we know it today. Instead, these men become "hired holy men" to do the work of God under the sponsorship of the "laymen" who assume lesser positions and too often become a "backup system" for the clergy.

Note that the clergy are the *equippers* and all the members of the Body of Christ are the *ministers!* The work of the clergy is to equip the ministers, not to do the ministry for them. The reason verse 16 is virtually unknown today is because the body has not been properly cared for, and is unable to function in its separate parts. Today's religious systems are simply not Biblical. They are encrusted with years of traditions, and many who wish to "protect their turf" continue to propagate the church as a campus with buildings, programs, and agendas that virtually *end* at the parking lot!

To verify the tragedy of this, note that scores of surveys of Pastors and Church Staff members admit they have no unchurched friends. Rarely do they have close fellowship with anyone who is not in a position of church leadership. We have made the church a "closed society," an island of religious activity within a secular society.

How can we possibly excuse this default? The "church" is the "body of Christ!" Jesus spent practically no time in the Temple (except to use whips in it!). How dare we claim that a series of programs which occur on a church campus is the work of the "body of Christ?"

Chapter 4 describes the place where the Body is to be ministering: among those who are "darkened in their understanding." *We are to "speak truth" in their midst.*

TO CORRECT A THIEF: 4:28

To correct a thief, let him work with his hands. A thief knows the *price* of things stolen (tin is never taken; gold is selected!), but does not know the *value* of anything. Working with the hands corrects the problem!

MORE ABOUT THE WALK: CHAPTER 5

Paul contrasts the church with the relationship existing between a husband and a wife—and gives us the Christian view of marriage.

CHAPTER 6: "STAND"

Finally, Paul deals with the warfare of the Christian. Note that the armor which is worn is all *defensive.* We simply stand upon ground claimed by Christ's act on the cross.

Note also that "in the heavenly places" there are also battles, and conflict with the Devil. *Do you believe in a personal devil? If you have not settled that issue, you may be sure the Evil One laughs every time your name is mentioned!* While some have gone overboard into demonism, no one is more "overboard" than Christians who deny the reality of Satan and his demonic forces. Ephesians 6 refers to a real world—*and you live in it.*

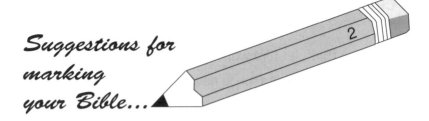

Suggestions for marking your Bible...

1. Copy the outline into your Bible.

2. Write beside Ephesians 1:3:

   "In heavenly places" —
   The sphere of spiritual,
   not physical, activity.

3. Write beside Ephesians 4:12:

   We are all ministers!

4. Add any other notes from the explanations which you wish to preserve in your Bible.

Unit Thirty Eight
THE BOOK OF PHILIPPIANS

OUTLINE OF PHILIPPIANS, "THE JOY WAY"

INTRODUCTION: 1:1-2

PART 1: PAUL'S THANKSGIVING AND PRAYER
    Thanksgiving—1:3-7
    Prayer—1:8-11

PART 2: PAUL'S SITUATION IN ROME
    Imprisonment and opposition—1:12-18
    Expectation of deliverance—1:19-26

PART 3: PAUL'S EXHORTATIONS
    To steadfastness—1:27-30
    To meekness and unity—2:1-4

PART 4: PAUL'S SUPREME EXAMPLE
    The humiliation of Christ—2:5-8
    The exaltation of Christ—2:9-11
    The "working out" of salvation—2:12-18

PART 5: PAUL'S MESSENGERS TO THE CHURCH
    Timothy—2:19-24
    Epaphroditus—2:25-30

PART 6: PAUL'S WARNING AGAINST HERESIES
    Judaism—3:1-14
    Carnality and lawlessness—3:15-19

PART 7: PAUL'S ENCOURAGEMENTS TO THE BODY
    Our new bodies—3:20-21
    Stand fast—4:1
    Be of the same mind—4:2
    Minister to the ministers—4:3
    Rejoice—4:4
    Moderation in all things—4:5
    Promise that prayer brings peace—4:6-7

PART 8: PAUL'S LOOK INTO THE THOUGHT LIFE
    The thought patterns of joy—4:8
    Follow Paul as a model—4:9

PART 9: APPRECIATION FOR THE GIFT
    Appreciation expressed—4:10
    Contentment is a choice—4:11-14
    Loving gratitude for missionary support—4:15-20

EPILOGUE—4:21-23

AUTHOR

Paul, with Timothy in his company.

DATE

A "Prison Epistle."

The date of the letter would be about 61-62 A.D., written from Rome. Read Acts 28:16-31 for Luke's report of those two years of imprisonment.

THEME

Paul had two themes in writing this book. One was PERSONAL; the other was to TEACH.

The financial support received from this Body of Christ was gratefully received by Paul, and he wrote this letter to thank them for it.

He dealt with the event of Christ's coming to earth in the most powerful of terms as he added teaching to the thanks...and, along with it, expressed his own views toward death. Perhaps he knew how quickly the Caesar of those hours could decide to snuff out his life!

NOTES

A LOOK AT PHILIPPI

Philippi was a city in the Province of Macedonia. It is about 10 miles inland from the coastal town of Neapolis (see Acts 16:11-12). Philippi was located on the Egnatian Way, a major overland route of Macedonia.

Note that Epaphroditus was sent back to Philippi from Rome: he would have journeyed over the Appian Way across Italy, then 80 miles by boat across the Sea of Adria, and then the Egnatian Way to Philippi.

This city became a Roman Colony in 42 B.C., and was a miniature Rome. It was exempt from taxation, because it was a military defense center. About 200,000 people lived there in Paul's time, mostly Greeks. Note Acts 16:13, where Paul held his first evangelistic meeting in the city.

THE CHURCH IN PHILIPPI

When Paul wrote this letter, the church was about 10 years old. You may recall that the first converts included Lydia, a seller of purple dye, and the town jailer (Acts 16). This church is considered the birthplace of European Christianity. The church was made up of Greeks, with some converted Jews. Their organization included bishops and deacons (1:1).

EPAPHRODITUS

LIFE AFTER DEATH

THE STEPS OF OUR LORD FROM HEAVEN TO EARTH AND BACK

THE STEPS OF PAUL FROM SELF PRIDE TO REALITY

NOTES

THE THREE ASPECTS OF SALVATION: 1:6

There is a *past tense* to our salvation first mentioned in this verse. Christ *"has begun"* a good work in us...and that points us back to the cross, the beginning place of our salvation. There, we were released from the *penalty* of sin.

There is a *present tense* to our salvation. Christ will *"carry it on..."* This continuing aspect of our salvation refers to the the daily activity of Christ within us, as He sets us free from the *power* of sin.

There is a *future tense* to our salvation: *"...to completion until the day of Christ Jesus."* (Do you remember our previous study about the term "the day of Christ?") In the future, Christ will not only set us free from the *penalty* and the *power* of sin, but also will release us from the *presence* of sin.

While there are those who seek to teach us we may, at this present time, attain sinlessness, the scriptures do not sustain this view. Such a teaching has skirted around the edges of Christian teaching for centuries. Don't be deceived by this doctrine! You have an old nature and a new nature, and you will continue to have them both until that final day of our redemption. One teacher even goes so far as to say 1 John 1:9 is not for the Christian—that it is written for unbelievers. Such a distortion to prove a doctrine wrenches the verse totally out of its context!

Foolish Galatian Christians and carnal Corinthian Christians help us realize sinless perfection is not verifiable.

PAUL'S RESPONSE TO FACTIONS IN THE CHURCH IN ROME...

Poor Paul! He had longed to visit Rome. His long letter to the church there has blessed centuries of Christians. But the church itself did not have the purity it should have had, and some within it were jealous of Paul. His reputation somehow clouded theirs, they thought, and when he finally arrived in the city, they delighted in his incarceration.

In 1:12ff, Paul sees this group of people through loving eyes. He admits that some are preaching Christ from envy and strife. Nevertheless, he rejoices that Christ is being proclaimed! He seems to be saying to us, "The Lord can hit a pretty good lick with a crooked stick!"

Those who demand perfection from others in ministry usually have a spiritually neurotic personality. Whatever God does with *any* of us, He must do in *spite* of us. Paul picks his fights carefully. One fight he avoids is with those not worth battling. He knew that "the main thing was to keep the main thing *the main thing.*"

HAVE YOU NOTICED THE CONTRASTS PAUL INSERTS BETWEEN BELIEVERS AND UNBELIEVERS?

In nearly all of his writings, Paul references the *PSUKIKOS* people, who live in rebellion against God, and reminds his readers that they used to be a part of that community. In Philippians 3:18ff, he again touches upon the condition of the unbelievers.

Sin leaves a swollen place in every life it stings. It is that painful area we focus upon when we bring the Gospel to them. That's why our message is "good news."

HAPPINESS IS A CHOICE!

In Paul's final chapter, he points out that happiness is not something we *receive*; it is something we *choose*. Note the eightfold path he outlines which will bring us happiness:

1. *Have a gentle spirit—v. 5*

Some folks get out of bed and put on boxing gloves. Letting the world know yours is a gentle spirit will create an inner peace. "You tell the size of a man by the size of what it takes to get his goat."

2. *Have no anxiety—v. 6*

Anxiety is a very serious emotion, which has physical symptoms. These include hyperventilation, sweating, nervousness, weeping profusely, etc. It is the result of deep fear. Those who feel they are controlled by circumstances, and that they have no control of what will happen to them, are victims of anxiety. The solution is clearly given. It is prevailing *prayer!* When we realize our Lord is in charge of all there is, we can then relax in the assurance that He—*not circumstances*—will control what happens to us.

3. *Let God guard your thought life—v. 7*

Satan is no fool. He knows he can slip into your subconscious and plant fear within you! Letting God guard thoughts is crucial.

4. *Meditate on positive thoughts—v. 8*

This verse is well worth memorizing!

348

5. *Focus on Godly behavior—v. 9*

Each time we choose a certain form of behavior, we generate happiness or sorrow from it. Only fools believe they will find happiness in practicing behavior out of keeping with Christ's Lordship.

6. *Divert attention from yourself to others—v. 10*

Instead of focusing upon himself, Paul speaks words of commendation to the Philippians. Folks who dwell on their own need, problems, or accomplishments don't collect much joy from the experience, do they?

7. *Make a job out of being content—v. 11*

Enjoy the half of the glass that is full, rather than complaining about the half that is empty.

8. *Remember the twofold activity in all I do—v. 13*

When I do *all things through Christ,* how can I *avoid* being happy? How can I be anything else *but* happy?

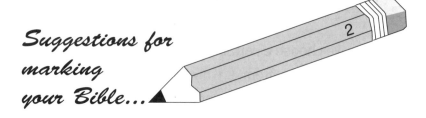

Suggestions for marking your Bible...

1. Copy the outline into your Bible.

2. Write beside Philippians 1:3:

   All 3 aspects of Salvation are in this verse!

3. Write beside Philippians 4:13:

   Note: 2-fold responsibility: <u>Mine</u> and <u>Christ's</u>

4. Add any other notes from the explanations which you wish to preserve in your Bible.

Unit Thirty Nine
THE BOOK OF COLOSSIANS

OUTLINE OF COLOSSIANS: "CHRIST IS ALL, AND IN ALL"

INTRODUCTION: 1:1-2

PART 1: PAUL'S THANKSGIVING AND PRAYER
    Thanksgiving—1:3-8
    Prayer—1:9-14

PART 2: PAUL'S DOCTRINE OF THE PERSON OF CHRIST
    His divine person—1:15-20
    His reconciling work—1:21-23

PART 3: PAUL'S PART IN GOD'S PLAN
    Rejoicing in suffering—1:24
    Proclaiming the word—1:25-29
    Concern for the saints—2:1-5

PART 4: PAUL'S WARNINGS AGAINST FALSE TEACHING
    Abide in the truth—2:6-7
    Beware of man-made theories—2:8
    The all-sufficiency of Christ—2:9-15

PART 5: PAUL EXPOSES A HERESY
    The fallacy of the teachings—2:16-19
    The folly of returning to bondage—2:20-23
    The superiority of the Christ-life—3:1-4

PART 6: THE NEW MAN IN CHRIST
    Vices to be put off—3:5-11
    Graces to be put on—3:12-17
    Family relations—3:18-25

PART 7: PAUL'S COMMENDATIONS
    Commendation of his messengers—4:7-9
    Greetings from friends—4:10-14
    Greetings to friends—4:15-17

EPILOGUE—4:18

AUTHOR

Paul, once again with Timothy in his company.

DATE

A "Prison Epistle." The date of the letter would be about 62-63 A.D., written from Rome.

THEME

About 6 years after this church was founded, an unspecified but dangerous error crept into this congregation. Epaphras visits Paul near the end of his imprisonment in Rome, and shares the disturbing news that certain false doctrines and practices threaten the faith of the Colossian Christians. They are in danger of drifting from the truth (1:23, 2:8). Paul writes to counteract these false teachings about the Person of Christ, and to give encouragement to their walk.

NOTES

A LOOK AT COLOSSI

Colossi was one of the "tri-cities" of the Lycus Valley. The area was about 100 miles inland from Ephesus. 500 years before Christ, it was called "The Great City of Phrygia." But, by Paul's time, it was a small town. When Paul wrote this book, there was a Christian congregation meeting in all three of the important regional "tri-cities"—Heirapolis, Laodicea, and Colossi. The inhabitants were mostly Greeks and Phrygians, with an unusually large Jewish community. The area was famous for its soft wool.

THE CHURCH IN COLOSSI

From Colossians 1:3-4, some have concluded that the members of the church were mostly strangers to Paul. Epaphras, who possibly was one of the converts of Paul in Ephesus, might have been the founder of the church (1:7), as well as the churches in the other nearby cities (4:13). He was a key member in the life of the congregation (4:12). Colossians 4:17 infers that Archippus was the church's pastor when Paul wrote the epistle (see Philemon 2). The church met in the home of Philemon, who was deeply devoted to its life (4:9 and Philemon 1, 5, 7).

LECTURE NOTES

THE MAIN THEME OF THE BOOK

THE HERESY IN THE CHURCH

WHAT DOES "CHRIST IN YOU" MEAN?

THE THREE ASPECTS OF SALVATION IN COLOSSIANS...

- Salvation past: 1:13

- Salvation present: 1:10

- Salvation future: 1:12

THE "COLOSSIAN FORCE"

In 1:16, we are told that all creation has occurred through Christ and for Christ. In 1:17, Paul goes on to say, "in Him all things hold together." Within nuclear science, this has spawned the term "Colossian Force," used to describe the unexplainable and mysterious force that keeps the atoms—and the very universe—from flying apart.

THE DEITY OF CHRIST

The powerful affirmations of Paul in this book about our Lord Jesus leave little to speculate about! Note 2:9-10. What more are we looking for? When God gives Himself and He has no more to give, some still wish for more proof from Him that He loves us, and that we can be joined to Him.

MORE ABOUT OUR MINDS...

In 3:2, we are reminded that if we set our minds on the things above, and not on the things that are on the earth, life will take a new direction.

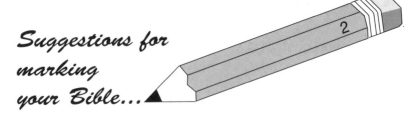

Suggestions for marking your Bible...

1. Copy the outline into your Bible.

2. Write beside Colossians 3:11:

   This verse gives the main theme of the book

3. Write as a footnote to Colossians 3:11:

   Paul does not preach a system or a philosophy, but a person—Jesus Christ.

4. Add any other notes from the explanations which you wish to preserve in your Bible.

Unit Forty

THE BOOKS OF
1 THESSALONIANS
2 THESSALONIANS
PHILEMON

OUTLINE OF 1 THESSALONIANS

INTRODUCTION: 1:1

PART 1: COMMENDATIONS TO THE THESSALONIANS
    For their faith and steadfast labor—1:2-4
    Word received with full conviction—1:5
    Became imitators of Apostles and the Lord—1:6
    Lived as Christian examples—1:7-9a
    Turned from idols to God—1 :9b
    Waiting for the coming of Christ—1 :10

PART 2: PAUL DEFENDS HIS CONDUCT
    Coming was not in vain—2:1
    Gospel proclaimed in boldness—2:2
    Words were entrusted to Paul by God—2:3, 4
    Delivered not with flattery or greed—2:5
    Or from vain glory—2:6
    But with gentleness and affection—2:7, 8
    And hard labor—2:9
    With devotion—2:10
    Exhorting and encouraging as a father—2:11
    So they might walk worthy of God—2:12

PART 3: PAUL'S CONCERN FOR THE CHURCH
Thanks God for the word received—2:13
Likens their sufferings to the Judeans—2:14a
Condemns the unrepentant Jews—2:14b-16
Blames Satan and Jews for his absence—2:17, 18
The Church his crown, hope, and glory—2:19, 20

PART 4: TIMOTHY'S VISIT
Timothy sent to strengthen and encourage—3:1, 2
Preparing them for afflictions—3:3-5
Timothy's good report of faith and love—3:6
A real comfort to Paul in his afflictions—3:7
Stand firm in the Lord!—3:8
Prayer of intercession—3:9-13

PART 5: PAUL REJOICES and PRAYS FOR THEM
To walk and please God—4:1
By the authority of Jesus—4:2
Abstain from sexual immorality—4:3-5
Not to defraud their brothers—4:6
God called them to sanctification—4:7
Rejecting this word is rejecting God—4:8
Increase your brotherly love—4:9,10
Tend to your own business—4:11,12

PART 6: THOSE ALREADY DEAD TO BE RESURRECTED
Don't grieve as those without hope—4:13
Belief in Jesus' resurrection the key—4:14
Those alive at His coming—4:15
Those dead at His coming—4:16
Those alive "forcefully caught up"—4:17
Use this knowledge as comfort—4:18

PART 7: THE "DAY OF THE LORD"

Coming as a thief in the night—5:1,2
As the birth pangs of a pregnant woman—5:3
Brethren are not of the darkness—5:4,5
Stay alert, sober, faithful—5:6-8
God has destined you for salvation—5:9-10
Therefore, encourage one another—5:11

PART 8: PAUL EXHORTS THEM TO BROTHERLY LOVE

Esteem your church leaders—5:12,13
Admonish the unruly, help the weak—5:14
Repay not evil for evil—5:15
Rejoice always—5:16
Pray continuously—5:17
Quench not the Spirit—5:19
Despise not prophecy—5:20
Examine everything carefully—5:21
Abstain from evil—5:22

PART 9: PAUL'S CONCLUDING REMARKS

For their preservation at His coming—5:23
He is faithful and true—5:24

EPILOGUE—5:25-28

AUTHOR

Paul—as validated by 1:1 and multiple personal references.

DATE

Approximately 52 A.D. We know the young church was established on his second missionary journey (A.D. 51), and that this first letter followed shortly after.

SETTING

Unbelieving Thessalonian Jews, angered by Paul's many Jewish converts, forced Paul to flee the city after he had been there for about three weeks (Acts 17:2). Not content to just chase him from their city, these Jews pursued him to Berea, 50 miles west, and again forced him to leave town. He then went 200 miles south to Athens.

From Athens, a concerned Paul sent Timothy back to Thessalonica to determine how the young church was faring. Timothy made the journey, catching up with Paul in Corinth with a most heartening report. This first letter was sent in response to that good report.

THEME

In many respects, this is a love letter. More than any of his other letters, it is characterized by simplicity, gentleness, affection, and intimacy.

Paul is genuinely pleased with the new church's growth and early maturity. Already they had become shining examples of faithfulness and steadfastness in the face of persecution. Gently, Paul admonishes them to remember how he came to them with affection, hard labor, and devotion, exhorting and encouraging them as a father. His earnest desire was that they might walk worthy of God. He reminds them that he had told them of their coming afflictions, and encourages them to remain steadfast in their faith when the persecution comes. He reminds them again that God will indeed deal with those who persecute His people.

At that point, his letter takes a radical turn. He first pleads with them to walk with God, to abstain from sexual immorality, and not to be guilty of defrauding their brothers. He reminds them that God has called them to sanctification (being set apart as holy vessels), and that those who reject this word are rejecting God Himself, who gave these words to Paul. He encourages them to mind their own business, and to increase in brotherly love.

Then, obviously responding to Timothy's report of his stay with them, he becomes their teacher. Their questions about the return of Christ are answered. He tells them not to grieve over those who have departed: they will be raised up first when Christ returns. Those who are still alive will be "snatched forcefully" from the earth, to meet them with Christ in the air. Therefore, they are not to grieve as the pagans, who see death as the end of relationships with their loved ones. Christ's return will come as a complete surprise to those who live in the darkness. Their prior knowledge should shape the way they will live out their lives.

NOTES

KEY VERSES IN 1 THESSALONIANS

4:16: Note 3 significant words:

"SHOUT"—given by the Lord as His resurrection command to the church.

"VOICE"—the voice of the archangel Michael; signals a gathering is taking place.

"TRUMPET"—in scripture, always signifies judgment.

5:3: NOTE...

" ...like birth pangs upon a woman with child."

This powerful prophetical statement is, in the scripture, always used in conjunction with Jesus' second coming and final judgment. It describes the travail of a pain-filled creation that is similar to childbirth pangs. That is, they start slowly, increasing steadily in intensity and rapidity until the actual moment of birth.

Most Bible scholars agree this accurately depicts the final 3 1/2 years of the "Great Tribulation," when the Lord permits the Antichrist to proclaim himself "god." This momentous blasphemy is the signal for the final countdown to Jesus' second coming. Then, like a woman's birth pangs, the world scene gets continually more wicked. Sin spreads pain in all directions! Jesus appears to herald a new order, a new birth. His coming ushers in a thousand year reign, called the *"Millennium."*

THE "MEETING IN THE AIR"
AND THE "RETURN OF CHRIST"

OUTLINE OF 2 THESSALONIANS

INTRODUCTION
> Thanksgiving and encouragement in their persecution and affliction—1:1-2
> God will repay those afflicting you—1:3-5

PART 1: THE DAY OF RETRIBUTION
> When Jesus is revealed from Heaven—1:6-7
> Delivering destruction to those who know not God —1:8
> Those banished forever from His presence—1:9
> When He comes to be glorified—1:10-12

PART 2: CORRECTIONS CONCERNING "THE DAY OF THE LORD"
> Don't be deceived: it has not come—2:1-2
> First must come the "Apostasy"—2:3
> The Son of Destruction will be revealed—2:3b-4a
> Displays himself as God—2:4b, 5
> The "Restrainer" removed—2:6-9
> Perishing of the unbelievers—2:10
> By delusion from God—2:11
> For the unbeliever's judgment—2:12

PART 3: SALVATION OF THE BELIEVERS
> Through sanctification and faith—2:13
> Called through the Gospel—2:14
> Stand firm: be comforted and strengthened—2:15-17

PART 4: EXHORTATION TO PRAYER AND STEADFASTNESS
> Pray for the rapid spread of the Gospel—3:1,2
> The Lord is faithful and will direct you—3:3-5

PART 5: EXHORTATIONS TO DISCIPLINE
Keep aloof from unruly and undisciplined persons
—3:6,7
As we taught, be an example—3:8, 9
No work, no eat!—3:10
Quit being busybodies—3:11, 12
Don't weary in doing good—3:13
Disassociate yourselves from dissenters—3:14
Admonish them as brothers—3:15

EPILOGUE
Peace and grace to you—in my own hand!—3:16-18

AUTHOR

Paul, as validated by 1:1 and numerous other personal references throughout the book.

DATE

Approximately 53 A.D., certainly not too long after his first letter.

SETTING

Paul hears that the first letter's teaching concerning Jesus' second coming has been misinterpreted by some of the church members. Some, it appears, presumed that the "Day of the Lord" was immediately at hand. Believing this, they were leaving their employment, sitting around, doing little except becoming busybodies and a general financial burden to the members who were employed.

Upon hearing this news, Paul writes the second letter. This time, the words are sterner and more urgent. Nevertheless, his overall approach is one of deep love and praise, with a generous portion of caution sprinkled in for appropriate preventative measures.

Paul opens by thanking them for their increased faith and love towards one another. He again mentions their steadfastness in suffering, and reiterates that God will indeed repay their tormentors with affliction, dealing out retribution to those who knew Him not. He describes the awful price of eternal destruction, separation forever from God's presence and glory.

Paul then focuses on the theme of his second letter: corrections pertaining to their erroneous beliefs concerning the "Day of the Lord."

That day has *NOT* come, he says, and *WILL NOT* come until (1) the "apostasy" comes; and (2) the Son of Destruction takes his seat in God's temple, declaring himself to be God. Further, he explains, the "restrainer" must be taken away so that the lawless one can be revealed—that is, the one who proceeds from Satan with power, signs, and false miracles. These false signs will be believed, Paul says, because God Himself will send upon those unbelieving people a deluding influence so that they might believe a lie, and be judged by their unbelief of the truth and constantly enjoying perverted pleasures.

Paul insists that God has chosen them not for this awesome destruction, but rather for salvation through sanctification by the Spirit and faith in the truth. It was for this, he says, that they were called. They are to stand firm in the truth and the Lord will comfort and strengthen them.

Paul then closes his letter, directing his flock to steer themselves away and remain aloof from any who lead unruly, undisciplined lives. He reminds them of his own disciplined walk while among them. He tells them that if any member of the flock will not work, they are not to eat! Further, he adds, they are to disassociate themselves from all who walk in this way, not to the point of making them an enemy, but for brotherly discipline.

NOTES

KEY VERSES IN 2 THESSALONIANS

> *1:10: "...when He comes to be glorified in His saints on that day, and to be marveled at among all who believe..."*

Paul here plainly teaches that Jesus' glory is in His *saints;* that is, those who choose to follow Him and receive His Gospel. We, who are by His grace, redeemed and given eternal life are His glory. We, in turn, will absolutely marvel at Him "on that day." Nothing we can now comprehend in the ripest fertility of our rich, God-given imaginations can prepare us for the awesome glory of His coming or His appearance.

2:7: "...only he who restrains will do so until he is taken out of the way."

Bible scholars have for years debated over the identity of the "Restrainer." The earliest church fathers thought it was the Roman Empire, which had for so long maintained law and order. However, this was proven to not be so. Today, many scholars point to the Holy Spirit as the Restrainer. However, this teaching presents us with a dilemma: if the Holy Spirit be removed, how can any person be *saved?* Unless we be indwelled by the Holy Spirit, we plainly have no chance for sanctification. Yet we know that during the tribulation, multitudes will be saved. Today many are asking, *"Why cannot the Restrainer be the Church?"* It is a case of reverse leavening, where we who are the Church are the "yeast" in the "bread" of humanity. It is the influence and prayer of the Christians that keep the light in the midst of the darkness of unbelief. If the true Church be raptured, what Godly influence will remain? Satan will, at that point, have full reign.

Still, the Holy Spirit *will* linger, waiting for those multitudes who, in the midst of the Great Tribulation, will see Satan and the "Lawless One" for who they truly are. Again, the Spirit will be waiting for the firm conviction of the Jewish remnant. They will be jolted by the unfolding prophecy that has come to pass in a most frightening fashion.

2:13:

"...God has chosen you from the beginning for salvation through sanctification by the Spirit and faith in the truth."

Here Paul refers to predestination. It is important that we understand that when the Bible speaks of predestination it does so in an ultimate sense of God's foreknowledge of events, choices, and decisions. It is crucial we understand the significance of time to God and to us.

God knows no such thing as "time." He Who has always been and always will be, the *Alpha* and the *Omega,* is of infinite existence. Therefore, the concept of time is to Him without meaning.

It is we humans, trapped now inside the envelope of time, to whom this concept is meaningful. In a sense, Adam invented "time." Without sin, he and we would live forever, and therefore would not be subject to such a limiting concept. But with sin came death, finite existence, and the entrance of "time." Now, all mankind is of limited duration.

A thrice Holy God, unable to even bear the sight of sin, has no such limitation. Therefore, He sees at a mere glance what *was,* what *is,* and what *will be,* because all are, to Him, all in the present.

It is from this dual view of "time" that predestination is to be understood. It does not mean that ages ago, before man was created, God selected certain persons for salvation and others for destruction. He simply knows who will, and who won't, be the "God Followers." In that sense, predestination is part and parcel of our existence.

Isn't it amazing? Knowing that man would sin—knowing that He would ultimately have to send His Son—*still* God elected to create mankind! Doesn't this fact fill you with wonder? Doesn't His grace appear, in this light, to be more awesome than we can conceive? The very concept of predestination should make us more appreciative of Him, our love deeper, our wonder more intense. Is it any wonder that *"in that day"* we will behold Him, and marvel?

OUTLINE OF THE BOOK OF PHILEMON

INTRODUCTION AND GREETINGS
　　From Paul and Timothy to Philemon—1:1
　　To Apphia and Archippus and the church in their
　　　　house—1:2
　　The "Apostolic Benediction"—1:3

PART 1: PAUL PRAISES PHILEMON: 1:4-7

PART 2: PAUL PLEADS WITH PHILEMON
　　By Christ's authority speaks—1:8
　　For love's sake pleads—1:9-12
　　Wanted to keep Onesimus—1:13
　　But not without consent—1:14
　　Onesimus' parting providential—1:15-17
　　Charge any loss or wrong to Paul—1:18-19
　　Pleads for acceptance and obedience—1:20,21

PART 3: PERSONAL REQUESTS
　　Prepare a lodging—1:22
　　Sends greetings from others—1:23,24
　　Sends grace from the Lord—1:25

AUTHOR

Paul, as verified in 1:1.

DATE

Approximately 62 A.D., from a Roman prison.

SETTING

Onesimus, one of millions of Roman slaves, had stolen from his master, Philemon, and had run away. Providentially, his flight took him to Rome, where he was eventually led to faith in Jesus Christ by Paul. Upon his conversion, he remained with Paul, serving him. Now he has faced his Christian responsibility of returning to Philemon and making restitution.

What a dilemma! Here is Paul, confronted with a situation tailored for explosion or exaltation. A slave (as are we to sin) has stolen from his master (as we have from God), and has run away (as have we). The slave Onesimus has become a willing slave to Jesus, his new Master, and to Paul, his mentor.

THEME

Christian responsibility and restitution are clearly in order, and it is to this issue this letter is addressed.

By Roman law, Philemon has the right to punish, even to put to death, his slave (the just punishment of sin). Would Philemon forgive the errant slave? Paul becomes the advocate (the Holy Spirit's role for us), pleading and persuading on behalf of Onesimus. He writes to a man who is his close friend and who has also been led to Christ by Paul. Thus, Paul finds himself in the place of being an earthly redeemer, but with the added problem of a redeemer trying desperately to serve both this slave and his dear friend.

Paul begins his case by addressing the letter to Philemon as a beloved brother and fellow worker. In addition, he also sends the letter to the local church. (A little peer pressure, perhaps!)

There is no hammer in Paul's words: he is pleading. He explains he could easily command Philemon, but wishes rather for his decision to come from his own free will. It is a letter filled with diplomacy and skill.

Note that Paul does not command or advise Philemon to get out of the business of slavery. Slavery is not the issue. Receiving a Christian slave as a brother is the real issue. The brotherhood in Christ went beyond that of a slave/master relationship. Would Philemon forgive his slave? Would he accept him as a brother, even while he remained as a slave?

The message is sensitive, yet important to the Kingdom! In Christ, there is neither bond nor free, rich or poor. Earthly position or status is of no importance in a Kingdom in which the greatest among us is the one who is a bondslave! With these facts in mind, Paul offers to pay the slave's debt himself.

This is Paul's most personal surviving letter. It shows his character and personality more clearly than any other letter. It also shows his grasp of the eventual impact of such letters being distributed among the young churches. The impact of it would help countless others who face similar circumstances.

KEY VERSE IN PHILEMON

1:14: "...without your consent I did not want to do anything, that your goodness should not be as it were by compulsion but of your own free will."

Ordering and commanding is easy, and there are times when safety or timeliness is of such importance that commanding or ordering is the only way to save a life, a soul, or someone from what is beyond his comprehension. God uses both commands and pleas. Clearly, He will always show us which is best. Just as clearly, He tells us that (if necessary) we are to jerk a brother out of the fire for the saving of his soul. God is first a God of love. Those who choose to obey Him because they love Him receive the greater rewards.

NOTES

IN RETROSPECT...

Paul's helpful explanations to the Thessalonians clear up many questions for us about the coming events of history. We are more prepared than ever to move shortly into the book of Revelation, which details the events of the end times.

Let us not miss the important stress made by Paul again and again as he wrote these letters: the time is short, and this is a time to live each day in the light of His soon coming.

In these times, we are observing world powers move in uncanny ways to take the positions predicted for them by the holy scriptures. Russia moves closer and closer to her final destiny as the dark force of Satan in the end times. China has come alive with international prominence after being a nonentity for millennia.

Do you realize the importance of using this time of personal Bible study to become equipped for your own personal ministry? *It's an urgent time.* We can ill afford to know more and more *about* the Bible, and be less and less involved in the redemption of our neighbors, our relatives, and our friends.

If these Bible books in Unit 40 make any sense at all, we must realize that the shortness of the days requires longer and longer outreaches of love to the lost!

Suggestions for marking your Bible...

1. Copy the outline into your Bible.

2. Write beside 1 Thessalonians 4:14-17:

    *This is another evidence
    that the early church knew
    no form of church life except
    the house church.*

3. Write as a footnote to 1 Thessalonians 5:1-11:

    *The Second Coming of
    Jesus Christ, separated
    from the Rapture by
    7 years.*

4. Add any other notes from the explanations which you wish to preserve in your Bible.

Unit Forty One
THE BOOKS OF
1 TIMOTHY
2 TIMOTHY
TITUS

GROUP	SETTING	EPISTLES	DATE	MAIN SUBJECTS	PURPOSES	
Travel Epistles	Between 1 & 2 Journey	Galatians	48	SALVATION - PAST, PRESENT, FUTURE	Evangelizing	TO CHURCHES
	2 Journey	1, 2 Thess.	52			
	3 Journey	1, 2 Corin.	55			
		Romans	56			
Prison Epistles	First Roman Imprison-ment	Colossians	61	CHRIST AND THE CHRISTIAN LIFE	Edifying	
		Ephesians				
		Philemon				
		Philippians				
Pastoral Epistles	Release	1 Timothy	62	THE CHURCH AND ITS WORKERS	Establishing	TO INDIVIDUALS
		Titus				
	2 Roman Imprison-ment	2 Timothy	67		Personal Farewell	

OUTLINE OF 1 TIMOTHY

PAUL GREETS TIMOTHY—1:1-2

PART 1: TRUE AND FALSE MINISTRY—1:3-20
    Warning against false doctrine—1:3-7
    The law and the Gospel—1:8-11
    Paul's thankfulness for mercy—1:12-20

PART 2: INSTRUCTIONS FOR CHRISTIAN WORSHIP
—2:1-15
Paul exhorts to prayer—2:1-8
The place and dress of women—2:9-15

PART 3: THE QUALIFICATIONS OF BISHOPS AND
DEACONS—3:1-13
Qualifications of Bishops—3:1-7
Qualifications of Deacons—3:8-13

PART 4: THE REASON FOR WRITING—3:14-16
Paul hopes to see Timothy—3:14-16

PART 5: ERROR AND ITS ANTIDOTE— 4:1-16
Predictions of apostasy—4:1-5
A good minister of Jesus Christ—4:6-16

PART 6: THE TREATMENT OF WIDOWS, ELDERS, ETC.
—5:1-6:2
Instructions concerning widows—5:1-16
Duty of elders—5:17-25

PART 7: THE TRUE and FALSE TEACHER CONTRASTED
—6:1-21
Warning against false teachers—6:1-10
The good fight of faith—6:11-21

AUTHOR

Paul, as validated by 1:1 and multiple personal references

DATE

Approximately 62 A.D.

SETTING

Paul, having been released from his first imprisonment in Rome, is instructing his beloved associate Timothy. The subject is how to deal with church problems in Ephesus.

THEME

Paul had left Timothy in Ephesus (1:3) to deal with problems, the greatest one being *FALSE DOCTRINE* (1:3). Note the attacks made by Paul in 1:4, 7, 19, and in 4:1-3, 7, along with 6:3-5. This is a deeply personal letter. His comments about church leadership and structures are vital to our understanding of how the church is to operate.

NOTES

TIMOTHY: A MAN AFTER GOD'S OWN HEART!

Timothy was a native of Derbe (Acts 16:1, 20:4). His name means "Honoring God" or "Honored by God." He was the son of a Gentile father and a Jewish mother (Acts 16:1,3). His mother was Eunice, his grandmother Lois (see 2 Tim. 1:5). Paul was 30-35 years old when Timothy was born, causing him to treat Timothy as he would a son (1 Tim. 4:12).

From childhood, Timothy had been taught scripture by his mother (2 Tim. 1:5, 3:14-15). Timothy's Gentile father evidently did not stand in the way of this training.

Timothy and his mother probably were converted when Paul visited Derbe (Acts 14:6-7, 20-21). As we study 1 Corinthians 4:14-17 and 1 Timothy 1:2, we may surmise Paul led Timothy to Christ as a young man, evidently in his late teens.

On the second missionary journey, Timothy was recommended to Paul as an associate (Acts 16:1-2). He was then circumcised. He was also set apart for ministry (see Acts 16:3-5, 1 Tim. 4:14). He served as Paul's assistant, doing many tasks, both significant assignments and simple "housekeeping" tasks (Acts 19:22, 1 Thess. 3:1-2). He served Paul while he was in prison in Rome (Phil. 1:1, Col. 1:1, Philemon 1, Hebrews 13:23). Tradition *(not the Bible)* tells us Timothy was martyred under Emperor Domitian or Nerva.

THE CHURCH AT EPHESUS

The congregations at Ephesus were 5-8 years old when Paul wrote 1 Timothy. Timothy had a full-time job, helping leaders of the various congregations fulfill their ministry. Paul, anticipating a long delay before he could get back there (3:14-15), wrote this letter of instruction.

KEY THEMES

SOUND DOCTRINE

PUBLIC WORSHIP
- Prayer
- Place of women

CHURCH OFFICERS
- Bishops
- Deacons

PASTOR/CONGREGATION RELATIONSHIPS
- Church and widows
- Church and elders
- Slaves and masters

OUTLINE OF THE BOOK OF TITUS

Greeting—1:1-4
Qualifications of Elders (Bishops)—1:5-9
Warning against false teachers—1:10-16
Domestic relations—2:1-10
The Christian life—2:11-15
Christian citizenship—3:1-2
The basis of the Christian ethic—3:3-8
The disciplining of factious men—3:9-11
Personal plans and greetings—3:12-15

AUTHOR

Paul, as verified in 1:1.

DATE

Approximately 62 A.D., from Rome

SETTING

Paul's young associate, Titus, is the recipient. Unlike his fellow worker Timothy, he was all Gentile. He served at Corinth and Crete. He had a strong and stern personality. He is not mentioned in Acts. He accompanied Paul and Barnabas to the Jerusalem Council in Acts 15 (See Galatians 2:1-4). He was Paul's representative in Corinth during Paul's third missionary journey (2 Cor. 7:6, 13-14), and collected money for the poor (2 Cor. 8:6, 16, 23). He was also Paul's representative to the churches in Crete after Paul was released from his first Roman imprisonment (1:4-5). He also had a ministry at Dalmatia (2 Tim. 4:10).

THEME

The theme of the book focuses upon proper relationships within the developing church. This "pastoral" letter speaks to pastors (1:5-9); the ethics of believers (2:1-10); the return of Christ (2:11-14); and, finally, the nature of salvation (3:3-7).

NOTES

ABOUT CRETE:

The towns of Crete were heavily populated. Morally and socially, Cretans had a bad reputation, as evidenced by the comment of Epimenides quoted by Paul in 1:12. Leonides said, "The Cretans are always brigands and piratical, and unjust."

SIGNIFICANCE OF BOOK:

1 Timothy and Titus are sometimes called "Twin Epistles." The book of Titus gives significant insights into the doctrine of God. He is shown as manifesting His word (1:3), revealing His grace (2:11) and His kindness (3:4).

OUTLINE OF THE BOOK OF 2 TIMOTHY

Personal Greeting—1:1-2
Thanksgiving for Timothy—1:3-5
Exhortation to endurance—1:6-18
A good soldier of Jesus Christ—2:1-13
Advice on personal conduct and relationships—2:14-15
People and situations to avoid—2:16-26
Difficult times to come—3:1-13
The central place of scripture—3:14-17
Exhortation to preach the word—4:1-5
Paul's hope—4:6-8
Personal concerns—4:9-22

AUTHOR

Paul, as validated by 1:1 and numerous other personal references scattered through the material.

DATE

Approximately 67 A.D., months or even weeks prior to his death.

SETTING

Paul was released from the imprisonment recorded in Acts 28:30. He then travelled to Ephesus (1 Tim. 1:3), Crete (Titus 1:5), Nicopolis (Titus 3:12), Miletus (4:20), and Troas (4:13). He returns to Rome as a prisoner (1:16-17). As he writes, he sees his death as very near (4:6-8).

THEME

This letter, Paul's last, gives his final words of instruction and encouragement to Timothy, who had a tendency to be timid (1:7-8, 2:1). He again warns about false teachers.

NOTES

1:6—Laying on of hands: Timothy is told to "stir up the *charisma*" (grace gift), a Spirit-given enablement for ministry. His usefulness began at the time he was set apart by Paul to be an equipper of the believers. This gift was bestowed by the laying on of hands. This was the symbolical act used by churches when setting apart (making holy) a person for ministry. In this way, the churches recognized the presence of the gifts of the pastor-teacher.

2:2—THE EQUIPPING PATTERN

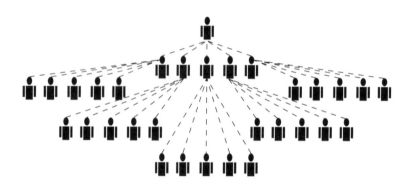

SOME THOUGHTS ABOUT MODERN DISCIPLESHIP...

Do we grow to go, or do we go to grow?

In today's way of thinking, young Christians should be matured before they are sent to minister. Thus, we have cloistered discipleship groups. Folks learn to memorize a hundred verses, outline their Bible six ways, take sermon notes three ways, and pray five ways. *After* their "quiet time" is fully developed, some think it might be time to reach out to the unreached persons around them.

The problem is that this form of discipleship has created a group of scholarly Christians who know more about discipleship *methods* than about *people who hurt, and how to help them!*

Jesus never gave his disciples a notebook. He never had a classroom. He walked with them for miles, constantly showing them how to heal, how to pray, how to love, how to react to evil.

Paul *never* gave his men a discipleship course. He took them to Cyprus, to Crete, to Athens, to riots, and to tough situations, but he never took them to a classroom.

Our generation believes you grow to go.
The New Testament pattern is to go to grow.

Cell Group Churches follow that pattern. For that reason, a vital part of your cell group life is reaching out to others through visitation and through Share Groups. (For further information, see my book *"Where Do We Go From Here?"*)

Suggestions for marking your Bible...

1. Copy the Outline into your Bible.

2. Write beside 1 Timothy 3:16:

   These 6 phrases are a quotation from an early hymn.

3. Write as a footnote to 2 Timothy 3:16:

   Literally, "All scripture, because it is God-breathed, is profitable..."

4. Add any other notes from the explanations which you wish to preserve in your Bible.

Unit Forty Two
THE BOOK OF HEBREWS

OUTLINE OF HEBREWS

THEME ESTABLISHED: 1:1-3

FIRST SECTION: INSTRUCTION: 1:4-9:28
(WHAT HAVE WE?)
Christ, greater than the Angels—1:4-14

> ### FIRST WARNING SECTION: 2:1-4
> *How shall we escape, if we neglect*
> *so great salvation?*

Christ, our Redeemer—2:5-18
Christ, greater than Moses—3:1-6

> ### SECOND WARNING SECTION: 3:7-4:13
> *Harden not your heart, as in the provocation...*

Christ, our High Priest—5:1-10

> ### THIRD WARNING SECTION: 5:11-6:20
> *Leaving the principles, let us go on*
> *unto perfection...*

Christ, Priest after the order of Melchizedek—7:1-10
Christ, Priest superior to Aaron—7:11-28
Christ's Priesthood summarized—8:1-5
Christ's New Covenant—8:6-13
Old and New Covenants contrasted—9:1-14
Christ's sacrifice establishes the New Covenant
    —9:15-28
The failure of the Old Covenant—10:1-18

SECOND SECTION: EXHORTATION: 10:19-13:25 (HAVING THEREFORE...LET US)

A plea to hold to the new faith—10:19-25

> **FOURTH WARNING SECTION: 10:26-31**
> *It is a fearful thing to fall into the hands of the living God*

Remember the former days—10:32-39
What is Faith?—11:1-40
Run the race—12:1-2
God's discipline necessary—12:3-11
Walking a straight path—12:12-17

> **FIFTH WARNING SECTION: 12:18-29**
> *See that you refuse not Him that speaketh*

Workings of Faith—13:1-17
Benediction—13:18-25

AUTHOR

The book of Hebrews is anonymous. Many believe its authorship is Paul (see Hebrews 13:19, 23-24). Because its authorship is so uncertain, Martin Luther placed it at the end of Paul's writings and at the beginning of the General Epistles. Thus, it can "fall" into either category. It is not necessary to know its authorship to know its true writer is the Holy Spirit! It is one of the most profound of all New Testament books.

DATE

Since Clement quoted from it in 96 A.D., it cannot be later than that date. However, it seems the Jewish sacrificial system was still functioning (7:8, 8:4, 10:1, 2, 8, 11). If so, no date later than the time of the Destruction of Jerusalem will suffice (70 A.D.).

Because the writer seemed to be presenting his materials to "second generation" Christians, a date of 85 A.D. is also possible. Those who see an earlier date would place it about 65-69 A.D. As with the authorship, its date is really unimportant to us as we glean truth from it.

SETTING

The earliest manuscripts have the title *Pros Hebraious* ("To Hebrews") for the title. From the internal study of the book, we learn that it was written to a single congregation of Hebrew Christians, living in a segment of the Roman world (2:3, 5:11-12, 6:9-10, 13:23-24). Some think it was written to the church in Jerusalem.

The readers were in a backslidden condition, in danger of apostasy and departure from the faith. Faith was waning (3:6-14); prayer, public worship, and even basic Bible study were being neglected (2:1, 10:25, 12:12-13). In 5:12, their infant-like state is described.

One of the reasons for their condition was the threat of persecution. They had earlier withstood severe persecution (10:32-34), but now were beginning to weaken before it.

THEME

The purpose of the book is to rekindle embers which are burning low! Dullness of hearing was an alarming condition. The writer carefully alternates between TEACHING and WARNING sections (see outline).

In a glorious declaration of truth, Jesus Christ is exalted as being greater than all, our only hope, our High Priest, and above all, the Son of God.

NOTES

HEBREWS IS A COMMENTARY ON THE PENTATEUCH

Hebrews has been called the New Testament's "Commentary on the Pentateuch," especially the Book of Leviticus. There are 86 direct references to the Old Testament scriptures, traceable to at least 100 passages. This book explains the significance of Old Testament rituals in the light of Christ's coming. The numerous ceremonial laws, the sacrifices, the Priesthood—all are explained as nothing more than "shadows" of Christ. He becomes, for the New Covenant, the Sacrifice, the Priest, and the true Mediator between God and man.

All the *TYPES* of the Old Testament are revealed as foreshadowing the coming Christ. Hebrews has sometimes been called "The Fifth Gospel," because it tells of Jesus' finished work on earth and His continuing work in Heaven.

KEY PHRASES TO THINK ABOUT AS YOU READ...

"What have we...?" (1:1-7:28)
> Found in 8:1, this phrase helps us focus on what we have in our Lord Jesus Christ.

"We have..." (8:1-10:18)
> Also found in 8:1, we have a High Priest! But the emphasis is on the word *"such!"*

"Having, therefore, let us..." (10:19-13:25)
> This phrase is found in the section listed above.

NOTE THESE CONTRASTS IN THE BOOK:

- Son and Angels—1:4-2:4
- Son and Moses—3:1-6
- Canaan rest and God's rest—3:12-4:13
- Christ and Aaron—4:14-5:10
- Spiritual infancy and maturity—5:11-14
- Apostasy and faithfulness—5:11-6:20
- Old and New Covenants—8:1-13
- Offerings of the Law and of Christ—9:1-10:18
- Faith and sight—11:1-40
- Mount Sinai and Mount Zion—12:18-29

CHRIST...

- The Son of God—1:1-2:4
- The Son of Man—2:5-4:13
- The High Priest—4:14-10:18

LET'S WALK THROUGH "THE FIFTH GOSPEL..."

Matthew, Mark, Luke, and John tell us all about the life of Jesus from the time of His birth until His resurrection. In Acts, we see Him ascending into Heaven. Paul has told us He is dwelling within us now, that we are literally His new body on this earth, and that He consequently carries on His work through us, flowing His power (spiritual gifts) into His activities.

Now, Hebrews will focus upon the life of Jesus following His ascension. We discovered that He is "seated at the right hand of the Father" in Ephesians, and that He is not only in *us,* but we are also "in Him," seated with Him in heavenly places.

In Hebrews, we are going to dwell on the life and activity of Jesus in those heavenly places, and see our own situation there as well!

First, we focus upon the character of Jesus...

He is superior to all others!

He is greater than the prophets (1:1-3)

These verses give us the Father's description of Him in the Heavenlies—appointed by God as heir of all things, the One through whom God made the ages, the total expression of God's character, the One who holds all things together, the purifier of sins, and at God's right hand.

He is greater than the angels (1:4-2:18)

He has, by inheritance as a *son,* a greater name than angels. He has a greater relationship to the Father. He reigns forever and ever. His righteousness is the sceptre of His Kingdom.

We then are warned not to disregard God's word

Note the five warnings in this book, bracketed in the outline. The first one makes a point flowing from the position of Jesus in the Heavenlies. If Israel faced punishment in the Old Testament for disobeying the word of angels, how much greater will be the punishment for us if we disobey the word spoken by Jesus!

The author then continues in 2:5-18 to show why Jesus is greater than the angels. The focus is upon the redemptive ministry of Jesus in His earthly life.

Why did He have to come to earth?

First, in order to recapture our lost destiny (2:5-9). Man was originally created to rule over all the earth. He was put into training, positioned a little lower than the angels. Because he sinned, he was unable to rule. Jesus came to make that rule possible again.

Second, in order for us to regain our lost fellowship (2:10-13). Because of His suffering, Christ now unites us to the Father and is our "older Brother."

Third, to deliver us from bondage (2:14-18). The power of death keeps us "locked in" to a bondage that limits our confidence to function properly.

He is greater than Moses (3:1-19)

The reason is that Moses was a servant, while Christ is the beloved Son.

The second warning relates to Moses' not entering the promised land...

Recall that Moses stopped short of entering Canaan because of his disobedience to God. Our writer extends his thoughts about Moses and further reminds us that an entire *generation* of Israelites died in the wilderness because of unbelief. Sin's deceitfulness can generate unbelief within us. There is a "rest" to the people of God, and we are urged to enter into it.

THE "REST"

The "rest" of Hebrews is "His *(God's)* rest." He enjoys it, and He gives it! He enjoyed it when creation was finished, and He now has it because of the completed work of His Son's redemption. It is intended for the People of God. See 4:10 for the great conclusion!

There are three "rests" in the Bible:
1. The rest from creation (4:4)
2. The rest from salvation (4:10)
3. The rest from consecration (4:11)

This *"rest for the people of God"* is a powerful truth. *It means there is nothing left for us to do.* Jesus has finished the activity required for us to be the children of God. By faith, the opposite of unbelief, we enter into that finished work.

While others may seek to gain "significance" before God, gaining "merit" by their works, we need only rest with Christ in the Heavenlies. He has completed our salvation and there is absolutely *nothing* we can add to it by good works.

He is greater than Joshua (4:1-16)

Jesus' rest is greater than the "rest" given to the Israelites by Joshua. The Israelites only had 25-40 years of "rest" in the land, while Jesus gives us a "rest" that is eternal.

Note the power of God's word (4:12-13)

This is a classic statement about the power of God's revealed truth. Think deeply about these verses...

He is greater than Aaron (5:1-10)

Have you noted the pattern used by the writer? He is comparing Jesus to all the "heroes" of the Jews. The comparison with Aaron is leading to a great truth...

Jesus possesses perfectly what Aaron only possessed in part. Like Aaron, Jesus was taken from among men (5:1). He was also like Aaron in that he was *chosen* (5:4), *compassionate* (5:2), *learned obedience* (5:8 and 2:10), *prayed* (5:7), and *suffered* (5:8). But, *unlike Aaron,* Jesus is God's unique Son, a priest like Melchizedek, and the author of eternal salvation.

The third warning is not to remain undeveloped in your spiritual growth (5:11-6:20)

Our great danger is that we might receive the precious salvation purchased by Christ's blood on Calvary and then not enter into all the *depths* of that new relationship! Without any question, this is the warning needed most by the typical Christian in our generation.

Slowly read 5:11-14. Here is a picture of stunted growth. Note that spiritual gifts do not develop *(teaching, v. 11; discerning true and false spirits, v. 14).* The lesson is powerful—it is not enough to accept Christ as your *Savior;* but you must also crown Him *Lord* of all you are. Only when we let Him be Lord, and we become His servants, will we mature in our faith.

If you are among those who have received Christ into your heart through faith, and now have no appetite for Godly things, you are being described in this passage. The writer says (6:1), *"GO ON! DON'T STOP HERE!"*

His explanation is very simple. Once you have passed certain milestones in the Christian life, there is no way to further develop at that point. For example, if you have already completed Algebra 1, why would you desire to take that class over and over? It would be logical for you to move on to Algebra 2, would it not?

In the opening verses of chapter 6, we are given a list of the truths that babes in Christ need to know about. In verses 4-6, the writer says, "How many times can you go to the cross and be saved by Christ? How many times can you *enter* salvation?" Only once! Therefore, if you continue to *stay at the cross,* you are saying, "Jesus, climb back on your cross and die for me again and again. One time was not enough. I have already *lost* what you gained for me by my first trip to Calvary. I want my salvation back again. *Die again for me!"*

The writer says, "Friend, if you do that, you put Christ to an open shame! You tell the world the work of Jesus was not a *finished* work! And, it *is a finished work!"*

His illustration is in the next verses. How do you know that a piece of ground has been seeded? *There is growth as a result.* When the rains come, the seeds grow and show the plants. But, if the rains come and nothing has been planted in the ground, only weeds will grow. This is positive proof that no seed was planted.

Now, if the readers have *not* had the "seed of Christ" implanted within them, then there might be good reason to continue to think about the basic salvation doctrines. But this is not true of them. In verses 9-12, they are told there *are signs of spiritual life within them.* Therefore, they have no reason to continue to dwell on basic truths.

The writer continues in 6:13-20 by comparing the promise God made to Abraham with His promise to us that He would give us much more than *just* the salvation experience received at Calvary. *All He has reserved for us is waiting for us!*

When God made His covenant with Abraham, it was a commitment based upon the integrity of God's own name. It could not be cancelled. Therefore, Abraham's patient waiting was justified. He could not possibly miss receiving God's promises. God could not swear by anything greater than Himself.

God has made an even *greater* oath than the one He made to Abraham! He has promised us full maturity in His Son. We are to "go on" until we have received it. This hope of full maturity is sure and steadfast.

Further, Jesus (v. 20) is seen as our "forerunner" in this guarantee of the maturity waiting for us. That is an interesting expression..."*forerunner!*" In ancient times, a large ship would throw its anchor, connected by a rope to its bow, into a smaller ship called the "forerunner." That little tugboat would then draw the ship into the safety of the harbor, carefully pulling it around hidden rocks. Jesus is doing this for us. And, says the author, He is doing it as our everlasting "High Priest...according to the order of Melchizedek."

The Superior Priesthood of Christ (7:1-10:35)

In chapter 7, His priesthood is a *royal* one. He is a King as well as a priest. Melchizedek was such a person. His priesthood is a *timeless* one. Melchizedek was such a person. His priesthood is an *independent* one. So also was the priesthood of Melchizedek.

(On your own, continue to study the comparisons and contrasts of the High Priesthood of Jesus which follows...)

Note the contrast of the COVENANTS of the old and the new priesthoods.

Three views concerning the identity of those who are within the new covenant:

1. The church has replaced Israel as the sole participant in this new covenant. (Paul refutes this in Romans 9-11!)
2. The covenant is only with Israel. (Thus, it does not fit chapter 8.)
3. The new covenant includes Israel, with the church a full participant with them in it.

In chapter 9, this new covenant is superior to the old one in the same way that the heavenly "temple" is superior to the earthly temple. In chapter 10, it is superior to the old one because the sacrifice of the heavenly "temple" is the Lamb of God, while the sacrifices of the earthly temple were endless animal lambs.

The fourth warning is about despising God's word (10:26-31)

These verses clearly refer to disobedient Christians. "Papa will spank His rebellious, immature child!"

The final section deals with the Faith Principle.

Chapter 11 is one of the greatest chapters in all of your Bible. Verse 1 tells us that "faith is believing something IS SO because you KNOW God is going to MAKE IT SO!"

In verse 39, we are told the justified will live by faith. Sandwiched between these verses are the heroes of faith in the Bible.

Chapter 12 outlines the pattern of faith. He tells us we are now on the playing field, and all those mentioned in chapter 11 are sitting in the bleachers watching us. We are to lay aside all that would weight us down, and run our race through total faith in Christ.

As every runner is disciplined to run more effectively by his coach, even so, our Father will discipline us. If we do not receive it, we are not His children! We can despise this discipline, as did Esau—who despised his birthright—or we can be stimulated by it.

The fifth warning: disagreeing with God's word (12:25)

The teaching about faith concludes in chapter 13 with a description of the *performance of faith.* Note the powerful benediction which closes this letter in 13:20-21.

Understanding Hebrews is not easy, but offers more "meat" than any book other than Romans in your Bible!

Suggestions for marking your Bible...

1. Copy the Outline into your Bible.

2. Write beside Hebrews 6:4-6:

    If one were to fall, reinstatement would be impossible. Falling itself is impossible!

3. Write beside Hebrews 11:1:

    Greatest definition of faith in Bible

4. Underline 4:16 in your Bible. This verse became the flag of Luther, Calvin, and Zwingli during the Reformation. In the margin, write:

    No sacrifice but Calvary; No priest but Christ; No confessional but the Throne of Grace.

4. Add any other notes from the explanations which you wish to preserve in your Bible.

Unit Forty Three
THE BOOK OF JAMES

OUTLINE OF JAMES

INTRODUCTION: 1:1

FIRST SECTION: GENUINE RELIGION
    Purpose of Trials—1:2-4
    Asking in Faith—1:5-8
    The Rich are Poor—1:9-11
    Testings and Temptations Compared—1:12-18
    Anger Discouraged—1:19-20
    Doing the Word—1:21-25
    Bridled Tongues—1:26
    Pure Religion—1:27

SECOND SECTION: GENUINE FAITH
    Favoritism Attacked—2:1-13
    Faith Without Works—2:14-26

THIRD SECTION: GENUINE WISDOM
    Teaching an Awesome Task—3:1-2
    The Bridling of the Tongue—3:3-12
    Bitter Jealousy and Selfish Ambition—3:13-18

FOURTH SECTION: GENUINE HUMILITY
    Source of Quarrels and Conflicts—4:1-3
    Adulteresses Admonished—4:4-10
    Critical Spirits—4:11-12
    Life's Length Unpredictable—4:13-17

FIFTH SECTION: GENUINE BEHAVIOR AWAITING THE
    LORD'S RETURN
    The Ugly Rich—5:1-6
    The Pricelessness of Patience—5:7-11
    Oaths—5:12
    Prayer for Healing—5:13-18
    Restoration—5:19-20

AUTHOR

The writer of this book is James, the half-brother of Jesus. He was one of four younger brothers of our Lord (see Matthew 13:55, Mark 6:3). He was slow to accept Christ (John 7:5), and was converted by the appearance of the risen Lord (1 Corinthians 15:7).

After Peter's activity in converting Cornelius the Gentile, the leadership of the Jerusalem church subtly shifts from him to James. (He never fully recovered from the suspicion left by his obedience to the Lord in that instance!). James then appears as the Bishop of the church in Jerusalem (see Acts 12:17, 15:13-29, 21:17-18, Galatians 1:19, 2:9,12).

DATE

The understanding of this book rests strongly on how we date it. The latest possible date for it must be 62 A.D., the year of his martyrdom. However, the letter does not refer at all to the Council in Jerusalem, held in 50 A.D. (Acts 15). The diaspora (dispersion) of the Jews mentioned in James 1:1 probably took place in 34 A.D. Thus, a dating between 34 and 50 A.D. seems to be in order.

Since the book is almost devoid of doctrinal content, it must have appeared before the writings of Paul (48-50 A.D.). Thus, James must be the earliest book written in the New Testament. When we read 1 Corinthians and see the strife and immorality within that early church, we can understand the emotions in James' heart as he hears of the "falling away" from a vital, true faith which is taking place in these scattered churches.

Assuming that it would take a couple of years for the scattered churches to become so carnal, we may position a date as early as 36 A.D.

THEME

Filled with sadness over the lack of pure love's expression, and concerned over the developing persecution by the Romans, James writes to the Jewish churches. If we assume Paul's ministry has not yet begun and Gentiles are not yet being added in large numbers to the Christian community, the salutation in 1:1 makes sense. In a word, James says, FAITH WITHOUT WORKS? **DEAD!**

NOTES

TRIALS AND TEMPTATION (Chapter 1)

HEARING AND DOING (James 1:19 ff)

FAITH THAT WORKS (James 2:14ff)

THE TONGUE (James 3:1-12)

THE BREVITY OF LIFE (James 4:13 ff)

HEALING IN THE BOOK OF JAMES (James 5:13ff)

Suggestions for marking your Bible...

1. Copy the Outline into your Bible.

2. Write beside James 1:22:

   Key to book

3. Write beside James 5:14:

   Note: the sick
   call for the Elders,
   not the Elders
   calling for the sick!

4. Add any other notes from the explanations which you wish to preserve in your Bible.

Unit Forty Four

1 PETER
2 PETER

OUTLINE OF 1 PETER

INTRODUCTION: 1:1-2

FIRST SECTION: OUR SALVATION

> Begotten by the Father—1:3
> Provided as an Inheritance—1:4
> Preserved by His power, not our works—1:5a
> Future salvation—1:5b
> Cause for rejoicing—1:6
> Purpose of trials—1:7a
> Future salvation, ours at His appearing—1:7b-9
> Prophesied by Old Testament authors—1:10
> Wrote, but did not understand—1:11-12
> Our response—1:13-16
> Our judgment—1:17
> Basis for redemption—1:18-21
> Love of the brethren—1:22
> Being "born again"—1:23
> The authority of the Word—1:24-25

SECOND SECTION: OUR SANCTIFICATION

> Change your diet—2:1-3
> The Church as "living stones"—2:4-8
> The Church as "segullah"—2:9-10
> Conduct as Christians—2:11-18
> Suffering's place—2:19-25

THIRD SECTION: HUSBANDS AND WIVES IN CHRIST

Words to wives with unsaved husbands—3:1-6
Words to husbands with unsaved wives—3:7
Words to husbands and wives alike—3:8-12

FOURTH SECTION: HOW TO SUFFER

Suffering for well-doing—3:13-17
Christ's suffering—3:18
His preaching unto the spirits in prison (the dead)
—3:19-20
The meaning of baptism—3:21-22
Suffering without sinning—4:1-5
Commentary on 3:19—4:6
Love and hospitality—4:7-9
Using spiritual gifts—4:10-11
More suffering to come—4:12-13
Suffer for Christ, not because of sin—4:14-19

FIFTH SECTION: GENERAL WORDS TO THE CHURCHES

To the elders—5:1-4
To the members—5:5-7
Resisting Satan—5:8-9
Apostolic Benediction—5:10-11
Final farewells—5:12-14

OUTLINE OF 2 PETER

OPENING BENEDICTION—1:1-4

FIRST SECTION: GROWING AND GROUNDING

> The steps of Christian growth—1:5-11
> Peter's awareness of his death—1:12-15
> The ground for his teachings: his own eyewitness
>   —1:16-18
> BUT...the scriptures even more authoritative!
>   —1:19-21

SECOND SECTION: ATTACK UPON FALSE TEACHERS

> Their danger described—2:1-2
> The surety of their judgment: past judgments—2:3-10
> The vileness of their inner character—2:11-22

THIRD SECTION: THE EVENTS SURROUNDING "THE DAY
    OF THE LORD"

> Remember Old Testament prophecies—3:1-2
> Dealing with the scoffers—3:3-4
> The "Word" that spoke creation...—3:5
> ...and caused the flood...—3:6
> ...is the "Word" which will act upon it again!—3:7
> The time frame belongs to God—3:8
> Reason for the delay—3:9
> The earth to be burned up—3:10
> How shall we then live?—3:11-12
> After the fire, a renovation—3:13
> *Again:* How shall we then live?—3:14
> Refers to Paul's writings—3:15-18

AUTHOR

Without any dispute, Peter wrote both letters, as evidenced by his many personal references.

DATE

The date for 1 Peter relates to his reference in 1 Peter 5:13, where he says he is writing from "Babylon." Some think Peter was speaking literally, and that he spent his last days in that city. Little evidence exists to confirm this view. The clearer meaning is that this Old Testament city's name has taken on a special meaning. It had always stood for a place of satanic power and deception.

One of the earliest writers of the church, following the death of the Apostles, was Tertullian. He said, "Babylon, in [the writings of] John, *is a figure of the city Rome,* as being equally great and proud of her sway, and triumphant over the saints."

Thus, Peter is considered by some to have been in Rome when he wrote. If this is true, the date would be during the reign of Nero in 63 or 64 A.D. Nero was responsible for the death by martyrdom of Peter, as Jesus had prophesied (John 21:18-19).

2 Peter was written shortly thereafter, from the same place and possibly within months. It was a final word from Peter to his beloved brothers and sisters as he expected his execution. Considering the fact that Peter had a child at the time he followed Jesus, he probably was in his sixties when death came.

THEME

In 1 Peter, he seems to anticipate the terrible persecution which may be unleashed by Nero, who was literally insane at the time of his rule over the Roman empire. He seeks to strengthen the readers by helping them see there are *future aspects* to their salvation and that death brings the joy of experiencing them. Many practical *"how to walk in Christ"* comments are made.

In 2 Peter, he is anticipating his own death, and is sharing three primary things. First, he wants the readers to know their authority is in the written Word of God, and that they should not follow the false teachings of contemporaries. Second, he wants them to face suffering for their faith in a different way than suffering for their own faults. Third, he wants them to recognize that the "Day of the Lord" will change every vestige of earth, and that a new Kingdom will be established here.

THREE ASPECTS OF SALVATION

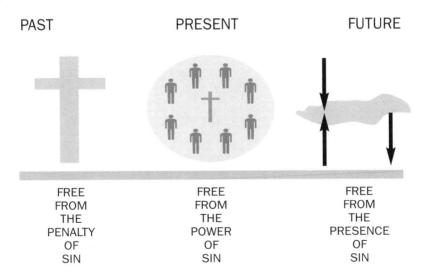

PAST	PRESENT	FUTURE
FREE FROM THE PENALTY OF SIN	FREE FROM THE POWER OF SIN	FREE FROM THE PRESENCE OF SIN

THE CHURCH AS LIVING STONES

THE CHURCH AS *"SEGULLAH"*

LIVING WITH AN UNBELIEVER

THE USE OF SPIRITUAL GIFTS

"PREACHING TO THE SPIRITS"

PETER'S VIEW OF INSPIRATION

THE "DAY OF THE LORD" AND THE RENOVATION OF THE EARTH

Suggestions for marking your Bible...

1. Copy the outline into your Bible.

2. Write beside 1 Peter 1:10-12, or as a footnote:

   *Bible authors read
   their own writings
   to see what God
   had said through them!*

3. Write beside 2 Peter 3:10-14:

   *The climax of the
   Day of the Lord:
   complete renovation!*

4. Add any other notes from the explanations which you wish to preserve in your Bible.

Unit Forty Five
1 JOHN
2 JOHN
3 JOHN
JUDE

OUTLINE OF 1 JOHN

INTRODUCTION: THE PERSONS OF
    THE FELLOWSHIP—1:1-4
    Testimony to Christ—1:1-4

FIRST SECTION: THE LIGHT OF FELLOWSHIP—1:5-2:27
    God is light—1:5-7
    Sin, its reality and remedy—1:8-2:2
    Tests of true knowledge—2:3-6
    The first love—2:7-17
    The danger of antichrists—2:18-27

SECOND SECTION: THE LOVE OF FELLOWSHIP—2:28-4:21
    The children of God and righteousness—2:28-3:10
    Love one another—3:11-24
    Trying the spirits—4:1-6
    God is love—4:7-21

THIRD SECTION: THE WAY TO FELLOWSHIP—5:1-12
    The New Birth: its threefold proof—5:1-5
    The witness concerning the son—5:6-12

FOURTH SECTION: THE CERTAINTY OF FELLOWSHIP
    —5:13-21
    The knowledge of eternal life—5:13-20

FIFTH SECTION: GENERAL WORDS TO THE CHURCHES
    —5:21

AUTHOR

The disciple John is the author. There is a remarkable similarity in vocabulary and style between the Gospel of John and the three letters in this section.

DATE

Writing from Ephesus, the location of John in the later years of his ministry, this letter dates between 85-95 A.D. He wrote to the churches in the region around that city.

THEME

This is a pastoral letter, dealing with several themes:
1. The Gnostic heresy
2. Dealing with sin
3. The marks of the true Christian
4. The assurance of salvation

OUTLINE OF 2 JOHN

INTRODUCTION: 1:1-3

FIRST SECTION: A NEW REASON FOR REJOICING—4

SECOND SECTION: A NEW LEVEL OF LIFE—5-6

THIRD SECTION: A NEW SOURCE OF DANGER—7

FOURTH SECTION: A NEW BASIS OF APPEAL—8

FIFTH SECTION: A NEW NEED FOR WATCHFULNESS—9-11

CONCLUSION: 12-13

AUTHOR

John, the beloved disciple, writing from Ephesus. He ministered to the people in Asia Minor after the destruction of Jerusalem (70 A.D.) until nearly the end of the century.

DATE

All three of these letters were written between 85-95 A.D.

THEME

A Pastoral Letter, written to encourage faithfulness to the truth of God.

415

OUTLINE OF 3 JOHN

SALUTATION—1-2

WITNESS OF THEIR WALK IN THE TRUTH—3-4

SERVICE TO THE BRETHREN—5-8

REBUKE TO DIOTREPHES—9-10

A GOOD TESTIMONY—11-12

CONCLUSION—13-14

AUTHOR

John, the beloved disciple, writing from Ephesus.

DATE

All three of these letters were written between 85-95 A.D.

THEME

Working together in love.

OUTLINE OF THE BOOK OF JUDE

SALUTATION—1-2

JUDGMENT ON FALSE TEACHERS—3-16

EXHORTATIONS TO CHRISTIANS—17-23

BENEDICTION—24-25

AUTHOR

Jude identifies himself as the brother of James (v.1); thus, he is one of the Lord's half-brothers.

DATE

Possibly between 80-90 A.D.

THEME

The threat of subversive teachers compelled Jude to write a strong letter contending for the faith. The entire letter is a warning against false teachers within the church, and contains strong words!

SPECIAL STUDIES:

ABIDING AND KNOWING

THE HUMANITY OF JESUS

CONFESSION

COMMITTING SIN

PROPITIATION

UNCTION

THE WITNESS CONCERNING THE SON

THE ASSURANCE OF ETERNAL LIFE

THE ELECT LADY

ANGELS WHO KEPT NOT THEIR FIRST ESTATE

FALSE TEACHERS

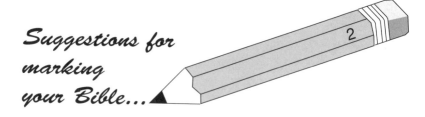

Suggestions for marking your Bible...

1. Copy the outline into your Bible.

2. Write beside 1 John 1:9
   (or footnote if room is needed):

   Confess: "to agree with God." It is viewing sin as God views it and to agree with His judgment against sin.

3. Write beside Jude 14:

   The return of Christ after the rapture: He comes with His saints.

4. Add any other notes from the explanations which you wish to preserve in your Bible.

Unit Forty Six

THE BOOK OF REVELATION—I

OUTLINE OF THE BOOK OF REVELATION

INTRODUCTION: CHAPTER 1

The Revelation of Jesus Christ—1:1-3

Destination: The 7 Churches—1:4

Description: The Bridegroom and the Bride—1:5-8

Author's Explanation—1:9-18

Outline of Book—1:19

Symbolism Explained—1:20

PART 1: THE THINGS WHICH YOU HAVE SEEN: CHAPTERS 2-3

Message to Ephesus—2:1-7

Message to Smyrna—2:8-11

Message to Pergamum—2:12-17

Message to Thyatira—2:18-29

Message to Sardis—3:1-6

Message to Philadelphia—3:7-13

Message to Laodicea—3:14-22

PART 2: THE THINGS WHICH ARE: CHAPTERS: 4-5

The Throne of God—4:1-4

The Worship of the Creator—4:5-11

The Seven-Sealed Book—5:1-4

Christ, the "Slain Lamb," worthy to open it—5:5-7

The Worship of the Lamb—5:8-14

PART 3: THE THINGS WHICH SHALL TAKE PLACE: CHAPTERS 6-22

1. THE BOOK OPENED, SEAL BY SEAL
    1. The first seal: False Christ—6:1-2
    2. The second seal: War—6:3-4
    3. The third seal: Famine—6:5-6
    4. The fourth seal: Death—6:7-8
    5. The fifth seal: Martyrdom—6:9-11
    6. The sixth seal: Terror—6:12-17

FIRST INTERLUDE—7:1-17

---

2. THE SEVENTH SEAL: SEVEN TRUMPETS SOUND
    7. The breaking of the seventh seal—8:1

    Seven angels with seven trumpets—8:2
    The prayers of the saints at the altar—8:3-5
    The angels begin sounding the trumpets—8:6

    1. First trumpet: 1/3 of earth burned up—8:7
    2. Second trumpet: 1/3 of sea becomes blood, 1/3 of marine life and ships destroyed—8:8-9
    3. Third trumpet: 1/3 of waters made bitter —8:10-11
    4. Fourth trumpet: 1/3 of universe smitten—8:12

3. THE LAST 3 TRUMPETS: THE THREE "WOES"

    Announcing of the three woes—8:13

    5. Fifth trumpet, First Woe: bottomless pit opened; locusts bring torment—9:1-12

6.   Sixth trumpet, Second Woe: army from the East
—9:13-21

SECOND INTERLUDE—10:1-11:14

The angel and the "Little Book"—10:1-11
The Two Witnesses—11:1-14

4.   THE SEVENTH TRUMPET: SEVEN PERSONS

1.   First person: Israel—12:1-2
2.   Second person: Satan—12:3-4
3.   Third person: Christ—12:5-6
4.   Fourth person: Archangel Michael—12:7-12

Satan persecutes Israel—12:13-16

5.   Fifth person: Jewish remnant—12:17
6.   Sixth person: Beast out of the Sea—13:1-10
7.   Seventh person: Beast out of the Earth
—13:11-18

THIRD INTERLUDE: 14:1-15:8

Vision of the Lamb and the 144,000—14:1-5
Vision of the Angel with the Everlasting Gospel
—14:6-7
Fall of Babylon announced—14:8
Doom of the Beast-worshippers announced—14:9-12
Blessedness of the holy dead—14:13
Vision of Armageddon—14:14-20
Before the Throne of God—15:1-8

5. THE SEVEN BOWLS OF WRATH

    Bowls released—16:1

    1. First bowl: sores—16:2
    2. Second bowl: Sea turns to blood—16:3
    3. Third bowl: Rivers turn to blood—16:4-7
    4. Fourth bowl: Sun scorches earth—16:8-9
    5. Fifth bowl: Darkness and pain—16:10-11
    6. Sixth bowl: Euphrates dries up—16:12

    Armageddon—16:13-16

    7. Seventh bowl: Hailstones—16:17-21

6. THE SEVEN DOOMS

    1. The doom of "Babylon"—17:1-19:19

    A divine view of Babylon—17:1-7
    Interpretation of the symbolism—17:8-18
    Warning to God's people to get out—18:1-8
    A human view of Babylon—18:9-19
    An angelic view of Babylon—18:10-24

FOURTH INTERLUDE: 19:1-10

Fourfold Hallelujah—19:1-6
Marriage of the Lamb—19:7-10
Second Coming of Christ—19:11-19
2. The doom of the Beast—19:20
3. The doom of the False Prophet—19:20
4. The doom of the kings—19:21

Satan bound—20:1-3
First resurrection—20:4-6

5. The doom of Gog and Magog—20:7-9
6. The doom of Satan—20:10
7. The doom of the unbelieving dead—20:11-15

7. THE SEVEN NEW THINGS

    1. New Heaven—21:1
    2. New Earth—21:1-2
    3. New Peoples—21:3-8
    4. New Jerusalem—21:9-21
    5. New Temple—21:22
    6. New Light—21:23-27
    7. New Paradise—22:1-7

FINAL INTERLUDE: 21:8-21

THE LAST MESSAGE OF THE BIBLE—21:8-19

THE LAST PROMISE AND PRAYER
OF THE BIBLE—21:20-21

AUTHOR

Five times the book is declared to be the writing of John, the beloved disciple: 1:1,4, 9; 21:2; 22:8.

An attestation to John's authorship also comes from these disciples:

JOHN discipled POLYCARP, the pastor of the church in Smyrna;

POLYCARP discipled IRENAEUS, who died in 190 A.D.;

IRENAEUS of Lyons, in documents written by him which we possess today, attested to John's authorship.

DATE

Revelation was written during the latter time of Domitian's reign (95-96 A.D.). One of the characteristics of this Caesar's determined attempt to destroy Christianity was the exiling of its leaders. Thus, John (the leader of Christianity at this time in Asia Minor) writes from the island of Patmos. It is a horseshoe-shaped rock island about 6 miles wide and 10 miles long. It is about 25 miles off the coast, due west of Miletus. He was a prisoner required to chip out rocks used for state buildings and pagan temples. John was a very old man, perhaps in his eighties, at the time of writing.

THEME

The Greek title is *APOKALUPSIS*: "Unveiling." At the heart of this book is our Christ. It unveils the future in much the same way the book of Daniel did. We may attest to the accuracy of this book by noticing the precision in forecasting the future found in that Old Testament book!

THE READERS

The letter is to be cycled among seven churches in Asia Minor. These churches are in their third generation of life, and have faced the vileness of a pagan culture since their beginnings. Slavery, idolatry, sexual promiscuity, and delusions of the Mystery Religions have always surrounded them. In addition, the terrible persecution of the Roman government is now at its height. Emperor Worship had been set forth in earnest; any who refused to worship Domitian were considered subversive.

APOCALYPTIC WRITING

Apocalyptic writing has well-marked characteristics:

- *Figurative style*
  Many of the phrases are drawn from Biblical writings.

- *Supernatural conveying of information*
  The announcements are made by angels, visions, and other supernatural means. The unseen world that lies behind the action of this present world is highlighted.

NUMERICAL SIGNIFICANCE

The use of numbers in Revelation is obviously a part of the symbolisms which must be understood. In Scripture, the numbers which commonly contain symbolic value include:

1: Unity, oneness (Deuteronomy 6:4)
2: Strength (Ecclesiastes 4:9-12)
3: God, the Trinity (Matthew 28:19)
4: The World (Revelation 7:1)
5: Man (Leviticus 14:14-16)
6: Evil, Satanic (Revelation 13:18)
7: Perfection, completeness (Revelation 1:4)

10: Five doubled; hence, completeness (Revelation 2:10)

12: God's perfection revealed to the created order (Revelation 21:12)

HOW TO INTERPRET

1. Take everything literally unless there is an obvious symbolism intended. (Example: 1:1-3)
2. Look for an explanation of the meaning within the book itself. *(Example: Revelation 1:20)*
3. Look for a further explanation of the meaning within the Bible itself.
   (Example: Revelation 4:3 with Ezekiel 1:26,27)

THE OLD TESTAMENT BACKGROUND OF REVELATION

This book assumes a good understanding of the Old Testament by the reader. Three hundred and forty-eight references to it are to be found! Of these, 95 are repeated more than once, so the actual number of *different* Old Testament passages are two hundred and fifty—*an average of more than TEN for EVERY CHAPTER in Revelation.*

Only a small number of these references include more than three or four words in sequence. One authority points out that of the 404 verses of the Apocalypse, 278 refer to the Old Testament.

SOME FINAL THOUGHTS ...

Revelation is the only book of prophecy in the New Testament, in contrast to *seventeen* in the Old Testament! It is also the only one in the entire Bible that promises a special blessing on those who study it, and a judgment on those who add or take away from it.

COMPARISONS WITH DANIEL

ITEM	*DANIEL*	*REVELATION*
ISRAEL	3:6	Chapter 12
ANTICHRIST	3:1-7 7:7,8,24-25 9:27 11:36-45	Chapter 13
LENGTH OF THE TRIBULATION	9:24-27	11:2 12:6 13:5 Chapter 14

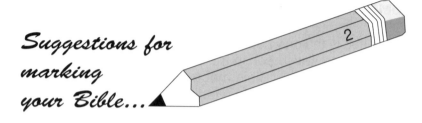

Suggestions for
marking
your Bible...

1. Copy the outline into your Bible.

2. Write beside Revelation 1:19:

    Key to outline
    of Revelation

3. Write beside Revelation 22:17:

    The final invitation
    of a loving Deity!

4. Add any other notes from the explanations which you
    wish to preserve in your Bible.

Unit Forty Seven
THE BOOK OF REVELATION—II
CHAPTERS 1-5

OUTLINE OF REVELATION 1-5

INTRODUCTION TO REVELATION: CHAPTER 1

The Revelation of Jesus Christ—1:1-3
Destination: The 7 Churches—1:4
Description: The Bridegroom and the Bride—1:5-8
Author's Explanation—1:9-18
Outline of Book—1:19
Symbolism Explained—1:20

PART 1: THE THINGS WHICH YOU HAVE SEEN:
       CHAPTERS 2—3

Message to Ephesus—2:1-6
Lost first love

Message to Smyrna—2:8-11
Persecuted

Message to Pergamum—2:12-17
Worldly

Message to Thyatira—2:18-29
Paganized

Message to Sardis—3:1-6
Lifeless

Message to Philadelphia—3:7-13
Missionary

Message to Laodicea—3:14-22
Lukewarm

ASIA MINOR

THE
AREA
WHERE
THE
SEVEN
CHURCHES
WERE
LOCATED

PATMOS

CYPRUS

MEDITERRANEAN SEA

FROM PATMOS, John could see Asia Minor. In his heart, he could see the spiritual condition of the seven church bodies he had nurtured for so many years. He felt their future was threatened by their poor relationships with their Lord, and saw their future in a vision.

PART 2: THE THINGS WHICH ARE: CHAPTERS: 4—5

The Throne of God—4:1-4
24 Elders: see 5:10. They are the Church, the Bride of Christ.

The Worship of the Creator—4:5-11
4 Living Creatures: see Ezekiel 10:20.
They are the Cherubim. Numerous eyes indicate spiritual perception. Both men and angels worship God!

The Seven-Sealed Book—5:1-4
This is the record of history yet unrevealed. It is not under the power of any man!

Christ, the "Slain Lamb," worthy to open it—5:5-7
V. 6 in the Greek describes a lamb with its throat slit, the head hanging awkwardly.

The Worship of the Lamb—5:8-14
Overwhelming! All creatures everywhere join in the mighty song of praise to the Lamb!

NOTES

THE FOUR MAIN SCHOOLS OF INTERPRETATION
OF THE BOOK OF REVELATION

SYMBOLIC, OR IDEALIST

PREMISE: Revelation is seen as only a series of pictures teaching spiritual truths. It sees no prophecy of specific historical events. It is held by those who have a low view of inspiration of scripture.

PRETERIST

PREMISE: All of the prophecies in Revelation were fulfilled in the First Century, with eternal destiny taught only in the last two chapters. It also is held by those who have a low view of inspiration of scripture.

CONTINUOUS-HISTORICAL

PREMISE: All of Revelation up to 19:1 applies to the centuries since the time of Christ. Only chapters 19-22 foretell events after Christ's second coming. Those who hold this view are widely scattered in their interpretations. For example, the Reformation is the mighty Angel in Chapter 10. Chapters 12-18 deal with the church internally, not chronologically. This view is typical of those who come to the book with prior decision to interpret it by personal projection, not by the direction of scripture itself.

FUTURIST

PREMISE: All of Revelation from chapter 4 speaks prophetically of "The Day of the Lord." It is the only interpretation that truly perceives the prophetic nature of the Old and New Testaments, and the perfect harmony which exists between them where prophecy is concerned.

Futurists divide into two camps in interpreting the Letters to the Seven Churches. One sees these churches representing seven periods of church history, leading up to the rapture in 4:1. The other sees these churches as describing literal churches in John's day, but descriptive of churches in all ages of history, up to the end times.

THE 3 VIEWS OF THE MILLENNIUM

POSTMILLENNIAL

PREMISE: Virtually extinct today, this view was popular among *Heilsgeschichte* scholars (do you remember what that means?) in the 1800's. It held that the Millennium was an age of peace and enlightenment, followed by the return of Christ. "Bringing back the King" would be done by educating the illiterates of the earth: literate people would be civilized to the point that they would no longer follow their animal instincts. World War I popped this bubble!

AMILLENNIAL

PREMISE: Commonly held today among neo-orthodox scholars, this view says there is NO *(A)* Millennium. The Millennium is a spiritual thing, taking place as Christ reigns with His saints in heaven at the present time. Further, God has ended all covenant commitments with the Jew. The church has replaced Israel as the chosen people. There is only the "spiritual Jew" today.

PREMILLENNIAL

PREMISE: Christ will come to the earth BEFORE (PRE) the Millennium begins, to rule the world with His saints, for a literal 1,000 years. Satan is bound and powerless during this time.

The period called The Great Tribulation precedes this Millennial reign. Its duration is 7 years, broken into two halves of 3 1/2 years (42 months).

The rapture, or taking away of the Church, is usually seen as taking place at the start of The Great Tribulation. While some minor schools of Bible scholars see the rapture as taking place in the middle (Mid-Tribulation) or the end (Post-Tribulation) of the period, the vast majority hold to the first view.

NOTES

THE WORLD'S LAST TWO BATTLES

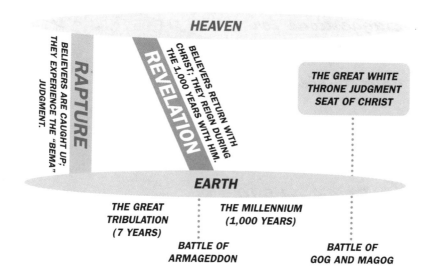

NOTES

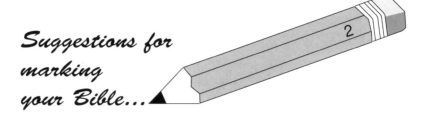

Suggestions for marking your Bible...

1. Copy the outline into your Bible.

2. Write beside Revelation 1:6:

    See 4:4 and 5:10,
    along with 1 Peter 2:5

3. Write beside Revelation 1:18:

    Hades—lit., "Gehenna"—
    the place of eternal
    confinement for those
    who have rejected God.

4. Add any other notes from the explanations which you
    wish to preserve in your Bible.

Unit Forty Eight

THE BOOK OF REVELATION—III
CHAPTERS 6—16

PART 3: THE THINGS WHICH SHALL TAKE PLACE:
CHAPTERS 6—22

AN OVERVIEW OF CHAPTERS 6-16

In chapters 6 through 11, we read about the breaking of the Seven Seals on the Book of History. The broken seventh Seal introduces us to 7 Trumpets, which sound in turn. The sequence of these two series is uninterrupted. They flow out of chapters 4 and 5.

THE SEALS deal with broad principles of judgment: war, poverty, pestilence, etc., true of all periods in history.

THE TRUMPETS deal with specific, concrete judgments, set into a more narrow interval of time than the seals. The first 4 trumpet judgments are physical in character; the last 3 are produced by spiritual forces.

BOTH deal with a real order of events. The seventh trumpet (10:7, 11:15-19) marks the establishment of the Kingdom of God over all lesser powers. With it, the period of the Great Tribulation comes to a conclusion.

In chapters 12 through 16, we find a detailed treatment of "signs," describing certain aspects of this period of Tribulation. In these signs "the wrath of God is finished" (15:1). There are three main "signs:"

1. The woman clothed with the sun, with the moon under her feet
2. The great red dragon (12:3)
3. The final judgments of the 7 bowls (15:1)

Thus, chapters 12-16 are a more detailed presentation of the period generally described by the trumpets. We see a powerful dictatorship uniting politics, commerce, society, and cults. It deals with the conflict between the dictatorship of the Dragon and the first Beast, and the loyalty of God's servants.

In chapters 12-16, we are introduced to a period of time described as 1,260 days (12:6), "a time, times, and half a time" (12:14), or 42 months (13:5). This measures the final 3 1/2 year span of the 7-year Tribulation period, a period in which the Woman (Israel) is persecuted by the Dragon (Satan).

THE DATING OF THIS PERIOD

These chapters cover a 7 year period, *The Great Tribulation.* With the completion of chapter 3, we leave the age of the Church, the time period in which we now live. In 4:1 the removal of the church, described in 1 Thessalonians 4:16-17, takes place: *"Come up here, and I will show you what must take place after these things."*

1. THE BOOK OPENED, SEAL BY SEAL

1. The first seal: False Christ—6:1-2
   The Antichrist has appeared! He assumes the posture of the Christ, who is the true wearer of the Crown.

2. The second seal: War—6:3-4
   He throws the world into war, taking peace "from the earth."

3. The third seal: Famine—6:5-6
   World famine follows...

4. The fourth seal: Death—6:7-8
   In the Greek, this horse is the color of green, rotted flesh. A fourth of the population dies...
   (Four=partial).

5. The fifth seal: Martyrdom—6:9-11
   This takes place in the middle of the Tribulation. These martyrs are also described in 20:4...

6. The sixth seal: Terror—6:12-17
   This passage introduces a dramatic, natural upheaval in the trauma of the Tribulation.

FIRST INTERLUDE—7:1-17

Back to the Throne (chapters 4-5) we go! Four angels are holding back the next holocaust. There we see 144,000 Israelites who have been martyred, along with a countless multitude of Gentiles. In this first period of Tribulation, Israel has recognized Jesus as the Messiah; the nation is sending Jewish missionaries to the ends of the earth. Finally, *finally,* the nations of the earth will receive the message of God's love, grace, and redeeming power through Israel.

2. THE SEVENTH SEAL INTRODUCES SEVEN TRUMPETS, SOUNDING JUDGMENT

7. The breaking of the seventh seal—8:1
    "Silence"—awe because of what will take place!
    Seven angels with seven trumpets—8:2
    Each angel's trumpet will release judgment.
    The prayers of the saints at the altar—8:3-5
    Do you recall our Tabernacle studies, and the fire taken from the altar where the lamb was slain? The Priest used it to ignite the incense, which burned inside the Tabernacle on the Altar of Incense (prayer).
    The angels begin to sound the trumpets—8:6

1. First trumpet: 1/3 of earth burned up—8:7
    In the context of Ezekiel 38:22, we see God's judgment falling through natural calamities upon the wickedness of those on earth.

2. Second trumpet: 1/3 of sea becomes blood, 1/3 of marine life and ships destroyed—8:8-9
    The judgment spreads from land to sea...

3. Third trumpet: 1/3 of waters made bitter—8:10-11
    Could this polluted water result from atomic fission?

4. Fourth trumpet: 1/3 of universe smitten—8:12
    This is unprecedented in history!

3. THE LAST 3 TRUMPETS: THE THREE "WOES"

    Announcing of the three woes—8:13
    Into this awesome scene comes the warning that
    the worst is yet to come!

    5. Fifth trumpet, First Woe:
        Bottomless pit opened, locusts bring
        torment—9:1-12
        These represent demonic angelic forces—(Jude 6,
        2 Thessalonians 2:6-7)—which are released to infect
        the activity of men with their evil power.

    6. Sixth trumpet, Second Woe:
        Army from the East—9:13-21
        This army of 200 million comes from China. They
        currently possess the largest army of footsoldiers
        on the face of the earth.

SECOND INTERLUDE—10:1-11:14

    The angel and the "Little Book"—10:1-11
    In Greek, a "scrap of paper," not a "book" as we
    think of one. *It is the Gospel:* sweet to the mouth,
    bitter to the stomach, speaking of the judgment it
    brings to those who do not confess Jesus as
    Lord.

    The Two Witnesses—11:1-14
    While some suggest these are Moses and Elijah,
    it is not necessary to identify them. Their death occurs
    in Jerusalem.

4. THE SEVENTH TRUMPET:
   SEVEN PERSONS—11:15-19

Once again, we start from the throne of God. In the introductory verses, we see the activity of the twenty-four elders. Then, in 12:1, we return to the earth's trauma. Note the "signs" referred to earlier in this lesson. We are not continuing a chronology of the Tribulation in this section. Rather, we are returning to specific persons who must be considered as important in the events already described.

    1. First person: Israel—12:1-2
        Israel, pictured as the "mother" of Jesus...

    2. Second person: Satan—12:3-4
        He awaits Christ's coming, to destroy Him...

    3. Third person: Christ—12:5-6
        A panorama of messianic history is unfolding...

    4. Fourth person: Archangel Michael—12:7-12
        In the panorama, an explanation of how Satan was cast out of heaven. The method of "overcoming" is the atonement of Christ!

Satan persecutes Israel—12:13-16
        Worse than Hitler's persecution by far, Satan is determined to exterminate Israel from the face of the earth!

    5. Fifth person: Jewish remnant—12:17
        These Jews remain faithful to Jesus in spite of the persecution.

6. Sixth person: Beast out of the Sea—13:1-10
    We are now introduced to two "Beasts." See Daniel
    7:7, 24-27. This is a revival of the ancient Roman
    Empire, greatly expanded. In Revelation 17, a "scarlet
    woman" will ride this beast. This world power will
    be the tool of Satan. Verses 1-3 refer to the *empire;*
    4-10 to the *emperor.* He will be called "The Beast"
    in Revelation 19:20.

7. Seventh person: Beast out of the Earth—
    13:11-18

    This deceitful beast is the False Prophet, the world
    leader of an apostate religion. He will align his evil
    powers to force allegiance to the Kingdom described
    in verses 1-3. He is the Antichrist.

    *NOTE: The "Unholy Trinity" is made up of Satan,
    plus these two evil beings...*

THIRD INTERLUDE: 14:1-15:8

In the midst of this trauma, John is again transported to the
Throne of God! No matter how bad things look here, there is
always a heavenly side to it...

Vision of the Lamb and the 144,000—14:1-5
These who have been martyred are lovingly portrayed in
their purity, before the Throne of God.

*Vision of the Angel with the Everlasting Gospel—
14:6-7*
There is a sense of excitement! We are now drawing close
to the "invasion" of earth by God's people...

Fall of Babylon announced—14:8
"Babylon" is Rome, the seat of the Antichrist and the world government controlled by Satan.
Doom of the Beast-worshipers announced—14:9-12
A judgment upon the wicked is coming!
Blessedness of the holy dead—14:13
...But precious are those in Christ.
Vision of Armageddon—14:14-20
Here is our first vision of the battle of Armageddon.

Before the Throne of God—15:1-8
This scene in heaven prepares us for the final "sign," the bowls of wrath...

5. THE SEVEN BOWLS OF WRATH

Bowls released—16:1
Direct judgment falls upon the evil of earth. We are reminded of the plagues which fell on Egypt!

1. First bowl: sores—16:2
    Some interpreters see this as referring to serious emotional disorders...

2. Second bowl: Sea turns to blood—16:3
    Note this is parallel to the Second Trumpet.

3. Third bowl: Rivers turn to blood—16:4-7
    Note this is parallel to the Third Trumpet.

4. Fourth bowl: Sun scorches earth—16:8-9
    The possibilities for explaining this are many!

5. Fifth bowl: Darkness and pain—16:10-11
    Is "Aids" a harbinger of things to come?

6. Sixth bowl: Euphrates dries up—16:12
   Preparatory for the marching of an army...

   Armageddon—16:13-16
   Once again, we come to Armageddon. Three unclean spirits inject a spirit of unrest and reprisal in the kings of the earth. They come from the mouth of the Dragon (see 13:4).

7. Seventh bowl: Hailstones—16:17-21
   To the very end, nothing deters evil men from cursing God and living in rebellion against Him! The heart of man is deceitful above all things, and desperately wicked...

NOTES

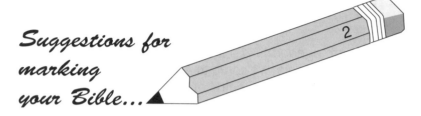

Suggestions for marking your Bible...

1. Copy the outline into your Bible.

2. Write beside Revelation 7:17:

   The precious promise about life after death

3. Write beside Revelation 15:3:

   Note the use of "Bondservant" here, referring to Moses

4. Add any other notes from the explanations which you now wish to preserve in your Bible.

Unit Forty Nine
THE BOOK OF REVELATION—IV
CHAPTERS 17—22

AN OVERVIEW OF CHAPTERS 17—22

Revelation 17:1-21:8 and 21:9-22:21—there are significant differences between these two sections of Revelation.

In the FIRST section, we deal with the forces of evil; in the SECOND section, the Glory of God. The FIRST section focuses on Babylon, the evil center for the final world power of Satan. The SECOND section ends with the New Jerusalem, the glorious capitol of God's eternal reign.

Note these contrasts:

SETTINGS: A Wilderness, 17:3; A High Mountain, 21:10

A WOMAN: A Harlot, 17:3; A Bride, 21:9

SUMMARY

The figure of the great harlot occupies chapters 17 and 18. Chapter 19, verses 1-10 are transitional.

The woman's identity is clear: she is a city, a ruling center described as "Babylon," the apocalyptic word for the city of Rome (17:18-19). But see also the spirit of rebellion connected to this city from the beginning of time, described in Genesis 11:4. It is revealed again in Daniel 4:30, where Nebuchadnezzar said Babylon existed to reveal his might, his great power, and "the glory of his majesty."

449

Harlotry in the Old Testament is used over and over to describe infidelity of man to God, especially in connection with idolatry (See Isaiah 1:21, Jeremiah 2:20). Thus, the description fits the world capitol of the Antichrist.

The Beast of Revelation 17 is identical with the first Beast of chapter 13. He is the dominating figure of the final world empire, evil to the core.

Chapter 18 deals at length with the overthrow of Babylon. A dual viewpoint of heaven and earth is shown. Note that the people of God are told to separate themselves from her.

Chapter 19 presents a scene of joy! The Marriage Supper of the Lamb is presented. The Second Coming of Christ follows. Such a full description is found in no other place in the Bible.

Chapter 20 shows the thousand year period known as the Millennium. Satan is bound in the "bottomless pit." Believers reign with Christ. Unregenerate men live in this period, but with their evil restrained. The curse of sin is removed from the earth. All the unfulfilled prophecies in scripture are now completed. Isaiah's vision of the Messianic period has come! The lion lies down with the lamb; men beat their swords into plowshares.

Among other facts demonstrated within the Millennium is that a perfect environment will not produce a perfect heart. In 20:7, the basic spirit of rebellion among unregenerate men (which has been latent for the Millennium) again erupts. The Battle of Gog and Magog takes place, the last war of history. Christ ends, for all time, the spirit of rebellion on this earth.

There follows the permanent abolition of Satan, along with the Beast and the False Prophet (Antichrist). They are thrown into the lake of fire. Then, all those from all time who lived in rebellion against God are brought to trial at the Great White Throne Judgment (20:11-15).

Think of the Millennium as the "Kingdom of Christ" (read carefully 1 Corinthians 15:23-28), which is to be followed by the "Kingdom of God." According to Paul's explanation, Christ must reign until He has put all enemies under His feet. Then, the Son shall surrender Himself and all the earth, "that God may be all in all." Thus, at the end of the Millennial period there follows the eternal Kingdom, with the total renovation of the earth.

Chapter 21:8 ends this first section, and we are introduced to this final, eternal period. The earth is destroyed by fire and renovation begins. The eternal Kingdom of the Father will have its headquarters not in Babylon, but in the New Jerusalem, described in 22:9ff. This awesome city is hard to imagine! It is 1,500 miles long, wide, *and high.*

Even the concluding verses (22:6-21) are charged with drama and power.

6. THE SEVEN DOOMS

1. The doom of "Babylon"—17:1-19:19

   A divine view of Babylon—17:1-7
   Babylon is pictured as a corrupt and immoral political system, godless and blasphemous. The "ten horns" send us back to Daniel. The awful persecution of believers is highlighted.
   Interpretation of the symbolism—17:8-18
   The beast is identical with the one in 13:1. Read 13:14, 17:8 and 11...note its parallel to the One "who is, who was, and who is to come" (1:8). The beast is the dominating figure of the earth's last empire.

   "Seven heads" are seven kings, one still to come. Various attempts have been made to identify these world empires. It is best to leave it to the future...

   The "waters" are people (17:15)

   Warning to God's people to get out—18:1-8
   Judgment "has" fallen in heaven upon Babylon before the fact! The people of God are told to separate themselves from the values of this society. Her culture originated in disobedience to God; she is doomed. The creation of a civilization pleasing to God must begin with a new life; it cannot ever be a revision of the old one!

A human view of Babylon—18:9-19

Note the suddenness of her destruction: "one hour!"
Those who sorrow at her parting are those who lived
for the luxuries within her.

An angelic view of Babylon—18:20-24

Six times the phrase "not be ....any longer" is used!
While evil men weep, the angel says, "Rejoice!"

FOURTH INTERLUDE: 19:1-10

Fourfold Hallelujah—19:1-6

This occurs after Babylon has been destroyed. We
are again at the Throne. The first announcement (v. 1,
2) declares the bride of the Lamb is ready, and the
wedding is to begin. From this point, God will bring
to pass His purposes which have been so carefully
developed from before the foundations of the
earth.

Marriage of the Lamb—19:7-10

"Bride" can scarcely mean anything other than "church"
(see Ephesians 5:23-32). Note the awesome contrast
between the previous stormy chapter and the peace
of this one!

Second Coming of Christ—19:11-19

He is followed by the armies of heaven. The next
series of events hardly needs comment: it flows from
the event of His return...

2. The doom of the Beast—19:20

3. The doom of the False Prophet—19:20

4. The doom of the kings—19:21

Satan bound—20:1-3

Temporarily (1,000 years), Satan's presence is removed from the earth. The Kingdom of Christ will not involve conflict with this fallen angel!

First resurrection—20:4-6

It would seem that those in the Church Age are resurrected from the dead at the time of the Rapture, and come with Christ. Now, those from the Tribulation Period who were martyred are brought to life, and reign alongside those from the Church Age for a thousand years.

5. The doom of Gog and Magog—20:7-9
    Satan's release proves that an unregenerate heart never changes. His attempt to rally another rebellion is permitted to develop only long enough to reveal those who will follow him. There is no "battle" between the saints and those in rebellion. God swiftly deals with it!

6. The doom of Satan—20:10
    Note the fact that there is no slight hint of a termination to this torment! Beware of all who teach such. It is in direct conflict with Scripture. Prevalent among all cults is the belief that the dead are simply annihilated...

7. The doom of the unbelieving dead—20:11-15
    This judgment closes all accounts, and brings ultimate responsibility to be faced by all who have lived in rebellion against God. Note the careful records of all deeds which are used, and the final destination of those whose names are not found written in the Lamb's Book of Life.

7. THE SEVEN NEW THINGS

1. New Heaven—21:1
   God's eternal renovation includes the universe! By then, man's clutter will be everywhere...

2. New Earth—21:1-2
   This new city, Jerusalem, is built by God!

3. New Peoples—21:3-8
   Once again, the promise of no more tears. The medical profession will have to be retrained for more suitable work!

4. New Jerusalem—21:9-21
   Nothing in our experience can prepare us to take this in. Some may ask, "Is this figurative?" Why should it be so interpreted...certainly not because it would seem more "rational" for us to do so!

5. New Temple—21:22
   God Himself is the Temple!

6. New Light—21:23-27
   God Himself is the Light! (He always has been...)

7. New Paradise—22:1-7
   The Bible began with a garden, and it ends with one.

FINAL INTERLUDE— 22:8-21

THE LAST MESSAGE OF THE BIBLE— 22:8-19
Tenderly read these verses. Catch the spirit of our God, who is not willing that any should perish!

THE LAST PROMISE AND PRAYER
OF THE BIBLE—22:20-21

Oh, come, Lord Jesus! Our hearts long for you!

NOTES

THE END OF YOUR SURVEY IS THE BEGINNING OF YOUR LIFETIME OF STUDY!

God's Word is so very, very rich! The treasures in it are not exhaustible. Those who have spent the most time in the study of it are those who continue to study it the most. You are now equipped, through the deliberate survey you have completed, to begin a book by book study.

As you close the book of Revelation, note the urgency of the final verses. Christ is coming soon! Even as we wait for His coming, we are told that the Spirit and the Bride say, "Come!"

Are you a part of that Bride? Are you a child of God?

Have you made that personal decision to confess with your lips that Jesus is Lord, and to entrust the ownership of your life to Him?

If not, the study of this inspired book has not penetrated your eternity. You stand in need of the blood of the Lamb of God we have studied about, and that precious blood is ready to cleanse you and make you God's child.

You are lovingly encouraged to share with your cell group if there is any area of your personal walk with Christ which disturbs you. Your cell group is ready to listen with concern, ministering to meet your needs.

Suggestions for marking your Bible...

1. Copy the outline into your Bible.

2. Write beside Revelation 20:11:

    The Great White Throne Judgment

3. Write beside Revelation 22:19:

    A warning to those who might tamper with this book...

4. Add any other notes from the explanations which you now wish to preserve in your Bible.

Unit Fifty
THE FIRST 300 YEARS AFTER THE BIBLE

PERSECUTION OF CHRISTIANS

Nero, having burned Rome, made the Christians the scapegoats. Some were sewn inside the skins of animals and torn apart by dogs. Others were crucified or doused with oil and burned as torches. Peter and Paul are described as being martyred during this period.

EARLY EVENTS

The collection of the writings of the Apostles began in earnest with the deaths of these two men.

Thomas went to India to preach the Gospel message. The Indian Church of Mar Thoma, numbering several million adherents, exists today as the oldest continuing church in history.

The earliest known Christian writing outside the books of the New Testament which we can date with certainty is 1 Clement, A.D. 96-97. It is a letter from the church in Rome to the one in Corinth, and describes a schism between the young men and the established presbyters. The rebels claimed special spiritual gifts and words of knowledge. Clement urges harmony among them.

A.D. 98-180

Trajan was the Roman Emperor. Martyrdom of Christians was a common occurrence during this time. Intense persecution of Christians broke out in Asia Minor, where Pliny was Governor. He writes of his orders to kill all those who will not recant their faith: "in any case obstinacy and unbending perversity deserve to be punished."

Ignatius of Antioch was a Christian sent to Rome as a condemned gladiator. He wrote seven letters while being taken in chains from Syria to Troas. At this time, Polycarp was the bishop of Smyrna. He also wrote letters which are in existence today, including one to the Philippian Christians. He was burned at the stake in A.D. 155-156 because he would not deny the Lord and King, "who has never done me ill during eighty-six years."

The next emperor was Hadrian. A brilliant defense of the Christians was written to him by Quadratus about 125 A.D. He wrote, "Christians are in the world but not of the world...Do you not see how (Christians) are thrown to wild animals to make them deny the Lord, and how they are not vanquished? Do you not see that the more of them that are punished, the more do others join their ranks?"

In 132, Hadrian decided to rebuild Jerusalem as a Roman city with temples to Roman gods. Jews in Judea revolted. Roman soldiers retreated from Jerusalem's area, and the Jews took it over. This was a brief rebellion, crushed as the Romans destroyed 985 villages and killed more than a million people in Israel. Jews were banished from the entire area of Jerusalem. The rebuilt city was called Aelia. The church within it was composed only of Gentiles.

JEWISH ANTI-CHRISTIAN SENTIMENT

It is about this period of time that the Talmud begins to record anti-Christian sentiment. Jesus' miracles were attributed to Egyptian magic; He was described as the illegitimate son of an adulteress. From this time forward, Christianity grew primarily among Gentiles, not Jews.

MARCION HERESY

About 139 A.D., a heretic named Marcion appeared within the church in Rome. He taught that the God of the New Testament was not the same God as in the Old Testament, and that Jesus was not born of a woman. He demanded that true Christians stop eating meat. He was excommunicated, gathered his followers in a separate church, and compiled a special "Bible."

Once when Marcion met Polycarp, he asked, "Do you know us?" Polycarp replied, "I know you, the firstborn of Satan."

JUSTIN MARTYR

Emperor Antoninus reigned from 138-161 A.D. During his reign, Justin Martyr, about 155 A.D., stands out among the early apologists (a defender of the faith). He had been a philosopher, whose search for truth brought him through several Greek philosophical systems before he became a Christian. His First Apology rejected the current teaching that Christians practiced gross immoralities under the guise of religious rites. He tried to reconcile faith and reason for those who considered it to be irrational. He also wrote Dialogue with Trypho the Jew, which sets Christianity as flowing naturally out of Jewish religious thought.

Marcus Aurelius reigned from 161-180. Justin tells of three Christians executed for nothing except their faith. He himself was beheaded in Rome about A.D. 165.

In the period immediately following the New Testament, a "bishop" and a "presbyter" were terms used interchangeably. In the second century (100-180 A.D.), the term "bishop" was considered to be above the "presbyter," who was, in turn, above the "deacon." The supervision of the clergy in the area became one of the chief functions of the bishop's duties. His territory was called a "diocese."

THEOPHILUS

Theophilus was born of pagan parents, converted to Christianity, and became the bishop of the diocese of Antioch about 168 A.D. He was a prolific writer, loved the churches and sought to protect them from the heresies of Marcion and others. He was the founder of Biblical chronology, dating the time of the Biblical record from his own era backward 5,698 years to Genesis 1:1.

By 180, the church was established in all parts of the Roman Empire and beyond its borders to the south and east. Missionary activities were carried out by the members and clergy of the local congregations through personal witness.

In London, Peter-upon-Cornhill is claimed to have been the site of a Christian church since 179 A.D. Ancient Christian ruins abound in Scotland.

IRENAEUS

Irenaeus grew up in Smyrna, where he saw and heard "the blessed Polycarp." Later, he moved to Lyons in Gaul (France), where there was a colony of Christians. He was ordained a Presbyter. He died about 200 A.D. He belongs among the outstanding theologians of the church's history.

MONTANISM

Montanism was a movement in the early church similar to modern day Pentecostalism. It was launched by Montanus in Phrygia. Their teachings looked toward an outpouring of the Holy Spirit, the establishment of a heavenly Jerusalem. They claimed the gift of "prophecy," involving continuing revelation beyond scripture. It was legalistic, commanded fasting, forbade remarriage. Penance was imposed on those who sinned, and those who lapsed from the faith would find no forgiveness. The movement was condemned by all of the Christian community. In one form or another, it continued as a submovement through the eighth century.

Actually, all we know about this movement is from its foes. Some feel it was a sincere desire to correct the stagnant forms which began to smother New Testament life, and the movement should be treated with respect.

TERTULLIAN, CLEMENT, AND ORIGEN

Tertullian of Carthage was the son of a pagan centurion. He was trained as a lawyer. He returned from Rome to Carthage after his conversion to Christ in 195 A.D. He was a prolific writer, and converted to Montanism in 207 A.D.

Clement of Alexandria (220 A.D.) and Origen (254), his pupil, are noted for their scholarship. They were the first "university men" of the early church. They were associated with the Catechetical School in Alexandria. This school combined philosophy, science, and theology, viewing all from a Christian perspective.

Although Clement was a brilliant theologian, he was outdone by his pupil, Origen. Some regard him as the most profound mind in the history of the church. Because of persecution, he had to flee to Caesarea. He wrote many volumes which have been lost. His *Principles* is a systematic presentation of Christian beliefs about God, man, free will, and the scriptures. He defended the faith against Celsus, who was a true "theological liberal." Celsus opposed the incarnation and criticized believers for looking to the cross for forgiveness.

As a result of Gnosticism, Marcionism and Montanism, there was a growing desire to settle the limits of inspired writings, called the Canon (Rule). In addition, as the church grew, there was more and more need for organization. The educating of future leaders began to take place in special schools like the one in Alexandria.

180-313 A.D.

With the death of Marcus Aurelius in 180, the Roman Empire entered 100 years of tempest. Corruption, pride, licentiousness, and cruelty marked the emperor's life styles. Heavy taxation destroyed the middle class. Inflation soared.

This same period among Christians was marked by the church becoming institutionalized. Marriages between Christians were solemnized by the church for the first time about 200 A.D. Veneration of martyrs and their remains became a cult. Penance was developed. Between 180-250, the bishop's power was increased significantly. The chief bishoprics were in Rome, Alexandria, Carthage, Ephesus, and Antioch. Rome was first because it was the seat of the Empire, but the Roman papacy would not develop for two more centuries. Power-hungry bishops were now on the scene—a far cry from the devoted men who had first led the churches.

A distinctive clerical class developed, all subordinate to the bishops. In Asia Minor, groups of bishops and clergy first met in synods to discuss points of doctrine and coordinate activities. This quickly spread to the other parts of the Empire. Alexandria and Rome were further elevated to the status of "Patriarchates."

DECIAN PERSECUTIONS; CYPRIAN

The time of the Decian persecutions began in 249. Many Christians were put to death. Many others denied the faith. Some Christians purchased certificates of participation in pagan sacrifices and did not actually participate in them.

Cyprian was elected Bishop of Carthage just 2 years after his conversion (248 A.D.). He died in 258. Although he violently opposed the power of the Roman bishop, his contributions to the development of Roman Catholicism were very great.

Due to the Decian persecutions, he fled from Carthage, only to give himself up later. He favored a lenient position toward Christians who had purchased the certificates of participation, suggesting a period of penance and probation. He was martyred in Carthage on September 14, 258 A.D.

NOVATIAN AND THE ROMAN CHURCH

Novatian was elected as a rival bishop in Rome, and opposed Cyprian's leniency. He demanded that purchasers of certificates should be subjected to lifelong excommunication from the church. His position was known as "Novatianism." He himself died as a martyr, and his followers continued in small groups for 200 years.

Rome had the richest and largest Christian congregation from 200-313 A.D. Victor I, Bishop of Rome (189-198), demanded the bishops of Asia Minor surrender to him. Extensive church properties in Rome developed, along with a far-reaching ministry to the poor.

The voluminous writings of Cyprian make it clear that the church was neither pure nor orthodox at this time. Schisms, heresies, arguments, and defections under persecution were frequent.

Late in this century, there was a phenomenal mass conversion of Armenians. Gregory, an Arminian aristocrat, was converted in Caesarea. Upon returning home, he won the king to personal faith. Following his lead, much of the population converted to Christianity.

The political situation of the Empire was crucial as 300 A.D. approached. Chaos in government and society ruled. It was considered necessary for religion to be unified in order to stabilize the state. It was this conviction that triggered the Decian persecutions. The demands for an outward agreement with paganism was pressed by the Emperor. Where Christians refused to conform, persecutions were terrible.

UNPRECENDENTED PERSECUTIONS

After Decius came Valerian (253-260 A.D.). He made it illegal for Christians to assemble. The deaths of church leaders were by torture.

Following his death, 40 years passed without further persecution. Then came Diocletian! From 284-305, an unprecedented persecution of Christians took place.

Diocletian was determined to restore the glory of Rome. In 303, all churches were ordered to be destroyed. All Christian books, including Bibles, were to be burned. All gatherings were banned. Church leaders were ordered to be put to death. These persecutions continued to 312 A.D. For a decade, Christians were under the constant fear of death for their faith.

CONSTANTINE BRINGS PEACE

In the struggle for the throne which followed Diocletian's abdication, Constantine emerged as victor on October 28, 312. His first act was to issue the Edict of Milan, which made Christianity a legal religion alongside non-Christian cults.

Perhaps 10% of the Empire was Christian at this time. He triggered the beginnings of what would eventually emerge as the "Holy Roman Empire." (It was neither holy, nor did it remain Roman, nor was it long to be an empire.) As he began his reign, he merged Christian and pagan festivals and calendars, thus creating a syncretized Christianity which laid the foundations for the Catholic church to emerge 150 years later.

Unit Fifty One
HOW TO BUILD YOUR OWN REFERENCE LIBRARY

1. LIST THE BOOKS YOU NEED

Study Bible

A leather bound copy. Wide margins! References are helpful but not as important as plenty of space to write, to underline. Suggested text: *New International Version Study Bible (NIV).*

Concordance

Get one to match your NIV translation. You can purchase a King James Concordance cheaper, but it's a problem using it with a modern translation.

Bible Dictionary

Many are on the market. The NIV Dictionary of the Bible is a good buy. Use mainly for quick references when the Encyclopedia will be too detailed for your question.

Commentary (Build slowly!)

You can purchase entire Commentaries. They will be heavy in spots, and thin in spots. Most Bible scholars prefer to purchase the best volume for each Bible book, instead of investing money in a full commentary. For example, Leupold's commentary on Genesis is without peer for conservative, scholarly study of the book. Perhaps no one has ever written a better commentary on Galatians than Martin Luther. Get the best! How will you know what is the best? Ask a Pastor who is a scholar of the Word of God. His eyes will light up and he will share gladly! Or, find a Christian book store with a "bookworm" on the staff, and you will get more help than you need!

Special Bibles
You may wish to add to your basic study Bible one or more of the following:

Nave's Topical Bible
The Bible, rearranged by topics. Great to follow themes through scripture.

The Layman's Parallel Bible
Combines four of the best known and most used translations in a 4-column parallel format which allows for easy comparison.

Paraphrases
A "paraphrase" is not a direct translation of the Bible. It is good to use for comparison, but not for a study Bible. Examples are the Living Bible and the Phillips Translation.

Amplified
The Amplified Bible gives several parallel words for the text of the Bible. It is slow to read but rich in study value! It's an excellent addition to your library.

Bible Encyclopedia
The best is, without question, the Zondervan Bible Encyclopedia. This five volume set has been written by over 200 of the most outstanding evangelical scholars. Photographs, illustrations, maps, and articles on practically any question you will ever ask when reading your Bible are all included. No library is complete until it includes this set!

Dictionary of Old and New Testament Words
Vine's Dictionary of Old and New Testament Words and Wilson's Old Testament Studies are most helpful. They will explain many of the words of the Hebrew and the Greek, and you can forgo the pain of learning those languages!

Bible Handbook

This is a small book that you can take to a group Bible study, containing many key facts about the books of the Bible. Two books here would be helpful: Unger's Bible Handbook (better than the others!), and the more detailed Eerdmans Bible Handbook. You may eventually want to own both.

Bible Atlas

A Bible Atlas is a good choice. It gives lots of maps of Bible times, and is most helpful in learning your Bible geography.

2. SET A SCHEDULE FOR THEIR PURCHASE

1. Budget on a monthly basis for a year.
2. Buy a book at a time.

3. AVOID "IMPULSE BUYING" UNTIL YOU HAVE PURCHASED THE BASIC BOOKS

1. Get the basic books first!
2. Setting priorities will make it easier to get the full library sooner.

4. SET ASIDE A REGULAR TIME TO USE YOUR REFERENCE LIBRARY

1. It's foolish to buy these books and not use them
2. How will you do it? Daily? Weekly?
3. Have a special place where they will be handy to take down and use. Avoid halls, living rooms, etc., where books are "stored." Don't "store" them...USE them!

5. KEEP A NOTEBOOK OR A REFERENCE FILE

1. A file, with one folder for each Bible book, is great! You can throw notes, sermon outlines, etc. into it.
2. A loose leaf notebook with dividers can serve much the same purpose.
3. Preserve your study!

6. DON'T ASK FOR HELP UNTIL YOU HAVE SEARCHED BY YOURSELF

1. From now on, don't "ask the preacher" until you have assured yourself you can't find the answer In your own library of reference books.
2. When you DO ask, try to find out the source for the answer you have been given. Consider adding that particular book to your library.

7. ADD SPECIAL BOOKS AS YOU STUDY

1. When you are going to study one special book of the Bible, purchase at least one good commentary for your library.
2. When you find a special reference book, buy it on the spot! (If you don't, it may be gone when you go back.)

8. MEDITATE AFTER EACH PERIOD OF STUDY ABOUT WHAT THE SPIRIT HAS TAUGHT YOU

1. You will appreciate the opportunity to simply sit and reflect on the new light you have gained by your study. Often the greatest value comes from these "Selah" periods!
2. Remember to write each reflection in your notes or file.

9. BECOME FAMILIAR WITH PUBLISHER'S DOCTRINAL POSITIONS

1. Avoid doctrinal type books which are published by presses which have a strong theological bias...at least in the beginning!
2. Learn which publishing houses you can trust, and which are unpredictable.

NOTES

Unit Fifty Two

PRINCIPLES OF BIBLICAL INTERPRETATION

Study your Bible in the same manner you would explore a magnificent mansion:

1. CAREFULLY SELECT YOUR GUIDE.

We have discussed the books you should add to your library. These "guides" should be trustworthy. As you build your commentaries and dictionaries, be sure you get ones you can trust.

2. USE THE RIGHT KEY TO ENTER.

Each book has a "key" which unlocks the theme or the outline for you. An example of this is in the book of Revelation, where we discovered the outline in 1:19.

Sometimes there are several "keys" which unlock intertwining themes. An example of this is 1 John, where "know," "love," "abide," etc., each present a new way to view the book.

In your class notes, you will find many of these "keys" included for your use. Pay attention to them.

475

3. BE FAMILIAR WITH THE FLOOR PLAN.

The divisions of each book are critical to understanding it. This is also true of the subdivisions, and frequently true of individual thoughts within a chapter. For example, our study of Revelation and Hebrews both required us to consider the "parentheses," or "interludes," inserted in the flow of the material.

The Psalms are grouped into sections. On a broader basis, the books themselves fall into sections: "The Pentateuch," "Minor Prophets," "Pauline Epistles." Knowing where you are in the outline of the book is important!

Do you recall the divisions of Ephesians?
*   *"Sit"*—Chapters 1-3;
*   *"Walk"*—Chapters 4-5;
*   *"Stand"*—Chapter 6.

What about Genesis? ...Ten divisions, with each one introduced by the phrase *"These are the generations of..."*

What are the two major divisions of Joshua?

How many "Books" are there in the Psalms?

What is the outline for Daniel?

What are the four "Beholds" for the four Gospels?

What chapters in Romans deal with the place of the Jew?

4. KNOW WHO LIVES IN EACH "ROOM."

The Bible is written to, or about, distinct classes of people. In 1 Corinthians 10:32, Paul refers to Jews, Gentiles, and the Church of God. Each passage in the Bible is written about or to one of these three classes of persons. Sometimes a passage will be addressed to all three, or have application to all of them. But there are books which belong to one class, rigidly excluding the others. Knowing the priority the writer has in mind as he writes is important!

This does not mean, however, that some scriptures "are for the Jew, and have no meaning for me!" For example, if a Jewish friend of mine is sent a letter, the primary meaning is for him. But, as he hands the letter to me and I read it, I may find some segments of it that speak directly to my own situation.

Failing to do this creates many of the problems found in different interpretations of the scriptures. For example, one of the basic errors of the Seventh Day Adventists results from their taking all the Jewish patterns of the Old Testament and applying them to Gentiles and the church!

Most of the Amillennial positions are developed by ignoring this principle. Promises given to Israel are taught as though they belonged to the church.

An example of this is to be found in treatments of Isaiah 60. This chapter speaks of the time when the Jew shall be the head and no longer the tail of the nations. Jerusalem will be exalted as the capitol of the whole earth, and the wealth of the Gentiles shall pour into it as a tide rises in the ocean. It is common to find teachers who will take all this and apply it to the church, and to Christians!

There is no reason for this. The Jew is never called a Christian any more than he is known as a Gentile. Mount Zion is no more the "church" than Mount Rushmore symbolizes Westminster Abbey in London.

When you enter a book or a section of a book, consider the people the book is written to or who are being talked about. For example, the book of Ecclesiastes is written by Solomon to describe a special kind of person: the man who tries to find meaning in life without recognizing the place of God. To develop theology about the Christian life from such teachings is deadly.

The Jehovah's Witnesses take you to Ecclesiastes to prove there is no hell, no life beyond the grave. They take you to Revelation and describe themselves as the Woman of chapter 12! Sad to say, it is not just cult groups who take such license with the texts. This is why it is important to know the credentials of your "guides" (commentaries).

5. CAREFULLY EXAMINE ALL THE "FURNISHINGS."

In each passage, phrases which may be similar to others should be prayerfully examined. An example of this is to be found in 2 scriptures:

Luke 21:24—*"...Jerusalem will be trampled under foot by the Gentiles until the times of the Gentiles be fulfilled."*
Romans 11:25—*"...a partial hardening has happened to Israel until the fulness of the Gentiles has come in..."*

The *"times of the Gentiles"* signifies the rule of the Gentile nations. That rule began with Nebuchadnezzar, as God set aside the Jews because of sin and evil, and brought in the Gentile governmentally. It will continue until Christ and His Church come to the Mount of Olives and overthrow it, bringing in "The Times of the Jew." (Study Zechariah 14:1-11, Zechariah 8:23, Deuteronomy 28:13).

On the other hand, the *"fullness of the Gentiles"* is referring to the filling up of God's purposes in this age, as He takes out of the Gentiles a people for His name: *"...God first concerned Himself about taking from among the Gentiles a people for His name."* (Acts 15:14)

The passage in Acts goes on to say, *"After these things I will return, and I will rebuild the Tabernacle of David which has fallen, and I will rebuild its ruins, and I will restore it, in order that the rest of mankind may seek the Lord, and all the Gentiles who are called by my name..."* (verses 16-17).

Thus, the Times of the Gentiles began centuries before the birth of Christ and will end only at His appearing to set up the Kingdom of Israel. The Fullness of the Gentiles began only after the resurrection of the Lord and may end at any moment, as the sudden secret rapture of the church takes place.

NOTES

6. CARRY IN LIGHT FROM OTHER PLACES.

In the study above, we have just seen how one section of the scripture (in Acts) sheds light on our study. If you have not yet discovered for yourself the thrill of suddenly getting insights into one passage of scripture through previous study, you will! As catching a 7-pound bass sends the fisherman back to the lake, so these insights send the Bible student back, again and again, for deeper looks at "familiar things."

NOTES

BIBLE STUDY

Passage: _____

1. CAREFULLY SELECT YOUR GUIDE:
Texts I will use in my study:
1._____
2._____
3._____

2. USE THE RIGHT KEY TO ENTER:
The key scripture that unlocks this passage is...

_____

3. BE FAMILIAR WITH THE FLOOR PLAN:
The outline I will use is found:
___ In my Cover the Bible Notes

_____

4. KNOW WHO LIVES IN EACH ROOM:
This book/chapter/passage is written to or about:
___ The Jew
___ The Gentile
___ The Church
___ General; applies to all
___ Other: _____

5. CAREFULLY EXAMINE ALL THE FURNISHINGS:
Word/phrase studies:

6. CARRY IN LIGHT FROM OTHER PLACES:
Other scripture references I found to help me:

BIBLE STUDY

Passage: _____

1. **CAREFULLY SELECT YOUR GUIDE:**
   Texts I will use in my study:
   1._____
   2._____
   3._____

2. **USE THE RIGHT KEY TO ENTER:**
   The key scripture that unlocks this passage is...
   _____

3. **BE FAMILIAR WITH THE FLOOR PLAN:**
   The outline I will use is found:
   ___ In my Cover the Bible Notes
   _____

4. **KNOW WHO LIVES IN EACH ROOM:**
   This book/chapter/passage is written to or about:
   ___ The Jew
   ___ The Gentile
   ___ The Church
   ___ General; applies to all
   ___ Other: _____

5. **CAREFULLY EXAMINE ALL THE FURNISHINGS:**
   Word/phrase studies:

6. **CARRY IN LIGHT FROM OTHER PLACES:**
   Other scripture references I found to help me:

BIBLE STUDY

Passage: _____

1. **CAREFULLY SELECT YOUR GUIDE:**
   Texts I will use in my study:
   1._____
   2._____
   3._____

2. **USE THE RIGHT KEY TO ENTER:**
   The key scripture that unlocks this passage is...

   _____

3. **BE FAMILIAR WITH THE FLOOR PLAN:**
   The outline I will use is found:
   ___ In my Cover the Bible Notes

   _____

4. **KNOW WHO LIVES IN EACH ROOM:**
   This book/chapter/passage is written to or about:
   ___ The Jew
   ___ The Gentile
   ___ The Church
   ___ General; applies to all
   ___ Other: _____

5. **CAREFULLY EXAMINE ALL THE FURNISHINGS:**
   Word/phrase studies:

6. **CARRY IN LIGHT FROM OTHER PLACES:**
   Other scripture references I found to help me:

BIBLE STUDY

Passage: _____

1. CAREFULLY SELECT YOUR GUIDE:
Texts I will use in my study:
1._____
2._____
3._____

2. USE THE RIGHT KEY TO ENTER:
The key scripture that unlocks this passage is...

_____

3. BE FAMILIAR WITH THE FLOOR PLAN:
The outline I will use is found:
___ In my Cover the Bible Notes

_____

4. KNOW WHO LIVES IN EACH ROOM:
This book/chapter/passage is written to or about:
___ The Jew
___ The Gentile
___ The Church
___ General; applies to all
___ Other: _____

5. CAREFULLY EXAMINE ALL THE FURNISHINGS:
Word/phrase studies:

6. CARRY IN LIGHT FROM OTHER PLACES:
Other scripture references I found to help me:

AFTER BIBLE STUDY COMES. . . MINISTRY!

These equipping materials are available form TOUCH OUTREACH MINISTRIES. For address and phone number, see the copyright page in the front of this book.

Seminars are offered from time to time by our ministry team members. If you would like to attend one, drop us a note and we'll notify you when we are going to be in your area.

JOURNEY GUIDE
A booklet given to each person who enters a Cell Group. It helps the Shepherd create a curriculum guide to equip each Christian for ministry and growth.

NEW BELIEVERS STATION
Provides your new Christians with practical guidance on walking away from the bondage of sin. Also, this title emphasizes a life of prayer, Bible reading, and community with other believers. The five weeks of daily study will ground your new believers in their walk with Christ and prepare them for spiritual battles ahead.

THE ARRIVAL KIT
Excellent follow-up for *COVER THE BIBLE* graduates! The *Arrival Kit* is great for use with new Christians. Eleven weeks of daily growth material deals with the value system of the Kingdom of God and contrasts it with the values of the world.

WHERE DO WE GO FROM HERE?
Compares the traditional style of church life with the Cell Group Church, and outlines how to create Cell Groups and Share Groups, Congregations (composed of 5 or more Cells), and the Celebration (composed of all the Cells and guests).

SHEPHERD'S GUIDEBOOK

Shows the Shepherd of a cell group exactly how to develop and lead a flock. Includes twelve weeks of outlines for Shepherd Groups, all the forms required to keep records. This book is being used around the world to shape the structures of cell group churches. You'll be filled with a vision of how *your* life can be used to reach others.

TOUCHING HEARTS GUIDEBOOK

An equipping module for those in a Cell Group who are learning how to share their faith using a special diagram based on John 3:16.

LIFE BASIC TRAINING

Helps sort out your values, often a mixture of secular and Christian. For use by small groups of five persons. Eleven sessions; *Daily Growth Guide* materials are included in the 136-page guidebook.